Strategic Management of Professional Service Firms

D1356458

Stephan Kaiser · Max Josef Ringlstetter

Strategic Management of Professional Service Firms

Theory and Practice

 Springer

Prof. Dr. Stephan Kaiser
Universität der Bundeswehr
München
Wirtschafts- und
Organisationswissenschaften
Werner-Heisenberg-Weg 39
85577 Neubiberg
Germany
Stephan.Kaiser@unibw.de

Prof. Dr. Max Josef Ringlstetter
Katholische Universität
Eichstätt-Ingolstadt
Wirtschaftswissenschaftliche
Fakultät
Lehrstuhl für ABWL, Organisation und
Personal
Auf der Schanz 49
85049 Ingolstadt
Germany
max.ringlstetter@ku-eichstaett.de

ISBN 978-3-642-16062-2   e-ISBN 978-3-642-16063-9
DOI 10.1007/978-3-642-16063-9
Springer Heidelberg Dordrecht London New York

Library of Congress Control Number: 2010938732

Cover design: WMXDesign GmbH, Heidelberg

Printed on acid-free paper

Springer is part of Springer Science+Business Media (www.springer.com)

Preface

Professional service firms, like corporate law firms or management consultancies, provide knowledge-intensive services for businesses. The entire professional service sector is gaining increasing importance both at a microeconomic and macroeconomic level in all developed economies. Among other things the growth of many professional service firms provides evidence of their increasing significance. On the other hand, this growth provides challenges both for firms' strategic development and their managements.

This book deals with these challenges. In it we attempt to contribute to the joint effort in combining academic and practical findings on the subjects of management and strategy in professional service firms and present the results to an interested audience. The book is thus primarily designed for partners and managers in professional service firms, but also addresses students and teachers working in this increasingly important field.

We would like to thank Simon Woll of the Catholic University of Eichstaett-Ingolstadt, who was responsible for the major project coordination tasks, for all his assistance and Adrian Bründl, without whose expert support we would never have been able to complete the book project in such a short time.

We hope that this book provides practitioners and academics with a major incentive to investigate professional service firms. We look forward to receiving critical comments and amendments and suggestions as to how this book might be improved.

Neubiberg, Germany   Stephan Kaiser
Ingolstadt, Germany   Max Josef Ringlstetter

Introduction

Professional service firms play a major role in today's business world. A few examples underline this:

- Influenced by strategic consultants, corporate groups realign their strategies and structures.
- IT service firms help to make corporate processes more efficient. Innovations, e.g., in the automotive industry, are highly dependent on firms of engineering services.
- Investment banks and corporate law firms are involved in big corporate mergers and takeovers and thereby influence the image of major corporate groups.

In spite of this high de facto influence and these numerous challenges, professional service firms have so far received comparatively little attention in management literature. This book examines all the essential facets of the strategic management of professional service firms. It both presents the latest academic findings in a comprehensible form combined with practical implications to provide a brief overview on the current status of research into professional service firms and it can be used as a kind of manual for making strategic management decisions. In its sound analysis of professional service firms it points out some of the special characteristics of the professional services sector to an interested public, it describes the most important challenges, presents useful management concepts and points up future trends. For this purpose the book is divided into three parts.

The *Part I* provides a basic introduction to the world of professional service firms. On this basis, it formulates the main strategic management *challenges* to professional service firms. The book then presents an overview of the *organization* of the professional services sector. General *types of business and forms of remuneration* are also examined at this point. It also examines the various *subsectors* and their individual characteristics, including corporate law firms, auditing firms, consulting firms, investment banks, recruitment agencies, communications agencies and engineering services firms.

The *Part II* focuses on the management of strategic resources of professional service firms.

- Service *quality* is a critical feature in the success of professional service firms. It also provides differentiation potential on the highly competitive service markets. For its part, perceived quality helps develop customer trust, another vital resource. The different aspects of the strategic resources of quality and trust are described and explained in detail.
- *Knowledge* is considered to be another core resource of professional service firms. It therefore seems obvious that knowledge must be professionally managed. However, the aim is to use corresponding knowledge management to generate *innovation*. Ultimately, it is innovative concepts and new services that make a professional service firm a market leader. The success factors of knowledge and innovation are introduced in detail, with emphasis on the strategic focus, the core tasks and the critical success and influence factors of knowledge management and the special challenge of generating innovation in professional service firms.
- In order to market innovative services, firms must be able to convince clients and customers to use them. This presupposes adequate *marketing* of the professional service provider and its services. The specific characteristics of the professional service sector requiring consideration and the marketing focus on prospective and existing clients are the main aspects illustrated in the last section of the Part II of the book.

The *Part III* of the book is devoted to the most important topics connected with the management of professionals. Because of their educational background and their vocational socialization they are a unique group amongst those working in this field. This is one of the issues that also need to be taken into consideration in the context of the management of professionals.

Since employees in professional service firms have a special role as knowledge bearers, the *fundamental concept of the management of professionals* is a vital issue. The objective of management of professionals is the supply of committed and competent professionals. The factors of acquisition, motivation and development of professionals are critical for this purpose. Before dealing with these factors, however, current performance and future requirements on part of the market and clients must be analyzed.

- The strategic management of professionals must be measured by its success. To increase the efficiency of HR measures, firms tend increasingly to concentrate and coordinate individual measures. Firms choosing such an approach are called *high performance work systems*. The systems, their origins and their respective elements are described at length. Finally, it is expected that this systematization of HR measures has a positive effect on the performance of the company as a whole; in such cases, employee motivation and commitment also play a pivotal role. Respective interdependence is also explained. Finally, the potential of high performance work systems for professional service firms is underlined.
- The *work-life-balance* of employees has become a particularly topical subject in the sector of management of professionals for professional service firms. This is

due to a change of awareness in society concerning the value of work in comparison to personal life, with a special focus on the family. Work in the professional services sector is generally linked with long working hours and a large amount of travel. It is therefore particularly important to understand how professional service firms deal with this conflict-laden issue.

- A large part of the success of professional service firms is the acquisition of new business. Contacts with former employees are a critical factor here. Professional service firms have recognized this and use their *alumni networks* to generate new business; one section of this book is therefore dedicated solely to this topic. In the process, the structure of such alumni networks and their strategic relevance for professional service firms is discussed. This forms the basis for extrapolate management implications and pointing out future trends.

In *Part IV* the book extends its focus and looks at the management of long-term strategic development goals of professional service firms.

- Initially three following *options for the strategic development* of professional service firms are introduced: strengthening core business, an international orientation and diversification. The selection of the right strategy can improve the use of the resources of knowledge and social competence and, at the same time, help meet customer requirements. When implementing the selected strategy, specific legal, cultural and organizational characteristics of professional service firms must be considered.
- Over the last few years there have been signs of change in the structure of the industry. Spin-offs and increasing market diversification has meant that the market is characterized by an increasing number of small and medium professional service firms; however, they are still competing with the large professional service firms. The *networking of small and medium professional service firms* provides an opportunity to overcome size and capital-dependent obstacles that prevent them from entering the market and which threaten their ability to compete. Network management gives small and medium professional service firms a chance to find new ways to make strategic use of the social capital, both on an individual and on an organizational level.

The right *strategies* in *times of crisis* are of particular importance. The basis of all crisis concepts is the realization that professional service firms organized on a partnership basis must generally keep growing in order to both maintain their profitable leverage structure and to meet career goals. More recently, such growth often has no longer been possible due to altered market conditions. However, there are three strategy options for sustaining provider profitability: a decrease in the pressure inherent in the career system, concentration on alternative, but similar growth markets in terms of project type, and the change to entirely new types of projects. The book concludes by illustrating the so-called archetype change in the professional service firm sector. This process is already partly complete but in most cases it is still on-going.

As part of this change, professional service firms have been increasingly introducing management practices and different types of organization structures. Finally, frameworks for classifying archetypes that allow the characterization of various archetypal professional service firms are presented, leaving room for speculation about future development trends.

Contents

List of Figures

Part I
Professional Service Firms

Chapter 1
The World of Professional Service Firms

As already mentioned, professional service firms play a major role in today's economy. They are generally associated with keywords like modern concept of work and service, high turnover and profit rates, but also with unpleasant decisions such as corporate restructuring measures. Hardly any bigger company has never resorted to a professional service provider – in whatsoever form. The reasons can be manifold: the non-existence of own resources or the desire for new external business impulses are just two exemplary causes.

That also explains why various research areas have begun to investigate this high potential sector more intensively. The definition of professional service firms does not only address readers with minor experience on the matter. Core topics are also being examined in greater detail and essential terms of the sector are being analyzed.

1.1 What Are Professional Service Firms?

Professional service firms like law firms, investment banks, consulting firms, auditing firms etc. are companies of the so-called tertiary sector. It includes all services, i.e. products, 'which require direct contact of provider and consumer and which appear mainly intangible prior to, during and after the contact'.[1] This allows services in connection with industrial goods to be particularly differentiated using two constitutive features: client immateriality and integration in the provision of goods and services. However, this definition of the term service summarizes a very broad and heterogeneous subsector and company spectrum which extends from cleaning service providers, fast-food restaurants to consulting firms.

To be able to differentiate professional service firms properly two other types thus need to be defined:

- Professional service firms providing *knowledge-intensive* services.
- Professional service firms providing services for companies.

Co-author: Bernd Bürger

S. Kaiser, M.J. Ringlstetter, *Strategic Management of Professional Service Firms*,
DOI 10.1007/978-3-642-16063-9_1, © Springer-Verlag Berlin Heidelberg 2011

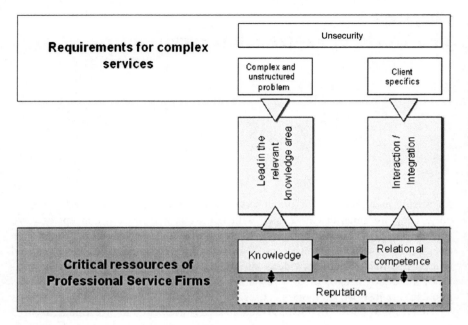

Fig. 1.1 Critical resources of professional service firms

Since attributes for professional services in most cases can be allocated simultaneously and are particularly distinctive, they are also described as 'pure and highly representative form of service'.[2] At the same time other (service) sectors can be differentiated via resources critical for success. There are three resources which significantly influence the success of professional service firms: knowledge, relational competence and reputation (see Fig. 1.1):

- *Knowledge:* Professional service firms have made it their business to work on unstructured problems for their clients. This is what distinguishes them from e.g. industrial cleaners, who deal with relatively clearly structured problems. Unstructured problems on the other hand require an excellent organizational knowledge, which allows the provider to gain competitive advantage in the relevant knowledge area in comparison to client and competitor knowledge. The value creation of professional service firms can furthermore be regarded as highly knowledge-intensive, since rather than machines or equity being needed, the expert knowledge, the experience and ability to solve problems of employees is required.[3] Problem solving is additionally complicated, since professional service firm clients are mainly companies, as well as public institutions and authorities.[4] These are much more complex systems than individuals[5] and thus require a more complex service provision.

- *Relational competence:* Comparable to other services the client is integrated into the service provision process as so-called 'external factor'. The provision of a complex, knowledge-intensive service, however, often presupposes a highly developed and multi-personal interaction between professionals and clients.[6] Only when using such an approach professional service providers are able to assess the internal and external client situation, generate a 'client-specific power of judgment' and provide solutions to company-specific problems. Different to the situation e.g. in a fast food restaurant, the relational competence of employees is hence the key to a successful interaction with and integration of clients.
- *Reputation:* Due to their high complexity and their economic significance for clients, professional services – as opposed to e.g. cleaning services – are deemed high quality credence goods. Such services are typically difficult to obtain, since clients have little means of selecting an adequate provider.[7] The service quality and the quality of the choice are often, if at all, revealed only after conclusion of contract. The consequently resulting insecurity on part of clients thus often leads to a focus on the quality feature reputation when acquiring professional services in exchange for 'security of choice'.[8] High reputation therefore can be deemed a 'door opener' and pre-condition for lucrative contracts. Ideally it reflects the company's knowledge and relational competence.

1.2 Management Challenges and Approaches for Professional Service Firms

So far, professional service firms have not been focusing too much on the management of their own businesses. This is mainly due to the self-image of many professionals. Particularly if they do not have economic background (e.g. lawyers), professionals often still today assume that their sole purpose lies in the provision of high quality services for the client. Even if this is naturally the main condition for the success of a professional service firm, it also proves that the profitability of the service provision and its management are first of minor importance. However, also the service provision of professional service firm needs to be profit-oriented in the long-term. Especially US experts have consequently found that professionals in principle have demonstrated increased management awareness throughout the last years. The changed trend from purely partner-managed professional service firms towards so-called 'Managed Professional Businesses' clearly reflects that.[9] In Chap. 14 of this book these aspects are being portrayed in detail under the keyword 'change of archetype'.

To guarantee increased service provision efficiency optimization approaches need to be found both for the factors turnover, as well as cost. This means that professional service firms – more intensively than other businesses – have to be active in and coordinated for two important markets at the same time: the market for professional employees and the market for professional services.[10] In other words employees and clients are core success factors.

- *Employees:* Highly qualified professionals are both carrier of (implicit) knowledge, and interaction partner of the clients. Their appearance and performance shapes the firm's reputation. That makes them mainly responsible for the company's success. To provide their service professional service firms require only little assets. They rather depend on their employees' quality and motivation. Professional service firms can thus be interpreted as 'ultimate embodiment of that familiar phrase "our asset are our people"'.[11]
- *Client:* The professional service market is shaped by individual client requirements. Clients demand high quality services tailored to their respective needs. Only when these requirements are met professional service firms are able to market their professional services and receive remuneration which is rather high compared to other sectors.

The main management challenge in professional service firms is to establish a balance between those markets and their specific requirements and constraints. For both markets positions have to be established and coordinated in parallel. The core idea hereby is the so-called *leverage*, which forms the core of the business model of professional service firms: in the context of a leverage relation also junior employees indirectly gain access to the knowledge gathered by the client contacts of partners and project managers of a professional service firm. This allows them to contribute to finding solutions for complex client problems. This, in turn, leads to the rather surprising situation that, e.g. young university graduates consult veteran managers. The possibility of using leverage in the areas of knowledge and client relations also allows professional service firms to charge higher rates when using their junior professionals and therefore increase the firm's profitability. The project team structure with expensive senior professionals and comparatively favorable junior professionals thus influences the remuneration and cost structure of the respective contract and is thus one of the main levers to increase profitability.

However, the project team organization cannot be changed arbitrarily, since it needs to meet the requirements of the professional service market. When using the degree of novelty and standardization as criteria, three project types can be identified in one continuum: the term *brain* projects is used in the case of highly innovative contracts with little room for standardization. In contrast to the aforementioned, *gray hair* projects have a low degree of innovation although they require a large amount of practical knowledge. The problems in *procedure* projects have often already been identified and the problem solving process can be standardized to a considerable extent. The team structure consequently needs to meet project requirements so that the various projects can, one the one hand satisfy the client, and be kept as profitable as possible on the other.

- *Brain* projects usually include problems with issues, which are strategically of particular importance to the client. Since such projects bear high risk on part of the client; the number of experienced and creative senior professionals has to be relatively high. If the project is carried out by many partners and few junior employees, the leverage potential is relatively low. At the same time, however, clients have comparably little remuneration sensitivity, which leads to high consultant fees.

- On the other end of the project continuum, the service provision in *procedure* projects is more standardized. Remuneration sensitivity is much higher here, which leads to lower hourly rates. The professional service firm can compensate for the resulting decline in turnover by using a higher leverage potential, though, i.e. the number of partners is kept low. Instead, junior employees with lower rates are used.

- *Gray hair* projects assume a middle position concerning remuneration sensitivity and leverage potential.

Against the background of these challenges the management's objective for professional service firms should be an optimal use and development of professionals as human resources for the company in line with their specific roles. There are three main levers to influence and align the behavior of employees to the business objective: the management of professionals, the design of the organizational structure and the development of corporate culture.[12]

1.2.1 Management of Professionals

As highly qualified employees the so-called professionals contribute substantially to the long-term success of a professional service firm.[13] Jeffrey Pfeffer, a well known expert in that area even goes as far as stating: 'the distinctive competence of a professional services firm is the skill of its staff'.[14] Why do employees in professional service firms have such a high significance? In the first instance this is simply due to the fact that the main services of a professional service firm – the provision of services in interaction with clients – obviously characterized by the commitment and the skills of an individual employee and/or a team of employees. In theory this can be verified by applying the so-called resource oriented strategic management approach to the human resources sector[15]: A superior amount of professionals matching certain criteria leads to long-term competitive advantage.[16] Competing professional service firms are not able to simply develop the same level of professionals and certainly not in the short term.

If the line of argument is taken one step further the significance of the management of professionals is obvious: The management of professionals becomes a strategic success factor, since the services of professionals depend on it at a considerable extend[17]:

> Many well-managed professional services firms emphasize recruitment, selection, and building strong cultures to retain the skilled employees who constitute the basis of their success. (Pfeffer 1994, p. 21)[18]

Thus the main issue at first is to recruit the best professionals from the external work market. Simply put, this ensures the basic availability of work. In addition the individual productivity of professionals needs to be developed on the one hand, the daily commitment must be secured and/or be increased on the other hand. Moreover, loyalty of professionals as core high performers of the company towards the professional service firm is to be maintained by offering e.g. special career development options. In reverse – especially in times of crisis – it can also be an option to let professionals go. This is ultimately the only way to retain a profitable leverage ratio. However, this does not only apply for institutionalized HR departments, but also for the management and career advancement of employees on a daily basis.

1.2.2 Design of Organizational Structures

The topic 'professionals' indirectly links to the second management challenge of professional service firms: the design of the organizational structure. Why? There is a strong correlation between professional staff and organizational structure: In general, individual professionals with specific individual skills form one professional service team to solve client problems. This leads to highly skill and at the same time individual dependent organizational structures. Ideally this precisely represents market and client requirements.

When discussing organizational structures of professional service firms, one needs to be aware that the organizational structures of the individual companies – especially across subsectors – vary considerably. However, there are two elements which allow a general classification. Firstly, most of the subsectors can be represented using a so-called professional pyramid. This pyramid particularly reveals vertical structures (1), which are generally based on the professionals' seniority. Furthermore additional management bodies and service areas can often be found. Secondly a detailed analysis of the professional pyramid also shows horizontal structures (2). These are mostly due to specializations and/or skills of individual professionals.

1.2.2.1 The Vertical Structure of the Professional Pyramid

Ideal-typically the pyramid-like organizational structure has three – in law firms mostly two[19] – levels: Partners, project managers and junior employees (see Fig. 1.2).[20] The partners are particularly responsible for the development and care of client relations and often own the professional service firm. This applies at least to professional service firms with a partner structure. However, recently also these firms can be divided into equity and non-equity partner businesses. Project managers are mainly in charge of coordination tasks, while junior employees provide more operative tasks to solve client problems.

Project teams, formed based on a specific client task, thus profit from internal synergies, since they consist of team members from the respective layers of the professional pyramid contributing their specific skills.[21]

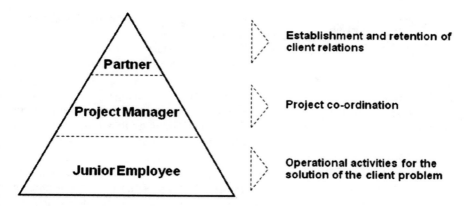

Fig. 1.2 Professional pyramid. (Source: Adapted from Maister 1982, p. 17)

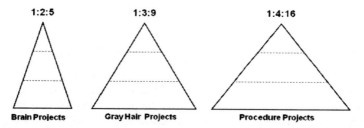

Fig. 1.3 Connection between project type and leverage structure

The ratio of the number of partners, project managers and junior employees on project or company level is represented by the so-called leverage ratio. A professional service firm with 4 partners, 8 project managers and 20 junior employees has a 1:2:5 leverage ratio. This ratio depends on market needs. It is obvious that a complex process, such as the legal consulting during an international merger, requires much more partner involvement than the relatively standardized implementation of an IT tool. The ratio of junior employees, project managers and partners in a team thus depends on the project type (see Fig. 1.3). Each project type hence requires another leverage structure.[22]

The leverage ratio typically varies across subsectors. Strategic consulting firms, mainly dealing with 'brain' projects, have a comparably low leverage ratio. If a professional service firm with such a leverage structure was implementing a 'procedure' project, professionals had to perform tasks which didn't meet their qualifications. Due to the different salaries of the three hierarchical levels profitability would be at risk.[23] In reverse professionals would carry out tasks exceeding their qualifications which would ultimately lead to quality risks. The point to be made is that the vertical hierarchical structuring is determined by the project type and vice versa.

Beyond the vertical structure, which is in a manner of speaking the structural core of the professional service firm, most professional service firms have management bodies.[24] These bodies can have rather legislative or executive character. While the actual shape of legislative bodies largely depends on the respective legal form of the professional service firm, many professional service firms have highly similar executive bodies.[25] Mostly these are so-called 'managing partners', irrespective of the fact whether they are the actual company owners from a legal point of view. In the context of an underlying 'democratic' ideology they direct the fate of the professional service firm together with 'executive committees'. Such executive committees are again formed by partners.

In the context of an increased trend towards a more professional management of professional service firms, companies have recently begun to resort to an ever increasing task sharing implementation between partners. This sharing can depend on regions, client groups, and knowledge areas or also economic functions, like funding, marketing or personnel management. In addition, at least bigger professional service firms have highly developed service areas, like e.g. HR, research and analysis departments etc.

1.2.2.2 The Horizontal Structure of the Professional Pyramid

To be able to better meet market and client requirements professional service firms also implement horizontal structures. However, since market and client requirements permanently change, it is beneficial for the professional service firm to have a flexible horizontal structure.[26] This structure is characterized by knowledge pools. Within these knowledge pools individual professionals of all hierarchical levels can be located based on their specialization and/or skills.[27] Depending on the professional service firm, specializations can be made concerning different objects. Strategic consultancies for example develop specialists for certain sectors (e.g. consumer industry), value creating functions (e.g. purchasing) or trans-sector issues (e.g. controlling). Large law firms have professionals for various subject areas, such as tax law, work law, etc.[28] Even if a change of specializations or multiple specializations is possible and often also desired, specialization limits project feasibility. A corporate law firm, with specializations in various areas can not automatically implement tax-related projects, even if the market required such service. The respective points of reference in terms of skills and knowledge thus presuppose a horizontal structuring of the professional service firm.

1.2.3 Development of the Corporate Culture

Corporate culture can generally be defined as the belief of employees in certain goals and values and an adequate strategy to achieve these goals or to live up to these values. Culture can never be fully defined via regulations or manuals; it is rather to be understood as an 'invisible guide' containing 'do's' – what employees are expected to do and 'don'ts' – implicitly forbidden things.[29] Strongly developed cultures can thus considerably facilitate the firm's management on the levels coordination, integration and motivation of employees[30]:

- *Coordination*: A strong corporate culture supports the coordination of different employee goals and interests with company objectives. It allows employees to cope with daily tasks also without detailed formal plans, programs and rules.
- *Integration*: The corporate culture can furthermore help to improve team spirit and thus promote solidarity of individual sub-systems in companies. Personal interests become less significant and culture shows its impact as 'social glue'.[31]
- *Motivation*: Norms and values of a corporate culture help employees to understand the entrepreneurial context of their actions. This leads to increased satisfaction and thus motivation on their part.

Corporate culture in professional service firms has a higher impact on the behavior of professionals than any codified job description or company regulation. In the provision of services professionals are highly autonomous and provide particularly much room for discretion. In companies, where employees enjoy such a high degree of freedom, the culture often considerably shapes their behavior towards colleagues and clients.[32]

Many studies have shown a culture to be particularly typical for professional service firms, the so-called 'one firm' concept.[33] This concept contains various cultural elements which can be found in companies like McKinsey, Goldman Sachs or Latham & Watkins. In the past these elements have had a crucial impact on companies' success and will surely continue to do so in future:

- A highly developed, sometimes cult-like, institutional loyalty
- Prevention of a general star mentality, which underlines the sole performance of an individual,
- High importance of team work and solidarity,
- Long work hours and high performance requirements,
- Acknowledgement of a mission, which prioritizes client concerns.

When considering management possibilities or options to coin corporate culture such approaches should not be based on 'an unlimited feasibility in the sense of a value or norm drill' or an 'indoctrination of attitude'.[34] In fact corporate culture is a dynamic system, which is shaped by decisions and actions on a daily basis.[35] There are nevertheless approaches to further develop culture, such as recruiting and training of new employees, corporate communication or the initiation of formative experiences. They can help to implement a new culture, or to change or strengthen an existing culture, i.e. to increase both the degree of anchoring, as well as the conformity of corporate values and norms with all members of the organization.[36]

1.3 Strategic Challenges and Approaches for Professional Service Firms

Beyond the briefly outlined challenges and approaches for the more or less daily management of the professional service firm, the question of the long-term strategic focus remains. Since the beginning of the nineties at the latest, the professional service market had been characterized by high growth rates and intensification of competition.[37] The huge growth was not only based on increased demand on the professional service sector, but also on the typical 'up-or-out' career system of professional service firms. Since professionals in such a system can only stay with a company, if they continuously advance and climb the respective steps on the career ladder, career and growth pressure in professional service firms inevitably start to rise. Nevertheless, directed career promises are made to recruit and make loyal new highly qualified employees. This systems works, since the chance to make it in the circle of partners is a vital incentive for many professionals in the long-term. However, if promises are held, the number of partners rises. Since partners often directly profit from company gains – due to their owner- or partnership – an extension of the circle of partners needs to be accompanied by an increase in company profits. The initial partners will probably not agree to give up parts of their commission in favor of succeeding partners and will rather try to maximize them. Against this background professional service firms have to grow strongly, to maintain a good balance between senior and junior professionals and to be able to meet their needs at the same time.[38] This phenomenon ('leverage ratio') is portrayed in detail in Chap. 11 of this book.

In parallel to these developments market penetration in the individual performance segments rises. The number of professional service providers increases, while existing businesses grow and expand their service spectrum. The auditing company KPMG is no longer exclusively limited to their core business, but – like other large auditing firms – has long begun to target other markets such as management consulting, financing and legal consulting. This convergence can be observed in various PSF subsectors[39] and leads to a highly developed competitive situation.[40]

In the last years phases of stagnation, recession and growth alternated. The above-average company growth rates and the increasing demand for professional services ended in the 1990s with a drastic drop in demand, which was caused by the general economic downturn. Professional service firms, which had previously built up considerable capacities, were suddenly facing an entirely new market environment. Since then professional service clients have become increasingly cost-sensitive. Many projects are cancelled or postponed against the background of such new cost awareness. The remuneration of professionals is being questioned and re-negotiated. This trend leads to professional service firms developing sales and/or pricing problems. Many consulting firms face less consulting contracts, while the number of new IPOs has sunk to a minimum, causing problems for investment banks, but also for many law firms and communication agencies. Auditors and tax consultancies might still be concluding new contracts, find themselves under

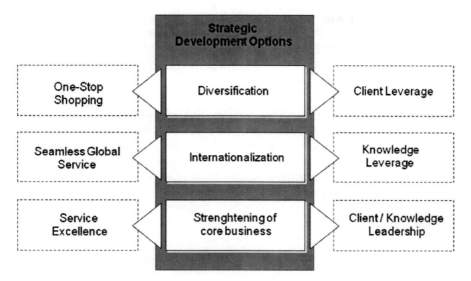

Fig. 1.4 Strategic development possibilities of professional service firms. (Source: see Ringlstetter and Bürger 2003, p. 121)

increased pricing pressure. Since professional service firms will typically try everything to improve utilization and to avoid letting professionals go, competition is additionally intensified.

In order to stay competitive in the long-term professional service firms have to create and develop specific competitive advantages to stand out from the competition. Critical long-term success factors are client relations and the company's knowledge base. Professional service firms can select three development strategies (see Fig. 1.4)[41]:

- *Diversification:* Diversification strategies imply expansion of the existing range of services. Clients are offered new services and thus have the possibility to use a 'one-stop shopping' service. In the context of 'client leverage' such diversification aims at using the existing clients base and at generating more turnover using an extended range of services.
- *Internationalization:* In almost all PSF sectors the leading companies have begun to internationalized – at the latest since the beginning of the 1980s – and have thus enabled their clients to work with the same professional service provider on a global scope ('seamless global service').[42] The international focus allows the provision of existing knowledge and problem solving capacity to a much broader clientele and leads to 'knowledge leverage'.
- *Strengthening of the core business:* Irrespective of the pursuit of either strategy professional service firms continuously have to strive to strengthen the core businesses since many segments no longer have potential for internationalization and

diversification or simply because competitive pressure rises. The main objective is an increase of quality, i.e. to improve 'service excellence' in the market. This can happen two ways. Either through the market differentiator competence (knowledge leadership) or via the client relation (client leadership). It is also possible to combine both approaches.

In this introductory chapter it has become clear that professional service firms represent a complex type of business with specific characteristics, which confronts the management with special challenges. Due to the fact that they have gained immensely increased economic significance in the last couple of years, strategic management tasks have recently become the focus of interest. These are particularly considered in the fourth part of this book.

However, at first the various subsectors professional service firms and their respective specifics shall be analyzed in detail to put the subsequent chapters on a holistic basis concerning the sectors and companies acting within them.

Notes

1. See Hentschel (1992), p. 26.
2. Stutz (1988), p. 50 outlines this using consulting companies.
3. See Alvesson (1995), p. 1.
4. See Müller-Stewens et al. (1999), p. 21.
5. See Worpitz (1991), p. 155.
6. See Weber (1996), p. 178; van Well (2001), p. 78. Not every professional service has interactive potential to that extent. Tordoir (1995), p. 139 et seq. in this context e.g. differentiates between highly interactive sparring and less interactive jobbing relations.
7. See Zeithaml (1981), p. 186.
8. See Vopel (1999), p. 45.
9. See Cooper et al. (1996).
10. See Müller-Stewens et al. (1999), p. 38 et seq. referring to Maister (1982), p. 15 et seq.
11. See Maister (1982), S 15.
12. See Süss (2001), p. 47.
13. See also Shapero (1985), p. 1.
14. See Pfeffer (1994), p. 21.
15. See Boxall and Purcell (2000).
16. See Wright et al. (1994).
17. See Kaiser (2001), p. 20 et seq.
18. See Pfeffer (1994), p. 21
19. See Sherer (1995).
20. See Maister (1982), p. 16 et seq.
21. See Maister (1982), p. 18.
22. See Løwendahl (1997), p. 45.
23. See Løwendahl (1997), p. 45.
24. See Müller-Stewens et al. (1999), p. 82 et seq.
25. See also Maister (2003), p. 292 et seq.
26. In this context Weber (1996) talks about "fluid organization".
27. Upon closer examination the structuring appears highly complex, since several knowledge pools can partially overlap.
28. See Sherer (1995) for a list of areas, p. 690.

29. See Lorsch and Tierney (2002), p. 143 et seq.
30. See Dill and Hügler (1997), p. 152 et seq.
31. See Albert and Silverman (1984), p. 13.
32. See Lorsch and Tierney (2002), p. 145.
33. See Maister (2003), p. 303 et seq.
34. See Dill and Hügler (1997), p. 143.
35. See Lorsch and Tierney (2002), p. 142.
36. See Dill and Hügler (1997), p. 144.
37. See Müller-Stewens et al. (1999), p. 24 et seq.
38. See Maister (1982), p. 22.
39. See Scott (2001), p. 16 et seq.
40. See Müller-Stewens et al. (1999), p. 30.
41. See Ringlstetter and Bürger (2003), p. 119 et seq.
42. See Müller-Stewens et al. (1999), p. 30 and Brown et al. (1996), p. 66.

Chapter 2
The Business of Professional Service Firms

As already outlined in the introduction, the professional service firm sector is characterized by a couple of commonalities, such as the critical resources. Despite all these commonalities it must be forgotten under no circumstances that there are considerable differences between individual companies within the sector. These differences on the one hand manifest in more differentiated types of businesses and remuneration forms. On the other hand they are based on the fact that professional services vary depending on the subsector. These subsectors will be portrayed in detail in the following chapter. When comparing the range of services of a management consultancy and the one of an insurance broker this is more than obvious. In the following types of businesses (Sect. 2.1) and remuneration forms (Sect. 2.2) are presented as can be generally found in the PSF sector.

2.1 Types of Professional Service Firm Businesses

The business basis of professional service firms in principle rests on the demand for additional qualitative or quantitative problem solving competence on part of clients. In some cases the involvement of professional service firms is a statutory obligation. Companies have to have their annual accounts performed by neutral parties, i.e. auditing companies.[1] The businesses, which professional service firms are able to conclude against this background, are often of highly diverse nature. There are three basic *types of business* (see Fig. 2.1):

- The first type of business is the *consulting business*. It tackles problems which can often not be clearly defined by clients. The objective of this kind of service is to develop ideas and concepts which form the basis of the client's decision-making. A typical claim of consultants is the development of constantly new specific solutions for each client. This is also referred to as 'expert economics'.[2] Whether firms like management consultancies are actually able to live up to this claim in the individual case remains questionable.

Co-author: Bernd Bürger

S. Kaiser, M.J. Ringlstetter, *Strategic Management of Professional Service Firms*, DOI 10.1007/978-3-642-16063-9_2, © Springer-Verlag Berlin Heidelberg 2011

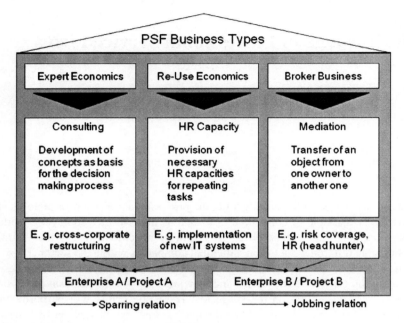

Fig. 2.1 Various types of businesses in the PSF sector

- When additional quantitative problem solving competence is required professional service firms which only provide *personnel capacities* are mainly used. With the help of these additional capacity client problems can be solved which are complex, but at the same time relatively similar. The term for this is 're-use economics'.[3] A classical example of such a case is the implementation of a new IT system.
- *Brokering*, or the so-called brokerage, has a main focus. Simply put, objects are transferred from one owner to the other on behalf of the client. The broker typically works as the mediator in a triangular relation between two companies. The brokered objects can have different form: In case of insurance brokers it is comprehensive risk coverage, for head hunters the 'objects of desire' are human resources.
- In practice the *combinations* of types of businesses are manifold. Often statements regarding this can be made only for specific companies or projects. The services insurance brokers provide for instance often exceed the brokering service. In addition clients often expect an individual consulting service and finally also general service and the administration of insurance products.[4]

The three different types of businesses can furthermore also vary in terms of the *relation*, in which the service is provided. In particular the so called *jobbing* and *sparring relations* are differentiated in that context (see Fig. 2.1).[5] The point of origin in both cases is a complex client problem.

- *Sparring* relations are often characterized by intensive reciprocal interaction. Client and consultant alternate taking on the role of guide and guided.
- *Jobbing* relations on the other hand are rather implementation oriented. The client outsources specific tasks and ensures the respective coordination.

Chapter 4 deals with quality management and looks at clients relations from a different perspective.

2.2   Remuneration Forms in Professional Service Firms

It can be concluded that a professional service firm can perform various types of businesses. However it depends on the agreed remuneration form whether every partial service provided is invoiced at the end of the day. The main *remuneration forms* are briefly presented below:

- The payment of a *commission* is a remuneration form with decisive parameters or percentages. In case of insurance brokers e.g. the broker fee depends on the amount insured as decisive parameter.
- *Profit sharing* is a special firm of commission payment. While in case of commissions the decisive parameter can be specified in advance, success orientation can be an element of uncertainty both for professional service firms and for their clients: Since success, directly allocatable to a certain project, is not always measurable or is sometimes not revealed unless several years have passed, the determination of this decisive parameter is problematic.
- The probably most common remuneration form is the *hourly fee*. Irrespective of the result the client pays pre-defined hourly rates to professionals involved in the provision of service. Partner rates are significantly higher than the junior employee rates. Such remuneration can be anticipated very well by professional service firms. Clients could face a problem though, if the productivity of professionals turns out to be insufficient.
- The remuneration in form of fixed prices, so-called *retainers*, is invoiced on a regular basis. Similar to hourly rates this form of remuneration can be well anticipated by professional service firms; however, for clients it also bears disadvantages.

It can be useful for the individual professional service firm to combine different remuneration forms. Furthermore remuneration forms are subject to strong temporal development dynamics. Over many years it was general practice for head hunters to receive commissions and for consulting firms to invoice hourly rates. Clients, however, have now begun to postulate profit sharing, not least due to the economic downturn.

After having introduced key terms and types of businesses as well as remuneration forms of professional service firms the following chapter takes a closer look at the individual subsectors.

Notes

1. See Gillmann and Ruud (2002), p. 21
2. See Hansen et al. (1999), p. 110.
3. See Hansen et al. (1999), p. 110.
4. See Griess and Zinnert (1997), p. 33 et seq.
5. See Tordoir (1995), p. 139 et seq. The 'sales relations' described by Tordoir are rather atypical for Professional Service Firms.

Chapter 3
The Subsectors of Professional Service Firms

The professional service firm sector contains a host of different subsectors and is thus rather heterogeneous. It therefore makes sense to see the sector holistically but to take a closer, systematic look at the characteristics and peculiarities of the individual subsectors. In this book the following subsectors are examined in more detail:

- Auditing companies
- Corporate law firms
- Consulting firms
- Recruitment agencies
- Investment banks
- Communication agencies
- Engineering service providers

The first six subsectors listed above, together with the market research companies not mentioned here, alone generate about 75% of the sector's total turnover[1]: Fig. 3.1 shows both the approximate subsector share of total revenue of the professional service market and also a possible subdivision of the services offered. It needs to be considered that the companies of the individual subsectors are often extending and enlarging their portfolio and provide services in the increasingly tougher and more dynamic competitive environment which exceed subsector boundaries. Correspondingly a fluent transition between individual subsectors can be assumed.

This book presents management challenges and sector developments in key subsectors. The bases for this are the characteristics and peculiarities of the eight subsectors listed in the following. For this purpose four issues have been identified:

1. What added value do companies offer their clients? What is the actual service provided?
2. How can the relationship between professionals and clients be described? Depending on interaction intensity highly interactive jobbing and less interactive sparring relations can be differentiated.[2]

Co-author: Bernd Bürger

S. Kaiser, M.J. Ringlstetter, *Strategic Management of Professional Service Firms*, DOI 10.1007/978-3-642-16063-9_3, © Springer-Verlag Berlin Heidelberg 2011

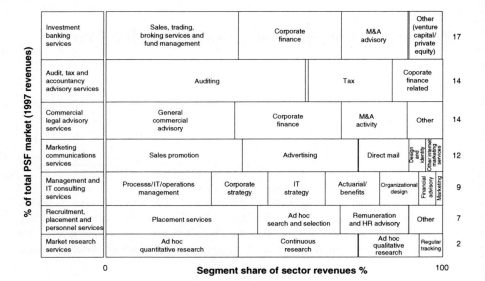

Fig. 3.1 Professional service firm subsectors. (Source: Scott 1998, p. 11)

3. How can the 'professions' of the respective sectors characterized and to what degree is the respective total of professionals institutionalized?
4. Who are the global 'key players' of the respective subsectors regarding turnover and/or number of employees?

Apart from the factor quality also the factor added value generated by a consulting service for the client can vary, depending on the PSF's size within the subsector. This is exemplary shown by different types of added value, generated by small and big consulting firms.

The existence of a problem is an essential trigger to use consulting services. Clients hope that mandating a consulting company will solve problems irrespective of the problem type. In general the added value created by the consulting company lies in the solution of client problems and of problems which emerged during the consulting process.

The assumption that the added value generated by consulting firms was specific has to be questioned in light of the downfall in growth at the beginning of the economic crisis in 2008. Renowned consulting companies like McKinsey, Roland Berger and BCG reported decreases in turnover and drops in profit. However, when taking a closer look at the numbers of the subsector, there are considerable differences regarding the company size. Small consulting firms with a specific focus for example where able to be commercially successful and grow. One explanation lies in a differentiated view on the added value provided by consulting companies of various sizes. Especially in economically difficult times it is necessary to use resources purposefully and as efficiently as possible. Client budgets for consulting services are consequently contracted out to professional service firms which have proven that they have already successfully solved a specific client problem – or ideally several problems – in the same context. Accordingly small consulting companies with precise focus on specific market niches and distinct areas can generate strong competitive advantages.

In view of the added value e.g. the cost basis can be used as an argument. The leading strategy consultancies invoice daily charges starting at about EUR 2000 for a junior employee, while professionals of smaller consulting companies offer their services for a daily rate of EUR 1000. However, price is not necessarily the main and/or decisive criterion for the selection and the generated added value. In case of strategically important problems, which decisively influence company success the key question is, who can address and solve the issue best. Most of the time large consulting companies use alternating team constellations with often less specialized professionals from project to project. Despite intelligently prepared knowledge databases and the pure man power this practice does not always lead to optimum results. Nevertheless image and reputation of generalists can justify mandating and provide added value. Specialist consultancies, the so-called hidden champions' on the other hand have outstanding reputation only in the respective niches they cover. The general public is often not aware of this image; however, it has major impact on the communicability of results. Small consulting companies can frequently profit from their improved market proximity and generate specific added value since the teams of professionals have often worked on comparable tasks in the context of various projects and are thus highly competent regarding their implementation.

3.1   Auditing Firms

The core service 'auditing' includes the audit of year end accounts and consolidated financial statements statutory for stock corporations and other large companies. It is also scrutinized whether the statements meet the respectively valid norms. As subsegment of 'assurance services' the auditing process intends to increase information quality and meet statutory requirements. The American Institute of Certified Public Accountants (AICPA) defines 'assurance services' as 'independent professional services that improve information quality or its context'.[3]

Apart from the year-end account also special audits, such as fraud audits, or audits of financial standing, company assessments as well as consulting with fiscal and economic questions are among the activities of auditing businesses. Many auditing firms have also entered new business segments like tax consulting, management consulting or legal advice as part of the diversification process. The entire service spectrum can be labeled as auditing and consulting with special finance focus.[4]

Globalised, economic processes increasingly require more company specific information, which financial key performance indicators alone cannot provide. What is rather needed is consulting on assessability and optimization potential in the areas financial accounting, internal revision and risk control.

Large and increasingly also small and medium auditing firms have established business areas for these audit-related consulting tasks. The so-called 'advisory' areas provide clients with differentiated services on economic, fiscal and regulatory issues. The consulting spectrum usually covers efficiency and securing of internal business processes as well as the protection and increase of values in a company through internal as well as external growth. The added value for clients can be seen in the combination of management, process, finance, IT consulting and sector know-how.

However, when professionals audit and consult at the same time, there is a risk that the double function endangers both their judgment and their independence. If the two functions are too closely connected this can cause serious problems since the annual statement should be based on a relation of distrust rather than on a personally close and collegial relation of trust.

The work of auditing companies is characterized by a triangular constellation. The auditor functions as an impartial entity between the management of the audited company providing information and the addressee of the statement using that information.[5] The auditing process can be standardized considerably. Standardization is limited though, since the interpretation of laws and accounting standards requires a well-founded judgment on part of the auditor.[6] To collect company information relevant for the audit professionals of the auditing firms cooperate with the company's respective specialist departments. The cooperation is strongly influenced by a jobbing relation (Fig. 3.2).

Many areas of the auditing profession such as training, membership in interest groups and the practice of the profession are subject to statutory regulations. At this point the German professional law shall briefly be outlined to provide an example:

• The entry to the auditing profession is strictly regulated in Germany. Apart from a completed university degree, 3 years of professional experience and a secure

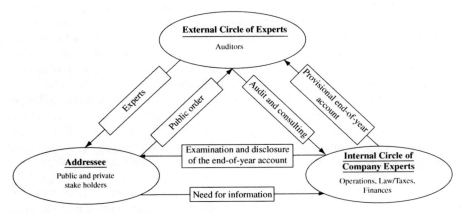

Fig. 3.2 Simplified representation of the triangular connection of auditing companies. (Source: Gillmann and Ruud 2002)

financial situation are expected. Only if these requirements are met, applications to take the certified accountants examination are accepted by the examination board, which is subordinate to the appropriate federal state authority in line with §5 of the auditor's code (WPO).

- Auditors and auditing firms have to be organized in the chamber of auditors. The chamber's responsibility lies in the professional self-supervision. Apart from the auditor's code, the chamber's statutes provide the legal basis in Germany.
- The auditing market is limited by special occupational duties, e.g. in terms of marketing possibilities and the establishment of interdisciplinary partnerships. Ethical norms, like discretion or 'professional conduct' are further requirements for people in the auditing business.[7] In case any rule is violated the chamber is able to apply sanctions. These range from a reprimand to disbarment.

Internationally people in the auditing profession can be seen as 'accountants' in a wider sense. According to the definition of the IFAC (International Federation of Accountants) accountants are 'those persons, whether they are in public practice, industry, commerce, the public sector or education, who are members of an IFAC member body'.[8] Apart from people auditing accounts the term 'accountant' thus includes all professional groups, which work in accounting and are a member of an IFAC organization. The IFAC consequently strives to harmonize national professional rules of conduct and auditing standards to guarantee the quality of international services in the public interest.

The international auditing market is dominated by four big, international auditing and consulting companies, the so-called 'Big Four' (PricewaterhouseCoopers, Deloitte Touche Tohmatsu, Ernst & Young and KPMG) (see Table 3.1).[9] These have to be differentiated from national and local and/or regional providers, which are less represented geographically and have much smaller auditing volumes.

Table 3.1 Largest international auditing firms in terms of annual revenue

	Company	Global turnover (2008 US $m)
1	PricewaterhouseCoopers	28.2
2	Deloitte Touche Tohmatsu	27.4
3	Ernst & Young	24.5
4	KPMG	22.7
5	BDO International	5.1
6	Grant Thornton International	4.0
7	RSM International	3.6
8	Praxity	3.2
9	Baker Tilly International	3.0
10	Crowe Horwath International	2.9

Source: http://www.worldaccountingintelligence.com/index.php (Last updated 7 August 2009)

3.2 Corporate Law Firms

Law firms are considered professional service firms, if their clientele mainly consist of companies, industrial groups or institutions. Their services include attorney's legal advice, in particular in the area economic and tax law and client representation in court, arbitration or before authorities.[10] Depending on the type 'full service firm' or specialized 'boutique' more or less commercial law areas are covered. There is a trend to expand competences with the objective to provide legal services for internationally operating clients. The increasing competition, primarily of British and American 'full service firms', which are moving into regional markets, leads to large corporate law firms developing into 'American-style law firms'. In addition to the classical legal advice and counsel before court they also offer transaction services to their clients. This trend is supported by another factor. Large international auditing firms, especially the 'Big Four', have started to found their own law firms. Furthermore the big players have their own big legal departments, providing services from legal counsel to drafting of contracts and estate planning.

The main interaction partners of corporate law firms are executives of client companies. The skills of the managers in the respective legal areas hereby shape the dominant type of relation. Highly professionalized managers rather work in a sparring mode with corporate law firms than less professionalized client. Interests and needs of client have to be analyzed and interpreted. Only then the question presents itself, what can be achieve from a legal point of view and what approach is economically attractive.

Many areas of the legal profession such as training, membership in interest groups and the practice of the profession are subject to statutory regulations. However, deregulation tendencies can be observed across the entire sector. Depending on the respective country this includes the possibility to take on non-lawyers as partners, the establishment of corporations, increased employment of marketing measures, etc.

In terms of number of lawyers the international top flight consists of the law firms Clifford Chance, Linklaters, Freshfields Bruckhaus Deringer and Baker & McKenzie (see Table 3.2).

3.3 Consulting Firms

Generally speaking consulting can be seen as interactive process with the objective to influence the behavior of clients in the context of a problem solution and – if necessary – also to support clients with the implementation. It can also include the verification and support of management decisions. This is realized by consulting firms providing access to resources and specific knowledge to their clients and by observing the system in question. The theoretical discussion additionally emphasizes the knowledge transfer function as a significant consulting task.

Client problems can be of different nature. To solve problems the client has to select consulting objectives, concepts and methods from a highly heterogeneous

Table 3.2   Largest international law firms in terms of annual revenue

	Company	Global turnover (2007 US $m)
1	Clifford Chance	2660.5
2	Linklaters	2588.5
3	Freshfields Bruckhaus Deringer	2358.5
4	Baker & McKenzie	2188.0
5	Skadden, Arps, Slate, Meagher & Flom	2170.0
6	Allen & Overy	2034.0
7	Latham & Watkins	2005.5
8	Jones Day	1441.0
9	Sidley Austin	1386.0
10	White & Case	1373.0

Source: http://www.law.com/jsp/tal/in_print.jsp (Last updated 7 August 2009)

spectrum. In general, a distinction is made between strategy and organizational consulting as well as IT consulting. While strategy consulting and organizational consulting can be associated with the superordinate management consultancy concept, IT consulting can be further divided in IT consulting in the strict sense and IT services. Admittedly the differentiation between IT service providers and management consultants has recently been softened. Management consultants also provide IT know-how, while IT consulting services meanwhile also contain company-strategic topics. Generally, an overlap of auditing and consulting activities can be found. The partly different focuses of the big international consulting companies as well as inconsistent market definition and intransparency make an international comparison very difficult. Apart from management consulting – in the wider sense – there are also recruitment agencies, IT consultancies and consulting engineers and their various subsectors among the consulting firms' core industry. The service structure in the consulting business can be characterized as follows:

The growing insecurity and dissatisfaction of clients with the quality of services of established consulting companies on the one hand and the profitability of services on the other hand leads to new competitors entering the market for consulting services. They are attracted by low market entry barriers to and relatively low investment costs.

The international big players in the management consultancy area are listed in Tables 3.3 and 3.4.

Client involvement with the provision of consulting services is always important both in case of the management and the IT consulting. However, interaction intensity can vary. The more standardized the consulting service, the higher the probability that the service is provided in the sense of a jobbing relation. Conversely, consulting services requiring strong individualization in terms of client-specific requirements and issues are rather provided in a sparring relation.

In most countries the term 'consultant' is not a legally protected occupational title. There is no standardized training and no discipline-specific academic degree is required. Especially some of the bigger strategy consultancies recruit graduates,

Table 3.3 Largest international management consultancies in terms of annual revenue

	Company	Global turnover (2007 US $m)
1	Deloitte Consulting GmbH	4,927.0
2	KPMG International	4,631.0
3	McKinsey & Co.	3,800.0
4	PriceWaterhouseCoopers	3,112.0
5	Mercer Human Resource Consulting	2,708.0
6	Ernst & Young	2,349.0
7	Accenture	1,912.0
8	Booz Allen Hamilton	1,755.0
9	Crowe Chizek/Horwath International	1,558.0
10	IBM	1,513.0

Source: http://www.consultant-news.com/article_display.aspx?p= adp&id=498 (Last updated 7 August 2009)

Table 3.4 Largest international IT consultancies in terms of annual revenue

	Company	Global turnover (2003 US $m)
1	IBM Global Services	42,636.0
2	Electronic Data Systems	21,502.0
3	Fujitsu	18,080.0
4	Accenture	13,020.0
5	Hewlett-Packard	12,305.0
6	Computer Sciences Corp	11,800.0
7	BT Global Services	11,300.0
8	T-Systems	8,402.0
9	Cap Gemini Ernst & Young	7,047.0
10	NTT Data	7,005.0

Source: http://www.builderau.com.au/news/soa/IT-services-giants-face-slowing-growth/0,339028227,339250363,00.htm (Last updated 7 August 2009)

who do not have economic background, but come with the necessary expertise as 'exotics' (e.g. physicians or theologians). Essential are general intellectual abilities, such as analytical skills and problem solving competence, but also certain other characteristics, like objectivity, discretion, willingness to learn, flexibility and the ability to cope with pressure and behavior, like e.g. communication skills. Due to these ambitious, but also rather general requirements for professionals the sector tries to accelerate the compliance with certain principles via professional organizations and associations. National associations for example can join the International Council of Management Consulting Institutes (ICMCI) to be able to award the CMC (Certified Management Consultant) to professionals. The connected quality standard might be of particular for small and medium consulting firms to increase their level of awareness and improve their reputation. Only in Austria and Canada professionals are subject to clear regulations in terms of qualification and market entry. Elsewhere the lack of professional laws often leads to the consulting subsector not being utterly approved of by the public.

3.4 Recruitment Agencies

At first sight the recruitment agency sector is difficult to define. For a deeper understanding of the sector it helps to differentiate recruitment agencies in a stricter and in a wider sense.[11] When talking about a recruitment agency in the wider sense, one refers to all consulting activities and services, which can be allocated to the human resource sector.[12] Recruitment agencies in the wider sense also contain advice in the areas remuneration systems, management, development, work law etc. Often such services are not only offered by specialized recruitment agencies, but also by broadly positioned consulting firms which also tackle HR related problems for their clients.

The recruitment agency in the stricter sense, offers its services predominantly in the recruitment area. Studies of the Bundesverband Deutscher Unternehmensberater (BDU) show for the German-speaking market that over 80% of the turnover of recruitment agencies is generated in that segment. The core service thus is the support of the client with the search and selection of specialists and executive staff.[13] Recruitment methods can be differentiated as follows:

- On the one hand there is the so-called direct search, where potential candidates are directly and actively contacted by the recruitment agency. Important factors here are the recruitment agency's personal contacts and databases as well as the identification and first contact of candidates.
- On the other hand there is the so-called media-supported search, where candidates are sought via classic ads and recently especially via the internet.

Various people are involved in the recruitment process, as search and selection of executive staff: consultants and employees of the client, but in the end also potential candidates. On the client's side there are board members and/or managing directors, other high-ranking human resource or personnel managers. Depending on the focus of the recruitment agency the candidates are employees of various hierarchy levels, as a rule, however, executive staff members. In total the recruitment agency in the stricter sense tends to have jobbing character, roles and tasks within the process are clearly allocated.

The agency's recruitment process furthermore consists of different phases, which ideal-typically can be summarized as follows:

- At first the structure and culture of clients and the requirements of the position to be filled need to be assessed.

- By referring to the existing or newly collected information potential candidates are identified, interviewed and pre-selected on this basis.
- These candidates are presented to clients and depending on client preferences a personal meeting is scheduled which is often joined by a personnel consultant.
- To support the decision of clients, often additional information on candidates is gathered and the client is accompanied during the final selection process.
- Additionally client contact is being maintained to monitor the success of the respective decision.

Recruitment has meanwhile become an independent service. The origins date as far back as 1926, when Thorndike Deleland in New York started the paid search for sales experts, which by the way coincided with the foundation of one of the most successful management consultancies to this day by James O. Mc Kinsey. During the 40ies and 50ies recruitment consulting turned into an independent subsector. In the 60ies American executive search consultancies started their first European subsidiaries. In the subsequent decades the sector experienced strong growth. Meanwhile 70,000 executive and specialist positions in Germany have been filled by 1800 recruitment agencies. Table 3.5 lists the ten largest international recruitment agencies.

In total the sector is characterized by a high degree of intransparency concerning the recruitment agencies' reliability and professionalism. This is in particular due to low market entry barriers. Neither high capital expenditure, nor a documentation of qualifications is necessary. However, some associations like the federation of German Executive-Search-Consultants (VDESP) in Germany or the association of Executive Search Consultants (AESC) try to accelerate the development of professional standards. As a rule leading recruitment agencies have expressed their commitment to comply with these standards.

Table 3.5 Largest international recruitment agencies in terms of annual revenue

	Company	Global turnover (2006 EUR m)
1	Korn Ferry International	552.90
2	Spencer Stuart	433.70
3	Heidrick & Struggles	415.20
4	Egon Zehnder International	376.10
5	Russell Reynolds	334.10
6	Ray & Berndtson	180.60
7	IIC Partners	107.30
8	Whitehead Mann	75.00
9	DHR International	70.10
10	Highland Partners	63.70

(Source: http://www.workforce.com/tools/hot_list/HotList_0607_17.pdf
(Last updated 07 August 2009))

3.5 Investment Banks

Historically, investment banks have acted as intermediates between supply and demand of capital and have issued and brokered securities ('underwriting'). That business has, however, increasingly lost in significance and at the beginning of the 1990s only accounted for 10% of investment banks' total turnover. A core characteristic of investment banks sill is, that they are allowed – contrary to so-called commercial banks – to perform security transactions, while being excluded from the loan and deposit-taking business.[14] Since the complexity of the services provided by investment banks, however, exceed these tasks by far, it is necessary to take a closer look, which reveals a host of various business segments[15]:

- *Mergers and Acquisitions:* Consulting of clients in case of mergers or takeovers of companies and or their prevention.
- *Corporate Finance or Financial Advisory:* Consulting of companies with funding issues, e.g. emission of equity and loan capital.
- *Structured Finance:* Consulting and management of project funding and financing by selling liability pools.
- *Capital Markets:* Issue and placement of securities, including consulting, takeover of securities and distribution to investors.
- *Sales and Trading:* Advice and support of investors, handling of the resulting trades.
- *Asset Management:* structuring and implementation of portfolio strategies for institutional clients.
- *Principal Investment:* Own investment department of banks within companies with the objective to increase value by influencing in-house business activities.

Depending on the (global) level of involvement in the business segments investment banks can be differentiated.[16] 'Bulge bracket' firms (e.g. Goldman Sachs, Merrill Lynch) work in the entire spectrum of the business, while 'major' (e.g. JP Morgan Chase, Lehman Brothers) or 'submajor bracket' firms (e.g. Bear Stearns) only cover a part of the spectrum and not always on a global scale. In addition there are specialized companies providing services as boutiques e.g. only in case of mergers and acquisitions (e.g. Lazard) or gathering and evaluating information as research firms (e.g. Moody's or Standard & Poor's). During the banking crisis in 2008 all large US investment banks lost their status. In September 2008 the traditional Merrill Lynch bank was taken-over by the Bank of America due to refinancing problems and Lehman Brothers had to file bankruptcy. In March Bear Stearns was forced to accept the sale to the J.p. Morgan Chase group. Also the investment banks Goldman Sachs and Morgan Stanley renounced their legal status as investment bank. Table 3.6 shows the ten largest international investment banks.

It is logical that the kind of cooperation with clients and the service provision process to a high degree depends on the respective business field. Partly the service is provided highly interactively (sparring relation), partly it can be characterized as jobbing relation. Irrespective of the business segments employees are, however,

Table 3.6 Largest international investment banks in terms of closed deals

	Company	Amount of deals 2008	Deal value (US $ b)
1	Goldman Sachs & Co	378	943.1
2	JP Morgan	423	878.1
3	Citigroup	374	847.0
4	Bank of America Merrill Lynch	376	698.0
5	Morgan Stanley	393	667.4
6	UBS	390	615.1
7	Deutsche Bank AG	316	510.2
8	Credit Suisse	358	508.7
9	Barclays Capital	114	382.9
10	Lazard	243	283.5

(Source: http://www.reuters.com/finance/deals/mergers (Last updated 7 August 2009))

the core success factor for investment banks. Recruitment by competitors and the loss of entire teams (including clients) have impressively demonstrated that in the past. Investment banks therefore face particularly high challenges when recruiting junior staff or retaining top performers.[17] There is no independent training-based profession, but there is a typical socialization as investment banker.

3.6 Communication Agencies

Communication, as 'transmission process of messages between a sender and one or several recipients', is the core service that communication agencies provide to their clients – companies or other institutions. Agencies use numerous communication instruments in the process which can be divided into 'above the line' and 'below the line' activities:

- Classical promotional activities like e.g. print, TV and radio advertising are called 'above the line'.
- 'Below-the-line' activities mainly include new communication instruments like e.g. event marketing, interactive media, public relations, direct mailing or sponsoring.

To be able to offer clients effective integrated communication, 'full service agencies' or networks, in which specialized affiliated agencies are providing a comprehensive range of service, have been increasingly developing. The work of classical advertising agencies is often still seen as the 'supreme discipline' of the communication sector.[18] They offer their clients advertising consultancy, planning and conceptual campaign design, as well as development and design of advertizing material and its subsequent implementation.

Since each measure needs to be developed both client as well as product specifically, communication services are to be regarded as 'highly complex consulting products'[19]. Their quality is not only based on specialist knowledge, but especially on creativity. The relations between clients and professionals of communication agencies can be of highly different nature. Primary interaction partners in the provision of PR services are executive staff members of the client, who either work with agency contacts in a sparring or a jobbing mode. In the classical ad sector services are mainly provided in the jobbing mode. Interaction partners in these cases are rather the advertising specialists of the client companies than the top management.[20]

The spectrum of tasks of advertising agency employees is very broad. A total of 25 professions, such as e.g. graphic designer, contacter or media planer can be identified in advertising agencies. The access to the profession and the term 'advertising agency' is not protected in any way. In particular to stand out among the many 'black sheep' operating in the sector, national professional associations offer their members a strong brand and a quality seal.

Due to the limited availability of international results of communication agencies a substantial listing cannot be provided at this point. It can be stated, however, that the group of the largest international communication agencies in 2007 is spearheaded by DDB Worldwide, McCann Worldgroup and Dentsu.

3.7 Engineering Service Providers

The engineering service provider sector plays an increasingly important role in industrial development. However, engineering service providers often work invisibly for the general public. Even for sector insiders it is difficult to gain an overview of the highly heterogeneous industry. This might also be caused by the fact that engineering service providers operate in a variety of fields. Engineering service providers offer their services in the areas engineering, chemical industry, oil and gas production, energy and water supply, microelectronics, paper and automotive industry etc. The spectrum ranges from the generation of product ideas and development and construction to detailing documentation.

The services are mostly provided in classical project business form. Based on client requirements, teams are created and the project is organized. Individual projects, however, can have different scopes. These range from the support by individual employees to the use of individually operating teams. Services are provided either with the client on-site or in the facilities of the engineering service providers. This mainly corresponds with statutory organizational forms for the project business:

- In the context of the supply of temporary work projects are implemented with the clients on-site. The engineering professionals are fully integrated into the client team; remain employed by the engineering service providers though.
- A service provision based on a work contract is also possible, if projects can be easily defined. In such cases the scope and the execution of services are stipulated prior to the project start between engineering service provider and client.

The outlined organizational forms ultimately also determine the interaction form. While intensive communication between engineer and client employees is typical when employees are temporarily hired (these therefore mainly tend to be sparring relations), service based on work contracts can be provided with lower interaction intensity (this kind of project implementation therefore can be rather characterized as jobbing relation). In addition, it needs to be mentioned that engineering service providers are also active in the recruitment sector. In such cases requirement profiles are generated for concrete positions and suitable candidates are sought. The clients are supported when selecting candidates and during their subsequent training period.

The employees of engineering service providers are primarily engineers with different backgrounds. In addition and as a rule, there are also larger numbers of technicians, technical draftsmen and designers. Due to academic degrees and training content the engineering profession can thus be well defined in principle. As a general rule the specific training guarantees a high level of quality of the service provision. Furthermore efforts have been made to catalogue and classify engineering services.

The objective of this chapter was to point out the heterogeneity of the PSF sector. The comprehensive overview of the individual subsectors suggests that strategic management of PSFs is not subject to a general set of rules. This fact, however, also explains the particular appeal of this topic.

The first part of the book provided a comprehensive introduction on the structures and characteristics of the PSF sector, the second part is now dedicated to the management of strategic resources.

Notes

1. See Scott (2001), p. 9 et seq.
2. See Tordoir (1995), p. 139 et seq.
3. See http://www.aicpa.org/pubs/cpaltr/mar97/scasrr.htm (last updated 14 July 2009)
4. See Gillmann and Ruud (2002), p. 18 et seq.
5. See Gillmann and Ruud (2002), p. 19.
6. See Gillmann and Ruud (2002), p. 20.
7. See Tordoir (1995), p. 146.
8. See §§ 9 und 10 of the Auditors' Code (WPO).
9. According to § 57 (1) of the Auditors' Code (WPO).
10. See § 52 Auditors' Code (WPO) and Strambach (1995).
11. See §§ 9 and 13 of the Auditor's Statutes.
12. See www.ifac.org/Members/DownLoads/IAASB_Handbook_2004.pdf (last updated 24 Aug. 2004).
13. On 1 September 2002 Arthur Andersen Deutschland and Ernst & Young merged and are now unified under the single name Ernst & Young.
14. See § 3 of the German Federal Legal Profession Act (BRAO).
15. See Tordoir (1995), p. 147 et seq.
16. See Kraft (2002), p. 19 et seq.
17. See Gaugler (1992), p. 1610 et seq.
18. See Dincher and Gaugler (2002), p. 17 as well as Herbold (2002), p. 195.
19. See Kraft (2002), p. 22.
20. See www.boyden.de (last updated 14 July 2009).

21. See Brinker (1998), p. 20.
22. See Achleitner and Charifzadeh (2001), p. 19 et seq.
23. See Achleitner and Charifzadeh (2001), p. 15 et seq.
24. See Schubert (2001), p. 189 et seq.
25. The term advertising agency is clearly defined neither legally nor factually.
26. See Tillmanns and Jeschke (2000), p. 128.
27. See Tordoir (1995), p. 148.

Part II
Management of Strategic Resources

Chapter 4
Quality Management

Service quality is a strategically important resource in professional service firms. It leads to business deals and – in a second step – generates economic profits. Strong market developments and company diversification have recently put more emphasis on the quality of the services provided as a possible differentiation aspect than before. Only if a professional service firm is able to stand out amongst competitors by continuously delivering quality services, will it be rewarded with the client's trust. This applies even if clients see the purchased service as commodity. Client trust is thus the results, but also the precondition for successful business relations of professional service firms.

Service quality is consequently more and more used as a differentiation characteristic. Driven by the emergence of numerous new businesses and the diversification of large companies the intensity of competition between professional service firms has risen and the 'battle' for clients today is fought significantly more aggressively. The consulting company Accenture, for example, pursues an approach that is new for professional service firms to differentiate themselves from competitors. In large-scale colored newspaper advertisements and even in TV spots the company markets services offered and career opportunities. In the differentiation strategy of many professional service firms the type of services offered increasingly fades into the background in favor of the quality of the service provision. However, it is not enough to simply provide high quality services; clients also need to be aware of the supposed quality advantage compared to competitors.

When selecting a professional service firm and its professionals the perceived quality plays the decisive role. A large part of the assignments is characterized by a complex problem, which is of particular strategic and/or economic significance for the client. At the same time, the results of services vary considerably, thus making it difficult to assess them in advance. With the rising quality of the service provider, the chances that an optimum solution for the company being found also increase.[1] Legal disputes such as Bayer's product liability case around the cholesterol reducer Lipobay in 2001 are a serious economic threat. It might be difficult for companies involved in such disputes to estimate the outcome of the proceedings; however, they

---

Co-author: Bernd Bürger

S. Kaiser, M.J. Ringlstetter, *Strategic Management of Professional Service Firms*,
DOI 10.1007/978-3-642-16063-9_4, © Springer-Verlag Berlin Heidelberg 2011

think that the prospects of success rise by contracting a high-quality law firm and are thus often also prepared to accept higher rates.

To focus the differentiation of the company to such client considerations, it is vital to be aware of the determinants of the quality perceived by the client. Service quality is best described as the result of an assessment process, in that course the client compares the expected service with the one delivered.[2] There are two core factors relevant for the evaluation and/or perception of quality:

- The *actual result* of the service provision decisively influences the perception of quality.[3] A high quality service e.g. would be the one of a headhunter, if the sought employee turned out to be the ideal candidate for the respective position. However, for clients it is often difficult to assess the performance of professional service firms objectively.
- The actual service quality is superimposed by the *subjective perception* of the professional service firm and its employees. The service is provided in close interaction and enables clients to evaluate comprehensively.[4] Furthermore the image and/or reputation of the professional service firm influence quality perception.

In addition to the continuous performance optimization the intermediation and/or communication of quality to (potential) clients thus play a decisive role when providing high quality services. Following the critical resources of a professional service firm the perceived overall quality can be influenced via three approaches (see Fig. 4.1).

Continues development of the knowledge base with targeted knowledge management can help to improve the quality of the service provision (1.1). Strengthening of the relational competence positively influences the quality perceived by clients on two counts. On the one hand it is the precondition in the service provision process that the interaction between client and provider is successful and the service is tailored to the client's needs. On the other hand it helps to convey quality during client interaction since it can also be seen as ability to display appropriate conduct

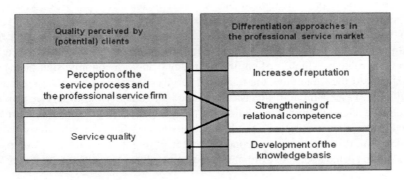

Fig. 4.1 Approaches to influence the perceived quality. (Source: Adapted from Ringlstetter et al. 2004, p. 143)

(1.2). The development of reputation in this context solely serves the purpose to improve the perception of the professional service firm with current and potential clients (1.3).

4.1 Increase of Service Quality

A central approach to improve service quality is strengthening and extending the knowledge base.[5] This knowledge base may not only be understood as abstract construct; it rather has to be outlined in light of the specific challenges in professional service firms (1). With the insight gained in the process it can be considered how the knowledge base can be further developed (2).

4.1.1 Knowledge in Professional Service Firms

Knowledge is a blend of skills generated by information and experience that, however, only gain relevance for a company, if it is action-oriented, i.e. bears fundamental significance for the business of the respective company.[6] Essential for professional service firms is a particular technical, but at the same time also client-specific knowledge. Technical know-how represents the essential basis, to develop methods and solve complex problems. It can be characterized with various features[7]:

- It is based on generally applicable, scientific knowledge, that forms the heuristics to analyze, assess and tackle complex situations and personal creativity that helps to solve complex problems as determinant of the generation of ideas.[8]
- The objective is to reduce the complexity of the client problem by breaking it down to various, less complex subtasks. The so called 'professional trick' is thus to split complex, unique tasks into subtasks that have already been tackled before and can hence be solved by implementing routines that have proven efficient.
- Complex tasks can only be comprehensively tackled if the expert knowledge of the professional service firm and/or of the professional is used in context rather than in an isolated perspective. That means that stimuli from related knowledge areas do not only have to be welcomed, but should also be used in a targeted manner.

Client knowledge is the second core component of the knowledge base of professional service firms. What is meant here is not the knowledge of clients that definitely contributes to the development of technical knowledge through learning from experience, but rather the knowledge about the client. This is required in particular to achieve 'client specific judgment' and to optimize client relations. Three categories have to be differentiated in that context[9]:

- General comprehension of the respective sector,
- Detailed knowledge about the client company and

• Personal knowledge on key staff members such as decision makers and information providers in the client company.

Technical and client specific knowledge can be available in companies or beyond at different levels. The direct interaction makes employees of professional service firms the first to acquire new knowledge about the client and from the client. However, knowledge can be on a higher aggregation and can thus be accessible as organizational knowledge to all employees of the professional service firm or in another stage to all members of a sector and/or profession (see Fig. 4.2). Of course not only individual professionals, but also all auditors are aware of the methodical approach of an audit due to the training standards monitored by central bodies such as the chamber of auditors

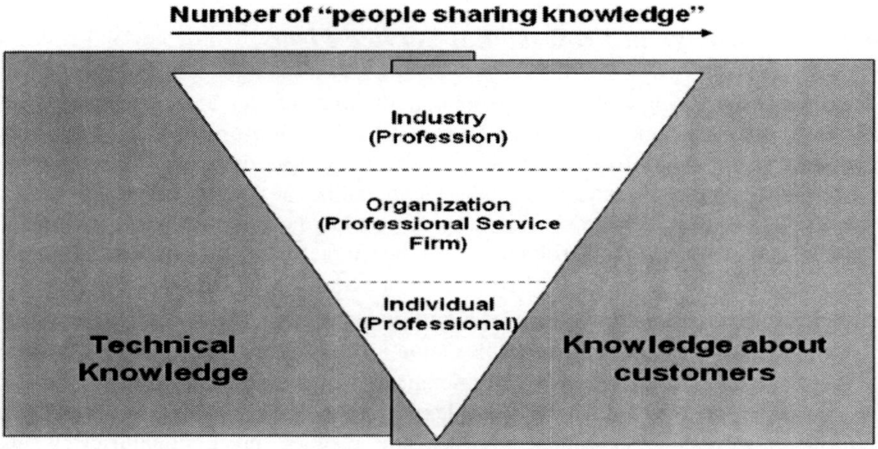

Number of "people sharing knowledge"

Fig. 4.2 Knowledge types and distribution in professional service firms. (Source: Adapted from Ringlstetter et al. 2004, p. 145)

4.1.2 Knowledge Strategies for Professional Service Firms

To avoid weakening of the knowledge work quality of a professional service firm and/or to improve it, the knowledge basis needs to be constantly renewed on an individual and organizational level. It is not the knowledge as such that provides competitive advantage via outstanding quality but rather the company's ability to create and distribute new knowledge to be able to use it to solve the problems at hand. This statement is currently underlined by a rapidly decreasing half-life period of knowledge, i.e. the duration in that relevance and validity of knowledge lose half their value.

A major precondition for the optimum use of knowledge is the exchange of knowledge between the people involved and the connected transition from individual to organizational knowledge. This firstly applies since intellectual assets profit from their use in contrast to capital assets. If such knowledge is adequately stimulated, it grows exponentially when in common possession.[10] Secondly, an early transfer can prevent employees from leaving the company as 'knowledge monopolists' and thus extract key knowledge. This is why knowledge management concepts tackle the issue of transferring knowledge in professional service firms.

The exchange of implicit knowledge is of special significance and at the same time represents a big challenge. It lies in 'personal experiences, subjective findings, values and emotions'.[11] Implicit knowledge, like the creativity of an employee or information on a vital decision-maker on part of the client contributes considerably to the solution of complex problems in professional service firms; however, it is embedded in the mind of the carrier and can only be activated by implementing the carrier's plans of action. Direct articulation is thus difficult. Explicit knowledge on the other hand, like facts or concepts, can be articulated and thus transferred more easily.[12]

Based on this concept of various knowledge types two different strategies can be used for the knowledge management in professional service firms[13]:

- The *codification strategy* focuses on the use of IT systems. Explicit – and as far as possible also implicit – knowledge is being systematically codified here and saved in databases so that any legitimized employee of the company can access it.
- When using a *personalization strategy* on the other hand implicit knowledge is mainly transferred via direct interaction of employees. This allows knowledge transfer as 'socialization process' based on observation, imitation and practice.[14] IT systems here only have a supporting role in the communication.

A *codification strategy* opens up possibilities to integrate scale effects via multiple use of knowledge and hence to expand business activities. Companies such as Ernst & Young or Accenture implement this strategy by using a 'people-to-documents' approach. Ralph Poole, director of the Ernst & Young Center for Business Knowledge (founded in 1993) describes this method as follows: 'After removing client-sensitive information, we develop "knowledge objects" by pulling key pieces of knowledge such as interview guides, work schedules, benchmark data, and market segmentation analyses out of documents and storing them in the electronic repository for people to use.'[15] The Ernst & Young intranet, also known as 'Ernst & Young Knowledge Web' (Kweb) is hereby of key significance. Here the employees of the company can access knowledge worldwide, without having to interact with other employees.

With the *personalization strategy* companies like Bain, The Boston Consulting Group or McKinsey concentrate on another point. The focus here lies in the interaction between individuals and not in the knowledge saved in databases. It can be transferred using various channels like brainstorming sessions, meetings, and teamwork or telephone conferences. When resorting to this strategy the implementation of interpersonal networks is essential. In the sense of 'know-who' relevant implicit knowledge can only be exchanged, if it is clear, who has the respective information. Many professional service firms thus try to further develop networks.[16]

McKinsey for example also supports employee transfer between individual locations to increase the contact network. In addition McKinsey's work is shaped by a 'rapid-response' culture. An unwritten rule is that all enquiries are supposed to be responded to with 24 hours. Technical solutions such as telephone, email, intranet or databases support the knowledge transfer process, by either simplifying communication or assisting in the search for experts with Bain's 'people finder' databases.

Both knowledge strategies are applicable in parallel, professional service firms should, however, decide on which strategy they favor. There are considerations on consulting firms concerning this matter that assume an 80:20 rule. Eighty percent of the knowledge is transferred using one strategy, 20% using the strategy the other.[17] In the Web 2.0 age the differentiation of strategies, however, increasingly plays less of a role.

As key knowledge carriers employees have to be mobilized to implement the selected strategy. To achieve this, knowledge transfer barriers have to be dismantled. Particularly difficult is the interdisciplinary knowledge transfer between professionals, who often regard themselves to be part of an elite with own cultural values.[18] On part of the knowledge sender the ability and willingness to share need to be increased. The recipient on the other hand needs to be able and willing to absorb the knowledge. This can be realized in different ways. Merryl Lynch employees are motivated to exchange knowledge – similar to the situation in other professional service firms – by connecting remuneration and evaluation of the professionals to peer relationship criteria.

4.2 Development and Use of Social Competence

Apart from a solid knowledge basis the development of client relations considerably affects the perceived quality. There are various client relation types and/or structures that are interdependent, however, vary in terms of organization (see Fig. 4.3).

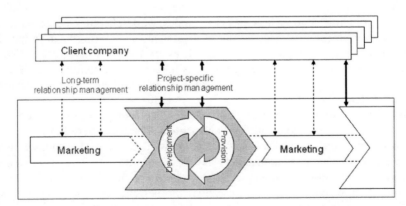

Fig. 4.3 Types and organization of client relations. (Source: Adapted from Ringlstetter et al. 2004, p. 148)

While *project specific relation management* solely focuses on organizational aspects when dealing with a specific client assignment, *long-term relation management* goes beyond such focusing on individual episodes.

Irrespective of the temporal focus there are two levers to increase the quality perceived by the client. On the one hand the actual service quality can be improved by optimizing the service provision and development (1). However, this does not suffice, if the client is not aware of the improvements. The client relation has thus to be used to communicate quality and hence to improve the perception of the service and of the professional service firm (2).

4.2.1 Approaches to Increase Service Quality

A constitutive feature of knowledge-intensive services is the close cooperation between professional service firm and clients, the integration of the client as an external factor. The information flow of the professional service firm to the client is equally important for the client-specific problem solution as the information flow in the opposite direction that in conclusion leads to reciprocal interdependence. The client becomes a 'temporal employee' since he contributes the necessary 'raw materials' to the service provision process.[19] Architects, for example, depend on client information when planning new company headquarters. No architectural office would get involved in the tendering process without having gathered information on the decision-makers' preferences, and the objective and problem areas of the construction project. To be able to integrate wishes and knowledge of clients in the service provision the consulting company McKinsey thus uses interviews with client employees as core method. Here the relational competence of the interviewer, his personal approach to the interview is crucial to the amount and quality of the information provided by the client.[20]

Although professional services are generally described as highly relation-intensive there are differences in the interaction characteristics. Two types can typically be differentiated in that context[21]:

- In a *sparring relation* the professional tries to put himself in the client's shoes to grasp his problems. He will then use technical and client knowledge to tailor a specific solution. The service provision process is often characterized by strong reciprocal interaction. Client and consultant alternate in taking over the role of the leader and the follower. Information is typically exchanged on the same hierarchical level.
- *Jobbing relations* can be observed in particular if the required knowledge is highly specialized and the client also has a decent amount of expertise in the respective area. In this case, the client is responsible for a complex project and uses professional service firms to outsource and coordinate subtasks in a targeted manner. The interaction in the service provision may (but does not have to) be equally intensive as in a *sparring relation*.

Often both relation types can be found in professional service firms. It was however possible to allocate various subsectors in an empirical study.[22] According to this study the work of strategy, organization, and financial consultancies is rather characterized by *sparring relations*. The services in auditing firms, marketing agencies, market research institutes, engineering offices and IT service providers are provided in a *jobbing mode*. The businesses legal consulting, recruitment, communication and PR consulting are hybrid forms. To improve the perceived service quality the client relation has to be analyzed and optimized regarding its intensity and the respective understanding of roles. It has to be intensive enough to develop 'client-specific judgment', it must not overused and thus become inefficient though.

The interaction with the client is however not the sole core factor for the service provision but it also considerably effects the development of the service offered. This has to be highly adapted to client requirements. The cooperation during the service provision process should therefore be used to identify and anticipate such needs and to generate ideas for new services in line with client requirements.

4.2.2 Approaches to Increase Quality Perception

High quality service provision does not automatically lead to client satisfaction; it has to be communicated between clients and professionals both in the long-term relation and in project specific-interaction.

One approach to systematize client relations and to improve the marketing of companies is *relationship marketing*. It provides a suitable basis to actively shape the relationship between professional service firms and their clients. It is based on the idea that key clients are focused on and continuously seen to and thus remain loyal.[23] The main objective is to influence both the current behavior as well as future intentions of a 'profitable' client towards a provider in a way suited to stabilize or extend the relationship.[24] This includes the possibilities of repeated assignments, cross-selling or recommendation. Such client loyalty is thus of vital importance since it opens up good growth and profit possibilities in the long term. On the one hand, it causes considerably lower sales and marketing costs as the alternative acquisition of prospects.[25] On the other hand, especially in the professional service sector that is characterized by a high level of insecurity, positive word-of-mouth advertising can help to generate new contracts. Such loyalty effects can be achieved if the client is aware of relation-specific advantages, the so-called 'relational benefits.' This can be of psychological and/or emotional, social, or economic type or be based on a strong dependence on the provider's knowledge.[26] Personal relationships among decision-makers of a client and employees of a professional service firm, for instance, or habits can have a decisive influence on the establishment of long-term and intensive cooperation. Since especially social and emotional aspects play a crucial role, investments in the development of such relationships pay off in the long term.

The considerations on *relationship marketing* merge the whole continuum from individual client transactions to long-term exchange relations in one concept.[27] To optimize the client relation management, it is vital to recognize individual relationship phases and to implement phase-specific measures. A division in assignment or project-specific and long-term relations provides a foundation in that context. In case of long-term relationships it is possible to further differentiate between the phase prior to and after the contract.

In case of the *project specific client relation* the quality perceived by the client is significantly influenced during the actual service provision. What is decisive here is 'any episode in that the client comes into contact with any aspect of the organization and gets an impression of the quality of its service'.[28] Due to its special significance for the provision of services, such client contacts are also called 'moments of truth.' Apart from 'non personnel-related' elements such as office equipment, personnel-related elements are of particular importance since they are tangible, i.e. directly detectable for the client.[29] The 'service experience' is determined to a considerable degree by the behavior, reliability, helpfulness, empathy and competence of employees.

When providing professional services, there are typically a large number of such project-related contacts that bear the chance, but also the risk, to have decisive impact on the quality image of the professional service firm. Competent performance can thus be a possibility to create trust and client satisfaction. In this context it should be noted that client expectations and preferences vary in terms of the appearance of professionals. This can manifest in sector- as well as in interaction-specific differences:

- The rules of conduct of the individual professional service firm sector can differ strongly from each other. While clients of investment banks, company consultants or lawyers are expected to wear a suit and to demonstrate an appearance that is often perceived as stiff, 'creatives' of the advertising agencies are rather expected to create an open atmosphere and to wear a 'trendy' outfit.
- Every interaction should be characterized by a clear role allocation to avoid misunderstandings and irritations. While the client rather takes on the role of the leader in jobbing relations, he should rather feel as a partner or follower in a sparring relation.

Supplementary to these transaction-specific deliberations, the *long-term client relations* also have to be shaped actively. These are developed parallel to the actual service provision, but also prior to and after individual projects. In the sense of indirect marketing, relationships can be consolidated and can support the long-term loyalty of strategic clients. In contrast to the service provision process, these interactions happen in particular among the decision-makers of the client and the partners of professional service firms, while the 'moments of truth' are rather experienced in the contact of project employees of all parties involved.

To generate long-term profitability, new (potential) clients should be rated concerning their strategic significance in three steps, also between various assignments. Firstly, client information can be gathered and analyzed, then a selection and prioritization can be chosen and finally suitable measures for the organization of the relation with the respective clients can be determined.[30] Apart from the criteria already outlined, such as possibilities of a new assignment, cross-selling or recommendation, also the questions whether the client or the specific project can help to increase the knowledge basis of the professional service firm or to improve its reputation should be considered when rating clients regarding their long-term significance. Numerous quantitative, but also qualitative methods, such as the 'client lifetime value' approach can be used when determining the long-term client value.[31] Only based on these considerations should it be determined that investments, both in terms of HR as well as financially be made in the respective relation.

The stage following the actual service provision is described as 'bridge phase' to long-term client retention.[32] Here the client satisfaction can be determined and even improved. Warranties, regular follow-up visits or ideally maintenance contracts are often door openers for further assignments and help to keep the professional service firm in the so-called 'evoked set', i.e. amongst the preferred providers of the client.[33]

4.3 Reputation and Trust as Long-Term Quality Criteria

Another approach to convey and/or communicate quality, towards existing and potential, new clients, is reputation. It has key significance for the selection process of the client as well as for professional service firms (1). There are numerous types of reputation and possibilities to convey quality information to the market (2). While the reputation of the professional service firm targets the client, trust reflects the positive client attitude towards the professional service firm. The development of trust is a complex and long process (3).

4.3.1 The Significance of Reputation in Professional Service Firms

'If you lose dollar for the firm by bad decisions, I will be very understanding. If you lose reputation for the firm I will be ruthless.'[34] With these words the world-famous financier Warren Buffet explained to investment bankers how important reputation was for the company's success when he was interim CEO of Salomon Brothers. Reputation is here the general assessment of the company by its stakeholders, like clients, investors, employees or society. Reputation can shape market differentiation for professional services for two reasons:

- Effects of reputation
- Suitability as quality surrogate when selecting a professional service firm

When complex and sometimes also unpopular decisions are made there can be uncertainty whether the company is on the right path and how this decision can be communicated to and/or legitimized towards employees, clients and others. Cooperation with a professional service firm, that has an outstanding reputation in the respective field, provides the possibility of avoiding such insecurity. In this case clients borrow the reputation of the professional service firm for a certain project.[35] When annual accounts have to be audited, renowned auditing companies are not only preferred due to their special qualifications, but also because the employment of such companies particularly helps to signal the correctness and regularity of the information to the outside world. Furthermore the employment of high-reputation professional service firms like McKinsey or Goldman Sachs can even help to improve the reputation of the client if the cooperation and/or the membership in this elite circle have positive effects.[36]

The main significance of reputation of professional service firms however lies in the role as quality surrogate in the selection process of the clients. Due to their complexity and the economic significance for the client professional services are considered high credence goods. Typically there are hardly any search criteria for such services that allow clients to select a suitable provider.[37] The service quality and thus the quality of the choice are revealed, if at all, only after conclusion of contract. The consequences of having hired a new employee through a headhunter or of a strategic reorientation of a company only show in the long-term and can thus not be assessed immediately after the project conclusion. In particular, since clients often do not have a reference value, i.e. the response to the question what result the competing provider would have achieved.

The resulting information advantage prior to the conclusion of contract concerning the characteristics of a professional service firm leads to clients often using the quality feature reputation as 'substitute code'[38] for correctness when purchasing professional services. The client bases his expectations regarding the performance of the professional service firm on the past experience of other clients and thus partly compensates his insecurity. In this context reputation is a feedback pool and thus the trust already gained by the professional service firm.[39] This indirect communication form between clients is particularly credible and valid for two reasons.[40] One the one hand, such non-commercial information is not influenced by the providers' interests and as a rule reflects the actual performance perceived by the client. On the other hand, they are suited for a realistic assessment of the company, since they are rather conservative. This is attributed to the fact that negative experiences are much more frequently communicated than positive experiences and thus allow a critical assessment.[41] Also, after conclusion of contract, the reputation of a provider serves as a guarantor for high service quality. Each client holds a part of the reputation collateral and could damage it by communicating negative information.[42] No professional service firm is willing to take this risk and will thus dispense with opportunistic behavior that can have detrimental effects on the client.

4.3.2 Types of and Approaches to Increase Reputation

With reference to their reputation in particular *generalists* and *specialists* and character–based and institution-based types can be differentiated.[43]

- *Specialists* built reputation by focusing. They are famous for their ability to offer a specific service often faster and better than competitors.

- *Generalists* on the other hand use a broad service spectrum to improve their reputation. They provide clients with the opportunity to receive several services in one go and thus to lower transaction costs.[44] Via diversification reputation already developed in one field can be expanded to new service areas. However, such broad focus also comes with the risk of losing the existing reputation. Jürgen Kluge, Head of McKinsey Germany, comments in that context: 'The bigger we become and the more broadly positioned we are, the higher the risk of losing our standing in an emergency.'[45]

The client perception, however, does not only depend on the focus of the service spectrum, but also on the role of individual professionals. Reputation can thus be either shaped by the institution as a whole or by individual characters that create a sense of identity.

The general image of some professional service firms is rather tied to an individual than to the institution. Roland Berger, founder of the consulting company Roland Berger Strategy Consultants, increased the reputation of the company with numerous public appearances particularly in Germany. Individual characteristics of a person and company reputation are highly interdependent. Bernd Michael, employee of 36 years and today the leading executive of the German branch of the advertising agency Gray shaped the company name unlike anyone else. His distinct feature, a red tie matches the logo and the connection is so close that he has already been addressed as 'Mr. Gray' more than 50 times.[46]

On the other hand, reputation is often characterized by the institution and is connected to a company name or a logo. In this case the whole staff and the work processes of the company help to change the public image. The consulting company McKinsey, e.g. is still today connected to the 'cost cutter' image and many still associate with the consulting company The Boston Consulting Group, the portfolio matrix of the early 1970s.

A number of approaches might prove to be an effective way to increase the reputation of a professional service firm. There are various possibilities to signal key information on the company to stakeholders.[47] Based on this information, stakeholders – in particular (potential) clients – are able to assess reputation. It is, however, essential to select measures matching the identity and the characteristics of the professional service firm so that stakeholders are presented with a consistent image. In particular, professional service firms that have a characteristic-based reputation will resort to other measures, namely focusing on the respective person as such with an institution-based reputation. A selection of approaches outlines the variety of possibilities:

- *Appearance of Employees:* Professionals are the figureheads of professional service firms, both towards clients but also for other interest groups. Their behavior when directly interacting with clients, as well as their involvement when giving speeches and launching publications or participations in contests or other popular appearances helps to coin the reputation.

- *Alumni Contacts:* Not only current but also former employees can consolidate reputation, image and the influence of the professional service firm.[48] A prerequisite for this is certainly a good relationship to the Alumni employee and his or her long-term satisfaction. Companies like McKinsey have also long been profiting from the targeted development of Alumni networks.[49]
- *PR Management:* Apart from current and former employees, the press decisively influences the public image. It is thus important to establish journalist contacts at an early age and to release information to the public in a targeted manner.
- *Performance Guarantees:* Professional service firms provide services that are often highly cost-intensive as well as of special economic significance for the client. Especially in such cases service guarantees or success-related remuneration can create trust and increase the reputation.[50]
- *Crisis Management:* Reputation is one of the key resources of a professional service firm. In case of a crisis it can make sense to pay fines and thus limit the reputation damage. In 1992 and 1993 the auditing firms Arthur Anderson and Ernst & Young paid millions of dollars in the USA to dispel any suspicions of negligent audit in public as fast as possible.[51]
- *Advertisements:* Also ads of professional service firms could recently be increasingly spotted in newspapers and even on TV. In particular the consulting company Accenture increases their presence this way and profits from the prominence. However individual professional service subsectors such as law firms, auditing firms or tax advisors only have limited possibilities to market their services. Tax advisors, for example, may solely address their clientele about their services in an informative and factual manner.[52]

When differentiating professional service firms, the quality perceived by the client is thus becoming ever more significant. Companies like investment banks have already taken a step towards a commodity and can no longer only use their service spectrum to stand out from their competitors, but have to demonstrate 'how hard they work, ... how fast they are and ... how ethical they are',[53] i.e. by presenting service quality. Any effort to improve the performance or to change the client perception should however be made in consideration of the proportionality. The reputation of the professional service firm can be damaged if the company is not able to implement the quality signals that were communicated to the client.[54]

If the professional service firm manages to provide consistently high-quality services, it is rewarded with client trust. This trust on part of the client is a key success factor for knowledge-intensive professional service firms, as the following paragraph shows.

4.3.3 Trust as Success Factor for Knowledge-Intensive Service Providers

As already outlined, professional services have a host of characteristics that make them susceptible to specific risks for the recipient. The success of professional service firms therefore depends not least on the *trust* of the recipient of the service. Despite the conceptual ambiguity of the concept trust it thus appears desirable for knowledge-intensive service providers to understand that mechanisms are suited to create and develop trust on the part of the client. This is at least the case when assuming that the development of trust can be influenced.

In the following it is outlined, based on the constitutive characteristics of knowledge-intensive services, why they are risk afflicted and why trust therefore plays a major role (a). Subsequently, a heuristic approach is suggested that helps to understand the development of trust in the provision of knowledge-intensive services. The interaction of service employees and clients is hereby of decisive significance (b).

4.3.3.1 The Risk of Knowledge-Intensive Services

The goods provided by professional service firms are at first only a contractually agreed commitment. The consequent implementation, however, is – ex ante – relatively open despite the contractualization. Even after the service provision – ex post – it is difficult to define the attributes relevant for the purchase of the knowledge-intensive service. Knowledge-intensive services are so-called credence and/or contract goods.[55]

Such goods typically are subject to special information and insecurity problems, since seller and client assess and agree on services that are not yet provided and that often remain unclear due to the complex and structured problems in connection with their provision. The high-quality character of the expected service implies that the information and insecurity problems (or this information and these security problems) are particularly relevant. A closer look reveals that the above-mentioned information and insecurity problems can be divided in two subcategories:

- Firstly the recipient of the service is systematically insecure when it comes to the actual performance of the professional service firm. The concrete danger lies in the suboptimal selection of a service provider. A poorly selected professional service firm might possibly not be able to provide the service with the desired quality or within an acceptable period of time. In this context this is called 'performance risk'.[56]
- Secondly the recipient of the service is confronted with the insecurity whether the service provider has sufficient commitment. There is the immanent risk of opportunistic behavior in the sense of a 'relational risk'.[57] The commitment of the professional service firm might turn out to be insufficient only after conclusion of contract and the service provider take advantage of dependencies already developed. Such dependencies can result from high switching costs that can be caused by investments already made, like, for example, in training measures of an external service provider for company-specific systems. A service provider, aware of these dependencies, can resort to client-adverse behavior (like renegotiation of rates etc.) and thus increase the total usage cost of external services.[58]

The outlined insecurities can be partly reduced by establishing institutional pro-fessions, as can be found e.g. in legal consulting or with auditors. The insecurity in these cases is attenuated through quality standard monitoring of controlling bodies or also the social acceptance of professional ethics. In other cases, however, like, for example, with consulting companies, such mechanisms to reduce insecurity do not exist.

Due to the above-mentioned insecurities concerning performance and commit-ment of professional service firms companies are only prepared to use the range of services, if they trust the performance and commitment of the professional service firm.

In reference to the term trust it can be said that in the application-oriented field of business studies the term has been causing a great deal of conceptual conmerger.[59] Trust is more than just the confidence in the performance of the professional service firm. Exceeding the mere attribution of performance the trust construct includes primarily relational aspects. This also applies for the expectations that the service providers and/or their employees refrain from displaying opportunistic behavior. Furthermore the discussion of the trust construct proves the existence of various reference objects that can be trusted. In this particular case these could be either individual employees and/or teams of the professional service firm, or in broader definition also the professional service firm as an institution.

Regarding the function of trust it can be stated that trust can, but does not have to be interpreted as instrumental-rational concept. Against the background of a social exchange model trust at the end of the day is a transfer of control rights in sit-uations, that are insofar as fraught with risk as knowledge on the actions of the person one is dealing with and a return service is temporally shifted.[60] This descrip-tion of the situation comes fairly close to the relationship of service provider and recipient. However, a point to bear in mind is that trust is not a coordination or control mechanism as generally understood. Trust rather allows coordination mech-anisms like spontaneous self-determination and self-organization in the first place. However, the inherent problems of these coordination mechanisms are not automat-ically solved in the process. Instead it is only to be expected that trust increases the motivation to improve the exchange of information and to display cooperative behavior.[61]

In literature, various ideas on the development of trust can be found. Three dif-ferent sources of trust are distinguished in the following that, to a greater or lesser extent, are based on information related to the past[62]:

- Firstly trust can be based on perceived personal characteristics and similarities (characteristic-based trust). This source of trust might probably only play a sub-ordinate role in case of knowledge-intensive services since characteristics are very hard to perceive and personal similarities in many cases do not exist.
- Secondly trust can develop from institutions stabilizing behavior (institutional-based trust). This might apply for professional service firms at least if institutions exist that guarantee professional organizations or bodies and quality features (e.g. bar associations).

- Thirdly, this is the reason for the particular relevance of the interactions process as source of trust (process-based trust). In this interaction-based perspective trust develops from personal information about past behavior.[63] Even if this source of trust – at least at firsts sight – does not appear relevant for the first contact between service provider and recipient, already the first encounter is a potential source of trust.

4.3.3.2 Development Mechanisms of Trust

The *service encounter* determines the interaction of the service provider with the client. It is often also called 'moment of truth'. In the following the term *service encounter* is outlined in a broader definition, which includes both person and non-person-related contact points.[64]

In this way, not only the person-related interaction is regarded an element of the *service encounter*, but also the environment in which this interaction takes place. The *service encounter* can thus be understood as entirety of the clients' interaction processes and resources with the employees and resources of the service provider. These resources can have both material and immaterial character. Furthermore the question of visibility is a decisive element for the client. The *service encounter* equals the entirety of all service processes, which can be observed by the client, i.e. the ones lying above an imaginary 'line of visibility'.

The process-based and visible character of the *service encounter* means that from a client perspective this is often perceived as the actual service. The perceived client satisfaction thus causally and directly depends on the experienced, individual 'moment of truth'. This is how the client assesses the service quality as well as the image of the company and thus determines the company development and profitability with repeated purchases in the long term. The interaction of the employees of the provider with the ones of the recipient plays a particularly important role in the development of past-related trust in the behavior of the service provider.

Based on the idea of the interaction-based development of trust heuristic approaches towards complex development mechanisms are developed in the following.[65]

Based on the proposed heuristic approach four interaction levels can be differentiated (see Fig. 4.4). Each element of a superordinate interaction level is constituted by the respective elements of the subordinated level.

The lowest level is formed by individual actions, i.e. phone calls or personal meetings between employees of the professional service firm and clients. These individual actions are only individual elements of an episode (e.g. a purchase negotiation) that results from the linking of interdependent individual actions and often contains typical exchange processes. Above the episode level there is another interaction level that is here named 'sequence'. Examples for a sequence are a joint project, the establishment of a facility or a joint product. Only a row of sequences forms and stabilizes a relationship between service and client company. In this connection it also has to be taken into account that professional service firms maintain a whole portfolio of relations with clients simultaneously or sequentially.

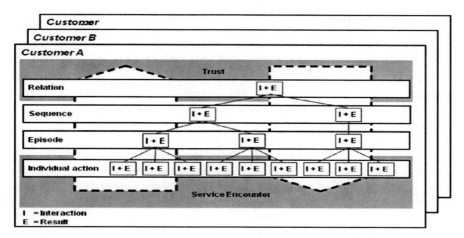

Fig. 4.4 Development of trust towards knowledge-intensive service companies. (Source: Adapted from Holmlund 2004, p. 281)

In addition to the differentiation of various interaction levels, a differentiation is also made regarding process aspects one the one hand and result aspects on the other. Each element, whether individual action, episode, sequence or relation, can be regarded as an individual interaction process (I) leading to a result (E) (see Fig. 4.4). At the end of the day trust therefore develops through the aggregated interaction results and processes reached with the respective partner on all interaction levels.

Key element in the development of trust remains an element of *externalization*.[66] In the context of the interaction the individuals involved can mutually observe and experience their cognitive and affective processes; foreigners turn into partners. The interaction processes, in particular on the level of individual actions, in this development model form the basic elements for trust. The leading role of every individual service encounter in the development of trust is hereby underlined.

The episodes consisting of several individual actions and/or the sequences consisting of various episodes have their significance particularly with a potentially reachable temporal *stabilization* of trust. They are virtually the cause of a *habitualization* over time. The client is building the trust that the service provider is able to solve problems in general, i.e. now and also in future (competence) while acting legitimately (omission of opportunistic behavior).[67]

Habitualization of trust is accompanied and complemented by the process of institutionalization of trust: The development of trust that at first is rather focused on personal relationship and subjective observations is stabilized organizationally over time. This trust difmerger leads to the existence of organizational trust on the interaction level of the relationship. In addition it should also be stressed that the communication of trust allows the development something exceeding the client portfolio of the service provider that is generally referred to as *reputation*.

The heuristics for the development of trust in the area of knowledge-intensive service considers both the level of the individuals involved as well as the organizational level. Due to the temporal and hierarchical linking of differentiable interaction processes and results both levels eventually merge. The development of mutual, organizational trust is thus an emergence process, i.e. a process of collectivization of personal trust in several organization members and over a longer period of time. This process is no longer completely reducible to the individual service encounter, however its origin with lies in it. Ultimately, it is the organizational trust that allows the client to handle information asymmetries and insecurities in the sense of a complexity reduction.[68]

Looking ahead, two implications for trust as success factor of professional service firms can be derived. Firstly knowledge-intensive professional service firms face the challenge to create experience and interaction-based trust on part of the client already at the first encounter. This applies at least if trust at the first contact cannot be substituted by reputation that already exists. The same applies subsequently for all other contacts between service provider and client, whereby personally experienced interaction replaces the general reputation a little at a time.

The fact that individual, negatively perceived interactions can suddenly destroy workiously achieved trust can be considered a problem. Professional service firms therefore secondly face the challenge, to avoid such negatively connoted interactions. If this proves impossible, the existence of the company can be at risk.

The second, rather critical comment regarding the success factor refers to the fact that trust only develops in the visible part of the service; at the same time however, a number of activities of the professional service firm remain invisible and thus unclear for the client. If the transparency level for the client is too high in an attempt to improve trust this can have adverse effects on the company's profitability. Building a trust relationship between a professional service firm and a client does therefore not mean to disclose all principles of one's own business model. This is ultimately the point where the line for trust as success factor for knowledge-intensive professional service firms has to be drawn.

Notes

1. See Ryoo (1990), p. 4.
2. See Grönroos (1984), p. 37 et seq.
3. Grönroos calls this quality component 'technical quality'. See Grönroos (1984), p. 38 et seq.
4. Grönroos describes this quality component as 'functional quality'. Grönroos (1984), p. 39. Gummesson examined numerous professional service firms in the context of a study and found that quality 'becomes a matter of a subjectively perceived quality ... also influenced by the professional's ability to sell himself and to sell his results'. In this sense the customer also buys trust; see Gummesson (1988), p. 4.
5. Also see Chap. 5 in this book.
6. See Rasiel and Friga (2001), p. 74 et seq.
7. See Tordoir (1995), p. 20 et seq.
8. The balanced application of factual knowledge and intuition is often described as the basis of McKinsey & Company's success. See Rasiel and Friga (2001), p. 50.
9. See Empson (2001b), p. 842.
10. See Quinn et al. (1996), p. 99.
11. See Seufert and Seufert (1998), p. 76.

12. Regarding implicit and explicit knowledge, see Nonaka et al. (1997), p. 71 et seq.
13. Hansen et al. (1999) outline the two different knowledge strategies using company consultancies as an example.
14. See Nonaka et al. (1997), p. 84 et seq.
15. See Hansen et al. (1999), p. 108.
16. See on this matter also Chaps. 9 and 13 in this book.
17. See Hansen et al. (1999), p. 112.
18. See Quinn et al. (1996), p. 100.
19. See Mills et al. (1983), p. 120.
20. See Rasiel and Friga (2001), p. 70 et seq.
21. See Tordoir (1995), p. 139 et seq. Apart from the two types sparring and jobbing Tordoir also describes a third type (sales), however he clla this type rather atypical for professional service firms.
22. See Tordoir (1995), p. 139 et seq.
23. See Filiatrault and Lapierre (1997), p. 213.
24. See Bruhn and Homburg (2000), p. 8.
25. See Eriksson and Vaghulg (2000), p. 364; Filiatrault and Lapierre (1997), p. 213.
26. See Mattila (2001), p. 92.
27. See Mattila (2001), p. 92.
28. See Albrecht (1988), p. 26.
29. See Stauss (1995), p. 382 et seq.
30. See Diller (1995), pp. 288–289, who divides the relationship management in four areas.
31. See Value Bruhn et al. (2000) on the topic customer lifetime.
32. See Filiatrault and Lapierre (1997), p. 219.
33. See Filiatrault and Lapierre (1997), p. 219.
34. See Fombrun (1996), p. 84.
35. See on this matter Fombrun (1996), pp. 331–332, where Fombrun describes the idea of borrowed reputation using investment banks as example.
36. See Fombrun (1996), p. 331 et seq. for the example of investment bankers and Gummesson (1988), p. 7 for the example of the consulting company McKinsey .
37. See Stauss (1995), p. 382.
38. See Vopel (1999), p. 45.
39. See Schmitz (1997), p. 45.
40. See Bone (1995), p. 213 et seq.
41. See Wilson (1991), p. 39.
42. See Büschken (1999), p. 1.
43. See Fombrun on the diffentiation of generalists and specialists (1996), p. 323. Fombrun applies this company-oriented differenciation to financial service providers.
44. See on this matter Müller-Stewens et al. (1999), p. 28.
45. See Balzer and Student (2002), p. 4.
46. See Richter and Hammer (2003), p. 28.
47. See Fombrun and Shanley (1990), p. 233 et seq.
48. See Sertoglu and Berkowitch (2002a), p. 8.
49. See hierzu auch Chap. 9 in this book.
50. See on performance guraantees and their significance for professional service firms Hart et al. (1992), p. 20.
51. See Fombrun (1996), p. 84. See also Chap. 12 in this book.
52. See also Chap. 9 in this book.
53. See Fombrun (1996), p. 327.
54. See Herbig et al. (1994), p. 23.
55. See Schade and Schott (1993), p. 16; Kaiser and Paust 2004, p. 29 et seq.
56. See Glückler and Armbrüster (2003).
57. See Glückler and Armbrüster (2003).

58. See Kaiser and Paust R. (2004), p. 30 et seq.
59. See Lewis and Weigert (1985); and for a multi-disciplinary discussion as representatives Bigley and Pearce (1998); McEvily et al. (2003).
60. See Coleman (1991).
61. See Dirks and Ferrin (2001).
62. See Zucker (1986), p. 60; Lewicki and Bunker (1996).
63. See Endress (2002), p. 53 et seq.
64. A respective interpretation of the term can e.g. be found with Solomon et al. (1985), who define the service encounter as 'face-to-face interactions between a buyer and a seller in a service setting' (p. 100).
65. This is based on a model for business relations by Holmlund (2004), that assumes that the interaction processes between two companies can be structured hierarchically-temporally und ultimately result in a business relation when aggregated.
66. See Langusch (2004), p. 72.
67. See Langusch (2004), p. 74.
68. See on this matter Luhmann (1989).

Chapter 5
Knowledge Management and Innovation

In the first part of the book the resource knowledge was outlined as one of the three strategic resources of a PSF among reputation and relational competence. The statements made in the previous chapter furthermore demonstrate that knowledge is the basis for service quality. This chapter now takes an even closer look and associates it with the important topic innovation (Sect. 5.1). In a second step, we assess how knowledge can be used in the targeted management in the context of the organizational characteristics in a professional service firm (Sect. 5.2). The innovation topic is tackled again in conclusion and hereby regarded as a special challenge for the knowledge management of a professional service firm (Sect. 5.3).

5.1 Knowledge and Innovation as Key Success Factors in Professional Service Firms

Knowledge is the key input and output factor of a professional service firm and is thus a decisive success factor. Not least for this reason the question how to manage such knowledge has been given particular consideration since the beginning of the 1990s both in scientific circles and in practice.[1] The starting point of scientific considerations however, at first created the discussion concerning a suitable definition of knowledge and the categorization of various types of knowledge (Sect. 5.1.1).

The rarely explicitly raised issue of innovations in professional service firms is also closely connected to the knowledge topic. In common PSF literature, the significance of 'innovations' is often pointedout,[2] however, these considerations rarely have concrete character and, as a rule, fail to establish direct knowledge references. In particular, the latter is surprising in respect of the fact that innovations in professional service firms characterized by knowledge intensity quasi ex definitione are probably strongly related to knowledge and a respective relation is thus natural. For this reason the subsequent examination of the term *knowledge* is followed by a deepened discussion of the term innovation in the context of the PSF theory (Sect. 5.1.2).

Co-author: Tilo Polster. We would furthermore like to thank Nicole Schonder, who provided valuable input to this chapter.

5.1.1 Knowledge – A Definition

The term *knowledge* today is seen in close connection, but also opposed to, related terms like 'data' and 'information.' While data per se is deemed to be understood as mostly context-independent abstract and objective fact concerning things or events, information is seen as individual and thus context-dependent interpretation of such data.[3] Knowledge, on the other hand, is ultimately the product of individually developing substantiated views and opinions about things or events on the basis of information. Therefore, knowledge implies an understanding of information that has developed over a certain period of time using analytical processes and that can never been seen independent of subjective perceptions and the social context of the knowledge carrier.

Following Nonaka and Takeuchi (1995) different types of knowledge can be categorized in two dimensions, i.e. the degree of aggregation and articulation.[4] Within the aggregation dimension a distinction is drawn between *individual* and *collective knowledge*. A person has only individual knowledge; collective knowledge on the other hand is embedded in a network of relationships within a group and cannot be disassembled into individual parts. Within the articulation dimension, knowledge is either attributed implicit or explicit character. *Implicit knowledge* in this context is deemed to be subjective, i.e. connected to the respective knowledge carrier, who does not necessarily have to be aware of the knowledge ownership. Such knowledge is very difficult to be formalized, which makes communication and transfer to other people more difficult or even impossible. Polanyi (1966) expresses the situation as follows: 'We can know more than we can tell' (Polanyi 1966, p. 4). *Explicit knowledge* in contrast to implicit knowledge, however, can be communicated to third parties.

Against the background of the outlined multi-dimensional definition of knowledge, two competing scientific perspectives have emerged that are the typical basis of topic organizational knowledge according to Empson (2001a).[5] Knowledge is thus either understood as 'asset' or alternatively as 'process.' For researchers of the first option, knowledge is an objectively determinable item that needs to be regarded functionally on an organizational level in order to be able to establish normative statements on the organizational approach towards knowledge. The other group of researchers, however, sees knowledge as social construct, that has to be interpretatively analyzed on the level of the social context of organizational individuals to be defined and understood.

In the context of the following explanation, none of the two perspectives is entirely rejected; instead selective aspects of both approaches shall be considered. However, independently of this, there is a risk to overemphasize the implicit character of organizational knowledge, that Donaldson (2001) figuratively also describes as 'remagnification of organizations' and thus as a countermovement to general rationalization.[6] It should be noted that as a result of the disregard of explicit knowledge as well as of a denial of the ability to transfer implicit knowledge into explicit know-how, the knowledge management concept ultimately becomes completely unnecessary. Since this is to be regarded unrealistic, in particular in light of numerous successful practical examples, a functional perspective usually dominates.

5.1.2 Innovation – A Definition

The interest in a targeted management of innovations both in practice as well as in science has been high for quite some time. Macroeconomically, innovations have been regarded carriers of growth and economic development since Schumpeter (1931).[7] On an individual company level they are understood as basis for the development and preservation of comparative competitive advantage. In the center of the accordingly numerous economic research efforts among the phenomenon innovation for a long time were especially industrially manufactured goods. Innovations in the service sector on the other hand have only recently been identified and focalized.[8]

Innovation research interests focus primarily on the management of innovation in the sense of a dispositive organization of both the innovation processes and the institution, within that such processes occur.[9] Innovation, as a rule in such case is regarded as the successful market implementation of something new.[10] The criterion 'implementation' serves to define and/or extend similar constructs like creativity or invention. While creativity in the sense of a human characteristic is viewed as a generator of new associations and/or ideas,[11] inventions are already deemed 'functioning' new ideas.[12] However, both only become innovation when implemented in the market, i.e. when the new idea or item is being commercial exploited. Roberts (1987) summarizes that with the formula: 'innovation = invention + exploitation' (Roberts 1987, p. 3).

Based on this first, comparatively abstract general definition of innovation, the question now is whether the definition can be specified more concretely for professional service firms. Reference to service research proves helpful, where innovation is divided into several dimensions (see Fig. 5.1):

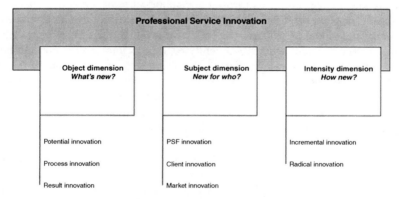

Fig. 5.1 Dimensions of service innovations. (Source: Adapted from Benkenstein and Steiner 2004, p. 31)

- *Object Dimension:* The degree of novelty of innovation can generally refer to various objects. Since the client experiences services usually within the three categories potentials (services provided), processes and results – contrary to classic goods – any of the three categories can be the object and/or the carrier of novelty.
- *Subject Dimension:* In addition to possible object of innovation, various subjects can furthermore be differentiated, i.e. different people or groups of people who perceive novelty. Differentiations thus need to be made between company, client or also market innovation, whereas in particular the latter are likely to be of interest to professional service firms with regard to the possibilities of economical exploitation of the innovation.
- *Intensity Dimension:* Since innovations can in particular also strongly differ from one another in terms of intensity, a distinction is often made between incremental and radical innovations. While the first type is regarded rather as further development of existing concepts, radical innovations have substantial impact and imply considerably larger potential for economic exploitation.

In summary, it can be stated that the definition of innovation is particularly multidimensional in the context of the PSF theory. Therefore, there are numerous options to specify the term. In view of the potential for economic exploitation, innovations are of special relevance for professional service firms that are perceived as radical by individual clients or also the entire market and that can refer both to the service potential as well as service processes and results.

5.2 Management of Knowledge

As already pointed out, the knowledge of a professional service firm is a key success factor for its economic success. For this reason, it is reasonable or even necessary for the professional service firm to explore the possibilities of managing the respective company knowledge. In this context the metaphorical term 'organizational knowledge basis' is often used describing the organization of the available knowledge base on an individual as well as on a collective level. Based on that approach, the knowledge management shall subsequently be seen as intervention concept targeting the organizational knowledge basis.[13] Knowledge management on the one hand includes targeted intervention in the organizational knowledge basis as consistent use and development of its inherent chances. On the other hand, the objective of knowledge management is also to define a realistic scope for intervention and to recognize the limits of intervention in the organizational knowledge basis, in the sense of self-reflection.

Based on the previously established understanding of the term knowledge management the subsequent subchapters first discuss two options of its strategic focus (Sect. 5.2.1). Afterwards, the key knowledge management tasks of a professional service firm are presented (Sect. 5.2.2) and critical influence and success factors are reviewed (Sect. 5.2.3).

5.2.1 Strategic Focus

Most sources in knowledge management related literature discuss tasks and methods of knowledge management without explicitly considering the question of an underlying strategic focus. Hansen et al. (1999) were finally among the first trying to fill this gap by examining the relation between company and knowledge management strategy in their empiric research endeavors.[14] According to their findings in practice, two basic strategic directions can be observed with regard to the management of knowledge: the codification and the personalization strategy (see Fig. 5.2).

Codification strategy pursues a 'people-to-documents' approach by trying to codify knowledge, i.e. to detach it from human resources and to make it independent of them, to guarantee the knowledge can later be used for various purposes. The use of databases where the codified knowledge is saved and made accessible using computer networks to ensure the use irrespective of time and location across the organization is hereby of core significance. In case of a codification strategy, the knowledge dominating within the organization should particularly have explicit character, since implicit knowledge can hardly be documented and/or codified. The leverage of the knowledge of the partners of a professional service firm (i.e. the increased use of this knowledge by junior professionals)[15] is potentially very high when knowledge is stored in databases, since it can be relatively easily accessed on the one hand, and access can be made in parallel. Organizational learning is accordingly focused on the exploitation of existing knowledge.[16]

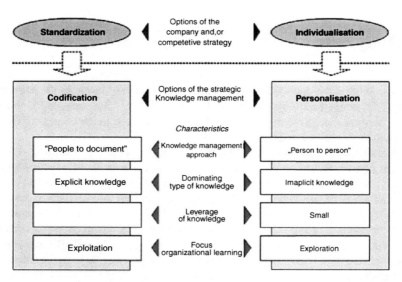

Fig. 5.2 Strategic focus of knowledge management depending on company and/or competitive strategy. (Source: Adapted from Hansen et al. 1999, p. 106 et seq.; March 1991, p. 71 et seq.)

Personalization strategy has a different perspective. The objective is to enable the use of knowledge throughout the organization and to promote dialogues in a 'person-to-person' approach between the human bearers of knowledge. Databases and computer networks are also used in this case; however, they do not serve as 'knowledge storage,' but are rather hints to establish dialogues with the respective (human) bearer of knowledge. Since the dominating organizational knowledge in case of this strategy is mainly implicit, codification can literally not be used. Instead, it is attempted to use the implicit knowledge in explicit form using dialogues in the sense of an exchange of experience. As a result of the necessity of personal and (time-) intensive communication, the potential leverage of partner knowledge is much lower compared to a codification strategy. Since the existing organizational knowledge first has to be made explicit and understandable before it can be applied in new and/or different contexts using adaption and further development, the focus of the organizational learning can also be described as explorative.[17]

As Hansen et al. (1999) emphasize in their findings, the decision for one of the two knowledge management strategies should not be made arbitrarily, but rather in strict accordance with the respective company and/or competitive strategy.[18] After all there is a big difference whether a professional service firm primarily provides services standardized to a great extent or highly individualized services. While standardized services imply a certain comparability of old and new 'problems' and thus of old and new knowledge, it is often not possible to understand and/or apply old knowledge in a new problem context in case of highly individualized services. For this reason, it seems adequate to pursue a personalization strategy concentrating on certain main points in case of highly individualized services and in case of standardized services a codification strategy.

5.2.2 Key Tasks

Irrespective of the strategic options outlined in the previous chapter, knowledge management on the operative level has a clear spectrum of tasks. In the subsequent paragraph, partly following Alavi and Leidner (2001),[19] five knowledge management core tasks are presented (see Fig. 5.3) and discussed in the context of the PSF theory with a practical orientation.

The key knowledge management tasks can ideal-typically be understood as subsequent phases: Based on a superordinate knowledge management controlling (1) at first, transparency regarding the organizational knowledge basis should be established (2), before (missing) knowledge can be acquired and/or further developed (3). After that the use and/or the application of the existing knowledge has to be promoted (4) and at the same time measures have to be taken suited to retain the organizational knowledge basis (5). As already mentioned, knowledge management in accordance with such concept is ideal typical. In practice, however, considerable feedback between the individual key tasks as well as temporal parallelism in their implementation is possible. It could happen that the transparency of specific knowledge can only be guaranteed when the knowledge is used and it can thus only be

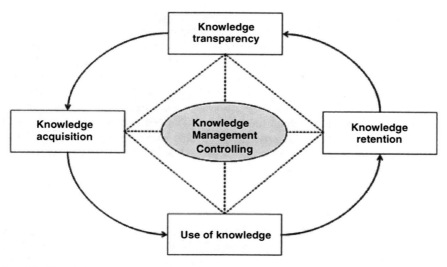

Fig. 5.3 Knowledge management key tasks

decided which measures have to be taken with regard to a necessary acquisition of knowledge subsequent to its use.

5.2.2.1 Knowledge Management Controlling

Contrary to the other four key tasks, controlling knowledge management is of superior meaning since it is focused on the organization, control, coordination and supervision. For this purpose, the controlling has to determine knowledge objectives and the degree of implementation of these objectives so that conclusions regarding efficiency and cost-benefit aspects of the knowledge management activities can be drawn.

The selection, formulation and determination of objectives are intended to ensure that the knowledge management does not become an end in itself, but is practiced demand oriented and focused on problem solving. In principle, knowledge objectives are nothing but a translation of strategic and operative organization objectives into a knowledge-oriented language.[20] In other words, it has to be decided what kind of knowledge the organization needs to achieve the set goals on a strategic as well as on an operative level. It is therefore possible that a professional service firm when entering a new market explicitly determines which knowledge relevant for this market is supposed to be available and/or established in which period of time.

However, it is possible that problems occur during practical implementation. It is not always clear what scope of knowledge a professional service firm could have, which would lead to potential knowledge being excluded from focus in advance despite possible relevance. There is furthermore a risk that the formulation of general goals which are difficult to implement makes it hard to derive precise conclusions regarding the other four key knowledge management tasks.

In addition to the determination of goals, a controlling system is also intended to supervise the achievement of set goals. In the knowledge management field this can be particularly difficult since the resource knowledge can often not be objectified or measured. In this context, e.g. the acquisition of implicit knowledge could be mentioned, which in individual cases can have a lasting impact on the company success and which, at the same time, can possibly not be converted into explicit knowledge, let alone be directly measured. For this reason, the costs of a knowledge management are often determined in practice, while yield and/or the results of the knowledge management are not quantified.

5.2.2.2 Knowledge Transparency

In another step, based on determined knowledge objectives, it is of vital importance to create transparency regarding the knowledge available in the professional service firm as well as in the external environment. The objective here is, one the one hand, to reveal (organizational) knowledge – if desired[21] – to avoid inefficiency and to facilitate and/or allow multiple uses of the knowledge.[22] On the other hand, possibly existing knowledge gaps have to be detected and the corresponding external sources of knowledge to fill these gaps have to be found.

In practice, numerous instruments can be found with which individual professional service firms try to create and/or to promote in particular internal knowledge transparency. As an example of a system to identify and distribute knowledge Ernst & Young's 'centers of business knowledge' have to be mentioned, which are interconnected and integrated in the company structure on a worldwide scale.[23] Amongst other things, it is the task of these centers to create project databases and coordinate national and international knowledge input in the sense of an in-company information service provider. The professionals of PricewaterhouseCoopers also use so-called 'working communities' for individual projects.[24] These are project-related databases that do not only allow the systematic generation of knowledge, but also the systematic and comparable filing of all work documents. McKinsey pursues a similar target by operating 'Practice Centers' staffed with thirty specialists, who provide, amongst other things, a so-called 'rapid response network' which guarantees that professionals making enquiries receive rapid answers and problem solving proposals.[25] These responses are generated by contacting people who are listed in databases and by using their project experience, which is automatically requested at the end of a consulting project as so-called 'lessons learned.'[26] McKinsey uses another form of 'knowledge tracking,' i.e. identification of knowledge structures by creating the possibility to locate, send and edit available charts as smallest units of knowledge and key communication media for analyses and proposals due to an individual coding worldwide.[27]

In the context of creating transparency of internal knowledge structures, also the positive efficiency of some of the classic HR measures ultimately needs to be mentioned. Job rotation, job enrichment, teamwork or participation in trainings or conferences can help professionals to exchange experiences (partly even across companies) and thus to develop higher but rather informal transparency regarding internal and external knowledge.

In conclusion, also limits and/or potential problems with the creation of knowledge transparency should be addressed at this point. It has to be considered, e.g. that individual positions of power of individual professionals with a professional service firm can be based on knowledge. In such circumstances the respective professional is not necessarily interested in making his knowledge fully 'transparent.' On the contrary, he will probably actively try to retain a certain degree of intransparency.[28] One approach to avoid this would be the targeted use of motivation and reward systems, which make a distribution of knowledge in the sense of positive incentive more likely. Yet another step would be the consideration of the individual willingness to create knowledge transparency in the context of the employee evaluation and promotion.[29]

5.2.2.3 Knowledge Acquisition

If, in the context of the knowledge transparency mentioned above, it turns out that certain knowledge objectives are not covered by the organizational knowledge basis the question arises how to fill these gaps by acquiring the respective knowledge. Against the background of cost and strategy considerations, non-existing knowledge can generally be acquired both externally as well as internally, while the latter is often also described as knowledge development. Knowledge is acquired internally if it is more cost intensive, strategically unacceptable or not possible at all to resort to external bearers of knowledge.

If the decision was made in favor of an external acquisition of knowledge, there is a variety of channels, such as newspapers, magazines, and books of reference, databases, studies and discussions with relevant experts. In large professional service firms like Ernst & Young such knowledge is often acquired via internal service providers in form of 'research & analysis' teams that acquire information upon concrete request and distribute relevant market information in form of regular newsletters.[30] Another possibility to acquire knowledge externally can be the direct access of client knowledge. Since clients often have relevant knowledge on the respective client problem, they are likely to be a 'cost-efficient' source of knowledge not to be underestimated.

However, in the focus of strategic considerations on the external acquisition of knowledge, there is above all, knowledge-oriented recruitment as well as externally provided personnel development services with the objective to ensure the availability of qualified employees at the right time and place. This is supposed to guarantee an adequate inflow of knowledge and to further the targeted development of the organizational knowledge basis with individual knowledge in the long term.

In contrast to the external acquisition of knowledge, the internal acquisition – as already mentioned – is an independent development of knowledge. Especially in larger professional service firms it can happen that the same or similar problems are tackled at the same time. To avoid unnecessary double work and the waste of resources, numerous professional service firms thus try to create transparency regarding the development of internal knowledge and to bundle and organizationally combine related activities. At Ernst & Young so-called 'communities of interest networks' take over the task of the knowledge development, by gathering organizational bearers of knowledge in 'centers of competence' and use them to solve concrete problems.[31]

However, internally provided personnel development measures are also of special significance in the context of the internal knowledge development. KPMG, e.g. has an internal 'Assurance Business School,' where junior employees receive training measures on KPMG auditing methods.[33]

In summary, it is to be noted that the knowledge acquisition is also subject to problems and internal obstacles. This applies in particular for acquisitions of knowledge, which are marked by having an especially strong novelty character. Since the successful acquisition of new knowledge especially in the context of an innovation management is highly significant, the subsequent Sect. 5.3 is referenced at this point.

5.2.2.4 Use of Knowledge

The efficient use of knowledge is the final goal of any knowledge management and not least serves the purpose to justify the amount of time and costs involved in the individual knowledge management activities. To make the actual use of knowledge more likely, (relevant) existing knowledge has to be communicated accordingly and made available. For this reason the task to create knowledge transparency – as already outlined – is automatically strongly connected to the goal to exploit the knowledge. The adequate and user-friendly use of information and communication systems also plays a key role, since they allow rapid and direct remote access to both internally and externally available (relevant) knowledge.

Another step to improve the knowledge exploitation is editing and/or processing existing knowledge. As already mentioned, it is often necessary to take specific knowledge out of context to ensure its general exploitation. As an example, the 'rapid response network' operated by McKinsey shall be mentioned once more.[34] A professional, who accesses the 'rapid response network' with a specific problem, receives a guaranteed problem-specific response, i.e. an accordingly processed use of the existing knowledge.

Of course the exploitation success of edited knowledge strongly depends on the quality of the editorial work and/or on the trust in its quality. For this reason the knowledge processing should be taken seriously and be subject to strict quality management.

Of major significance is also how the knowledge is used. What kind of knowledge is used in which form and intensity in the context of a project, e.g. depends – among other things – on team organization and the structure of the organization's knowledge culture. Team organization with a focus on diversity in combination with a knowledge culture focusing on a free, creative use of knowledge can result in a different treatment of existing knowledge and, e.g. promote the development of innovative services. Due to the close relation to the topic innovation further information on this topic will be provided in Sect. 5.3.

5.2.2.5 Preservation of Knowledge

Another key task of knowledge management in professional service firms is maintaining organizational knowledge. Since acquired knowledge does not necessarily and permanently have to stay with the company, it makes sense to apply measures to protect the organizational knowledge basis against unwanted erosion. Knowledge erosion is particularly possible in three major respects:

- There is a risk of employees leaving the company and thus the respective knowledge is also lost.
- Furthermore (e.g. strategic) knowledge can lose its value and thus quasi get completely lost, if it is not sufficiently protected against difmerger and competitors.
- However, also without actual 'external' drain knowledge can erode. This is the case if project teams or also individual professionals do not internalize (implicit) experiences or convert them into explicit knowledge or document them thus causing that information to be quickly forgotten.

To prevent unintended loss of knowledge in form of employees leaving the company the potential of carriers of critical or even irreplaceable knowledge should be gathered in a knowledge carrier portfolio as a preventative measure. In the context of a knowledge-oriented fluctuation management, it can be attempted subsequently to protect the organizational knowledge basis by preventing critical bearers of knowledge from leaving with increased incentives.

Difmerger of organizational knowledge to competitors or third parties is in particular critical if strategically important or strongly client-related knowledge is concerned. Since the value of the organizational knowledge basis as well as the reputation and thus the strategic resources of a professional service firm can persistently deteriorate, unnecessary risks of such knowledge difmerger have to be avoided. This can be ensured by providing critical knowledge to a select group of users only or by removing (critical) characteristics from the organizational knowledge. In this case, a restrictive control of knowledge transparency can be assumed since too much transparency can also carry the outlined risks. Another possibility to prevent difmerger is to mark critical knowledge as 'confidential' and ask employees to handle such knowledge with care and not to disclose it to third parties.

Systematically recapitulating and documenting experiences made, thus attributing explicit character, can particularly limit knowledge erosion in the sense of internally 'forgetting.' The documentation, one the one hand, supports the internalization, i.e. the learning process with the documenting person, and at the same time, enables other organization members to access that knowledge on the other. A measure often used in consulting companies in that context is the already mentioned systematic production of 'lessons learned.' Similarly, it is also common practice in corporate law firms after conclusion of a larger mandate, to apply so-called 'post transaction reviews,' in which the involved professionals, the organization, the communication processes as well as details of the legal advice are critically reflected.[35]

5.2.3 Critical Influence and Success Factors

In addition to the already discussed key tasks of knowledge management there are various critical factors, which can substantially influence the success of the knowledge management activities. Numerous studies have shown that, in particular factors like corporate culture, management style as well as recruitment can persistently affect the development of the organizational knowledge basis.[36]

Knowledge-oriented corporate culture can serve as social infrastructure[37] of the knowledge management and thus positively influence the willingness to share personal knowledge and to take on external knowledge in addition to the formal incentive systems. The development of such a corporate culture, e.g. involves the requirement and/or the promotion of a productive exchange of ideas throughout the entire company, which leads to the participation in knowledge management activities being regarded a matter of course.[38] With similar targets, PwC Consulting e.g. regularly carries out a culture assessment using workshops, checklists and questionnaires to evaluate the knowledge-management culture of the company and gather proposals for change.[39]

Also closely connected to a knowledge-oriented corporate culture is the issue of management style. Efforts to setup a specific culture fail if the management and/or the managers of the company fail to comply with such a culture or even act in opposition. Since executive staff members are role models for their employees, it is of crucial importance that the management promotes individual knowledge-management activities and also sets an example.

The significance of knowledge-oriented recruitment was in particular already tackled in the context of the key task 'knowledge acquisition' in Sect. 5.2. As outlined, gaps in regard to strategic knowledge objectives can be decreased or filled – amongst other things – by acquiring human resources, which leads to further development of the organizational knowledge basis. Apart from the individual knowledge that potential new human resources contribute, their skills in dealing with the respective knowledge should also be considered. For individual companies it can be desirable, for example, to confront the organizational knowledge basis with a certain dynamic approach. Since professional service firms are regarded as 'learning' organizations, their development depends on internal opposition, diversity of opinion and competition. Corresponding recruitment is thus able to promote and manage the necessary organizational diversity with targeted measures in combination with a strong, internalized corporate culture with regard of the respective company objectives.[40]

5.3 Innovation as a Special Challenge

Innovations of professional service firms were rated in particular as economically relevant in Sect. 5.1.2, if they are regarded as radical by individual clients or by the entire market. The idea is that radically new professional services allow the professional service firm to disassociate themselves from competitors and to receive 'innovation awards' at the same time.

In the following, this is going to be briefly outlined using the consulting sector as an example: If a client company seeks to purchase (radical) innovative consulting services,[41] it is likely to apply specific criteria when searching and selecting a consulting company. The consulting companies, regarded as particularly innovative by the client in this situation have an advantage over their competitors regarded as less innovative. It can furthermore be assumed innovative consulting services tend to take more time and are often followed by follow-up and/or implementation assignments. As a result, the consulting company can possibly generate additional 'billable hours' [42] and thus monetize the respective profits.

Against this exemplary background it can be interesting for the professional service firm not to leave innovations to chance, but to manage them. According to the authors, such management is to be regarded as subsector of a superordinate management[43] and bears 'only' specific and/or special challenges. In view of the five knowledge management key tasks presented in Sect. 5.2.2, this applies in particular for the tasks knowledge acquisition and knowledge use, since the acquisition as well as the use of radical new knowledge raise interesting questions.[44]

Moreover, the question arises how innovations and/or new knowledge develop in the first place. This applies in particular if specific knowledge does not exist ex ante, i.e. it can also not be acquired via external sources of knowledge and is thus quasi unknown. Following Rammert (1988) something new and/or an innovation exists if at least one element is renewed or if the combination of elements is changed.[45] New knowledge can thus either develop by completely new creation or by the new combination of existing knowledge. Both new creation and new combination have an initiating and/or creative moment. The critical question regarding the acquisitions and use of innovative knowledge therefore is: how can a creative environment be created in which knowledge elements can be newly created or newly combined and thus successfully used? There are various approaches to answer these questions, which shall be briefly described in the following:

- *Original individual creativity:* The individual and personal creativity of the individual professional is the original source of creative performance within an organization.[46] Already in the recruitment process the applicant's ability to creatively solve problems and/or to deal with certain tasks can be considered. Such 'screening' in particular seems important in light of the limited possibilities to compensate poor creativity skills with personal development measures.
- *Use of creativity techniques:* In addition to the individual personal creativity there are also targeted techniques, which do not necessarily intensify creative work results, but make them more likely though. In this context, classic techniques such as brainstorming, morphologic analysis and synectic shall be mentioned.[47] However, also the conscious organization of project teams, which can often be found in professional service firms – the so-called 'staffing' – can have major impact on the future creativity of the team. Since successful teamwork also depends – amongst other things – on the fulfillment of possibly opposing team

roles,[48] these have to be filled as fully as possible depending on the individual skills of the respective team members. If, in individual cases team creativity is particularly needed, more creative professionals could be involved.

- *Overcoming internal obstacles:* The development of new knowledge can fail due to organization-internal obstacles irrespective of the existing degree of creativity. Especially in professional service firms it can occur that the development and/or use of innovative knowledge is deliberately prevented due to power displays. In comparison, professional service firms are organized rather decentralized due to the broad existence of partner models,[49] with several or many partners, who in turn seek autonomy and control in regard to their client base.[50] If they see their client base at risk, e.g. due to the development of innovative knowledge by another partner, they can interfere, by not granting organizational resources for example. At this point, contrary to 'normal' companies, the necessary central body can be missing in a professional service firm, which provides the resources required to generate innovations against the background of a superior constitutional authority. For this reason, organization-internal barriers should be identified as fast as possible and dialogue with the respective partners and/or employees should be sought.[51] Under certain circumstances existing fear, prejudices and thus existing obstacles can be removed through communication.
- *Overcoming obstacles on the part of the clients:* On the part of the client there are often reservations and thus obstacles for (unexpected) innovative solutions for the respective client problem. To avoid this, it can be attempted to involve the clients into the service provision at an early stage, as co-producer and to 'commit' him for future results. In case of radical innovative services, in principle stronger implementation orientation can be recommended. Consulting companies often face accusations that their consulting results are far from the client reality and that they neglect challenges and/or obstacles of future implementation. The risk of such criticism on the part of the client probably tends to grow with the degree of innovation of the respective service, since the implementation and/or enforcement of novelties often implies organizational changes which can lead to a shift in power structures and general insecurity. Against this background it seems wise to anticipate potential obstacles opposing the novelty service at an early stage and to overcome them in the context of targeted implementation considerations.

As these facts show, the topic of innovation in professional service firms is not only interesting from a scientific perspective, but in particular in regard to its practical application connected to various knowledge management challenges. With focus on the acquisition of knowledge, creative methods also have to be fostered in the field of using innovative knowledge to overcome internal and external organization obstacles. If this succeeds, innovation awards can be received and other positive effects on the firm's reputation can develop which at the same time is the basis for future success potential.

Notes

1. See Empson (2001a), p. 811.
2. See Maister (1982), p. 24; Bürger (2005), p. 32; Anand et al. (2007), p. 407 et seq.; Nissen (2007), p. 4.
3. See Choo et al. (2000), p. 30; Watson (2003), p. 7.
4. See Nonaka and Takeuchi (1995), p. 57.
5. See Empson (2001a), p. 813 et seq.
6. See Donaldson (2001), p. 956.
7. See Schumpeter (1931), p. 100 et seq.
8. See Sundbo (1997), p. 432 and Anand et al. (2007).
9. See Hauschildt and Salomo (2007), p. 32.
10. See Roberts (1987), p. 3; March (1991); Morner (1997), p. 12.
11. See El-Murad and West (2004), p. 189 et seq.
12. See Roberts (1987), p. 3.
13. See Alavi and Leidner (2001), p. 107.
14. See Hansen et al. (1999), p. 106 et seq.
15. See Ringlstetter et al. (2004), p. 15 et seq.
16. See March (1991), p. 71 et seq.
17. See March (1991), p. 71 et seq.
18. See Hansen et al. (1999), p. 107.
19. See Alavi and Leidner (2001), p. 115 et seq.
20. See von der Oelsnitz and Hahmann (2003), p. 109.
21. In practice sometimes also critical knowledge is relevant, for example, in form of sensitive client data that should only be used restrictively and which is thus not made transparent, or disclosed at limited extend only (see also consideration on the retentention of knowledge in Sect. 5.2.2).
22. It would, for example, be inefficient if the necessary expert knowledge for a specific project was available within the PSF and project participants could not access it, leading to a time and cost-intensive new acquisition of that expert knowledge.
23. See Widmer and Brun (1999), p. 247.
24. See Thiesse (2001), p. 86.
25. See Probst et al. (2006), p. 153.
26. 'Lessons learned' are generally systematically processed experiences of completed projects.
27. See Balzer (2000), p. 52.
28. See Anand et al. (2007), p. 413 et seq.
29. See Davenport and Probst (2002).
30. See Probst et al. (2006), p. 194 et seq.
31. See Ofek and Sarvary 2001, p. 1443.
32. See hierzu auch Chap. 7 in this book.
33. See Kühnel (2004), p. 180.
34. See Probst et al. (2006), p. 153.
35. See Wollburg (2004), p. 221.
36. See Gupta et al. (2001), p. 19.
37. See Mertins et al. (2003), p. 66.
38. See Thiesse (2001), p. 75.
39. See Alvesson (1993), p. 39.
40. The reasons stated in literature for purchasing consulting services are manifold. Amongst other things consultants can assume management, restructuring, intervention, facilitation, legitimation, or mediation functions with clients (see Caroli 2007, p. 117).
41. 'Billable hours' are hours which can be invoiced to the client. See Maister (1982), p. 18 et seq.

42. As already outlined in Sect. 5.1, innovations in knowledge-intensive PSFs ex definition have a strong connection to knowledge and thus are automatically allocated to the area knowledge management.
43. The other three core tasks transparency, retention and management-controlling of knowledge are subsequently largely disregarded, since they hardly imply specific challenges for particular innovative knowledge.
44. See Rammert (1988), p. 18.
45. See Landau (1969), p. 17.
46. See Barrett (1978), p. 27 et seq.
47. See Robbins (2001), p. 318 et seq.
48. Partnerships are companies owned by the managing employees. See Greenwood and Empson (2003), p. 914 et seq.
49. See Anand et al. (2007), p. 407.
50. See Anand et al. (2007), p. 413 et seq.

Chapter 6
Marketing and Relationship Management

The product range of professional service firms is characterized by specifics like the predominantly immaterial operational variables, by quality which can hardly be assessed ex-ante, collective problem solving and a relatively complex procurement decision. This applies in particular for the marketing of professional services. A unique feature of a professional service firm from the client's point of view is at first the quality commitment. If the self-conception of a brand meets client expectations, the client regards the quality commitment to be fulfilled. In the long term the resulting client trust and the reputation of a professional service firm are decisive success aspects.

Modern and effective professional service marketing covers all hierarchical levels and functions of a professional service firm. When operatively implementing the relationship marketing strategy it is essential to determine the connections between existing and new clients and to coordinate the marketing activities accordingly. Classical marketing approaches do not hold much promise when marketing professional services. These can only be effectively marketed, if sector characteristics are considered and understood. For what reasons do clients require the assistance of external professionals in the first place, how professional is the selection of a professional service firm and who is involved in that decision? An according professional services marketing and a professional service provider selection can already lead to a trust relation based on mutual advantage at the beginning of business relation.[1]

In this chapter at first factors are presented which influence the procurement decision (Sect. 6.1). The second part focuses on the basics of effective marketing of professional services (Sect. 6.2). In the third part operative aspects of a professional services marketing in regard to the implementation of strategies for new and existing clients are tackled (Sect. 6.3).

6.1 Criteria when Purchasing Professional Services

To successfully market professional services it is vital to recognize key criteria which clients apply during the procurement decision process. In other words, aspects of the organizational procurement in relation to professional services need

S. Kaiser, M.J. Ringlstetter, *Strategic Management of Professional Service Firms*,
DOI 10.1007/978-3-642-16063-9_6, © Springer-Verlag Berlin Heidelberg 2011

to be understood. In principle organizational procurement is characterized by the following aspects[2]:

- *Multi-personality*: The involvement of several people in the selection process
- *Rationality*: The attempt to actively generate an objective general view by systematically gathering information
- *Multi-organization:* Involvement of third organizations – like banks or professionals – in the procurement decision
- *Interaction:* Regular and intensive contact for the exchange of information and agreement on common and performance objectives

Moreover, the procurement of professional services is subject to special rules.[3] These can be summarized with three elementary characteristics:

- At first the high *degree of insecurity* in connection with the procurement decision has to be reduced.
- The way professionals *understand an issue* is also of major importance, since it helps to offer a tailor-made approach to tackle a specific client problem.
- Another point is the close connection of the service with the implementing *professional.*

Only when having the competence to implement the service, it can be effectively sold and foster trust on part of the client necessary for the procurement decision.[4] Trust is the key component when procuring professional services. It does not only mean to purchase a service, but to enter into a mutual relationship with the professional,[5] which again underlines the high degree of insecurity, connected with the decision making process. Since the acquisition of professional services usually means considerable investment without guarantee to reach a successful result, the decision to procure professional services is subject to high risks.[6] One possibility for clients, to lower this risk, is an improved internal company communication or contacts with other companies.[7] In many companies the procurement decision today is centralized and concentrates on specialized employees. Therefore this process is often also called client professionalization. It is therefore assumed that inter-company communication works relatively well. The communication between companies is thus of major importance and since the word of mouth recommendations are an integral part of the marketing of professional services, the *referral networks* developing between companies are an important acquisition factor.[8]

Indicators for the required or desired characteristics of a professional are of decisive significance for the marketing of professional services.[9] Various studies underline in particular the important role of reputation of the professional service firm and the personal qualifications of the professional.[10] Image, recommendations and experiences thus are key factors to reduce insecurity and in the selection of the service provider.[11] Three main factors which influence the procurement decision can be identified:

- *Market Reputation:* Can be influenced by professional service firms. In particular reference projects and the view of a specific problem are key factors for the target group.
- *Personal Reputation*: Is of the utmost importance for the procurement decision and can only be developed with recommendations of colleagues and business partners.
- *General Quality Indicators for Professional Services:* The academic reputation of key figures in consulting and the innovativeness of consulting approaches as well as the membership in an association, which is connected to certain quality requirements, provide decision-makers with a basis to assess the *quality* of the consulting service.

6.2 Effective Marketing of Professional Services

The following section describes the fundamentals of an effective marketing of professional services. At first the frequently implied marketing aversion of professionals is discussed (1). Subsequently professional service marketing is classified within the more comprehensive *service marketing* sector (2). This is followed by the development of marketing specific implications as foundation of a relation marketing strategy from *specific characteristics of professional services* and the *procurement strategies* of clients (3).

6.2.1 Marketing Aversion of Professionals

In many professional service sectors the idea of marketing was not only strange; it was even perceived as indecent.[12] In accordance with an occupational class mentality well trained professionals consider it beneath their dignity to get involved in sales or marketing activities.[13] Many professionals assume that high quality work is enough marketing. In their view, the quality of service and the client care suffice for a sustainable growth of turnover.[14] This attitude on the one hand and the fact that a professional service firm is in serious difficulty without marketing efforts on the other hand leads to a dilemma.[15]

Another reason for this opposition is average marketing success which is often related to an *inefficient marketing approach*. Here marketing is often seen as purely functional task without strategic relevance and is managed by employees who have little knowledge of the operative business of the professionals. In addition clients, especially new clients, are often the single focus of the marketing strategies.[16]

As a matter of fact, marketing is one of the most important functions for a professional service firm to rise to the ever changing market challenges. Therefore, the marketing aversion of professionals has to be met with a professional marketing concept, tailored to the requirements of consulting firms.[17]

6.2.2 Professional Service Marketing as Special Service Marketing

The difficulties of professional service firms to guarantee continuous and especially sustainable growth can often be explained with insufficient marketing activities.[18] Professional service firms thus have to market their provided professional services with an equally professional marketing management and have to pursuit competitive advantage in the market by taking a clear strategic position.[19]

This responsibility does not only lie with the marketing department of the consulting firm. Modern and effective professional service marketing covers *all hierarchical levels and functions* of a company.[20] It is of particular importance that professionals are actively involved in the acquisition process.[21] Since the strategic relevance of the professional service marketing is obvious, the question arises, how professional service marketing needs can be met best. Professional services are a particularly pronounced and pure form of service. It is thus logical to look for the fundamentals of professional service marketing in *service marketing*.

The core of excellent service marketing is reliability. This implies that the client receives exactly the service promised in a precise and reliable manner. Even if huge efforts are made, mistakes in the service provision can unfortunately never be completely excluded. For this reason professional service firms should always strive to increase reliability to pursue outstanding achievements especially when correcting mistakes made in the provision of the service. The ultimate goal of the service marketing is the control and outperformance of client expectations.[22] In addition, the simultaneity of production and sale and a close connection of the marketing with the actual service is an essential condition.[23]

6.2.3 Fundamentals of a Relationship Marketing Strategy

The reflections on the elementary differences between products and services already made have the logical consequence that professional services in particular require marketing mechanisms,[24] which are in many respects different from product marketing requirements.[25] For a marketing strategy of a professional service firm to be successful, the characteristics of the professional services thus have to be particularly considered. This means most of all that the derived critical resources have to be used for marketing purposes.

The resource *knowledge* on the one hand is suited to identify the need for consulting on part of the client, on the other hand it helps to communicate that external know-how is required in the process. His skills and knowledge are the only means of the professional to influence the client's procurement decision.[26]

The professional service business is commonly referred to as 'people business'. This underlines the relevance of the factor *relational competence* of professionals. Only if it is highly developed, rapport – an essential factor for the development of sustainable trust – can be created with the client. These inter-personal skills can

Convincing clients to outsource
certain tasks
Identifying new service needs

People Business: Creation of a
Personal level
Continuity of contact persons

Mutiplication of successful
projects
Use of the strong networks
between clients

Fig. 6.1 Marketing implications of critical resources of professional service firms

be identified as the most important tools to retain existing clients and to gain new clients (Fig. 6.1).[27]

Apart from knowledge and relational competence *reputation* beyond doubt is the most important tool to market consulting services. In a successful project the interconnection of clients acts as disseminator and thus as driving force in the prospect acquisition. Reputation is a key element of the relationship marketing approach and thus of major strategic relevance for the marketing of professional services.

It is difficult to acquire new contracts, if one does not understand how, why and when people make procurement decisions.[28] The previously mentioned reputation in ideal situations leads to the client actively approaching the professional which makes a pre-selection obsolete. A professional service firm has the best chances to skip these selection steps if it actively informs the client about the service requirements in his company and at the same time provides the respective solution. In this context it is also vital to encourage satisfied clients to actively recommend the services within their network. Thus new clients can be acquired by using their 'referral networks'.

Interesting for the marketing of professional services is the fact that one can speak of a predominantly professional procurement even if the actual selection is often made highly subjectively. A professional service firms has to adapt to these procurement processes accordingly. Key sales argument for professional services is efficiency.

Another interesting detail is the fact that the level of innovation of the concept has considerable impact on the procurement decision. A professional service firm with an innovative concept can thus definitely make a name for itself and hence increase the willingness of clients to pay.

The traditional transaction-oriented marketing approach turns out to be inadequate for complex and knowledge-intensive services, as provided by professional service firms.[29] *Relationship marketing* is an adequate marketing strategy in that context. On the one hand it is based on an understanding of the client's procurement and added value processes[30] and on the other hand on the finding that multiple market forces influence the success of a company.[31] Starting point for the *relationship marketing* approach is the *business relation* between the professional and the client system. In relation to the marketing a traditional and an interactive function can be

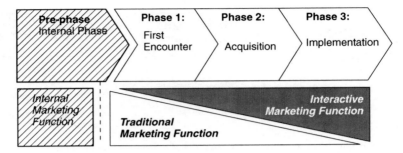

Fig. 6.2 Three stage model. (Source: Adapted from Grönroos 1982, p. 10)

differentiated. The classical marketing mix – product, price, promotion and distribution – and thus the traditional marketing functions seems too production-oriented
and neglects the client interaction. The interactive marketing function on the other
hand is supposed to represent the influence of marketing in the implementation process where the client typically interacts with systems, physical resources and the
employees of the service provider.[32] A business relation accordingly consists of
three phases. It is essential to stimulate the interest of the client in the context of a
first encounter. If this was successful the resulting *acquisition phase*, is supposed
to persuade the client to award the contract. The subsequent *implementation phase*
is crucial for the long-term business relation and according follow-up contracts. As
Fig. 6.2 shows traditional marketing instruments can at least partially be used for
the first two phases. For the third phase, which is essential for a long-term client
relation and thus for follow-up contracts, these instruments completely useless and
interactive marketing instruments are required. Due to the enormous significance of
the staff in contact with the client, the entire service company is targeted to meet the
client requirements in the *internal phase*.[33]

Relationship marketing can be understood in a market-oriented approach as
a concept which exceeding the client focus involves all stakeholders and shifts
focus rather on client retention than on the acquisition of new clients. Marketing
is regarded a *cross-functional company function*. Successful business relations are
thus based on a mutual contribution to added value. The client receives added value
from the business relation, which results in an added value for the professional service firm in form of client loyalty. Such added value on part of the client can only be
guaranteed by continuously providing high quality services.[34] The aforementioned
expansion of the client focus to all stakeholders of a company is implemented via
the so-called 'six markets model' (see Fig. 6.3).[35]

The *client market* is still at the centre of the model. Different to focusing on
individual sales transactions, the emphasis here lies on a short-term orientation on
client relations and requirements. Prior to a long-term *business relation increased
commitment to the client requirements* and mutual trust play a leading role. On the
recommendation market network contacts are actively used to acquire new clients
and it is attempted to establish long-term partnerships on the *supplier market*, based

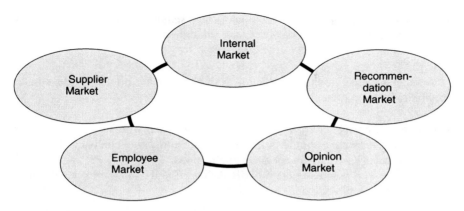

Fig. 6.3   Six markets model. (Source: Adapted from Payne and Poulfelt 1992, p. 163)

on the idea of mutual 'added value'. On the *employee market* relations are maintained with the respective educational institutions and new employees are selected matching the strategic focus on sustainable client relations. In the *opinion market* relationships with opinion leaders are nurtured and lobbying measures are taken in form of skilled PR activities. Ultimately a marketing culture prevails on the *internal market* within the company. Open communication guarantees the unimpaired flow of information and thus relationship marketing becomes a company-wide function[36] to overcome information asymmetries between professional and clients in the acquisition phase.

6.3   Operative Professional Service Marketing

Different marketing instruments have to be considered to motivate clients to retain a sustainable and continuous business relation.[37] The subsequent section outlines how the strategic focus on relationship marketing can be operatively implemented in professional service firms. First a basic overview on the various *marketing instruments available* is presented (1). Subsequently their benefits for the acquisition of *new clients* (2) and for projects of *existing clients* (3) are addressed in particular detail.

6.3.1   Implementation of the Relationship Marketing Strategy

In principle a consulting company can market their services either directly, via classical advertising or public relations:

- In case of the *direct marketing* strategy the consulting company either directly or personally approaches existing or potential clients or reacts on client requests.
- In addition a consulting firm can also resort to *classical ads,* e.g., in print media.

- *Public relations,* e.g., the organization of client seminars, networking, publishing of books and articles, newsletter etc. are suitable measures to develop long-term reputation.[38]

Another differentiation of marketing activities provide the categories contact, credibility and corporate level marketing[39]:

- *Contact marketing* hereby equal all marketing activities with direct client contact.
- *Credibility marketing* should properly market a consulting company, their skills and competences e.g., with adequate publications.
- *Corporate level marketing* is primarily dedicated to the long-term establishment of reputation and/or a brand.

Irrespective of the chosen marketing mix of a consulting company it is vital that it is selected in accordance with certain professional ethic standards. The so-called 'hard sell' marketing, which e.g., involves the creation of unrealistic expectations concerning the service performance on part of the client or the defamation of competitors, should be avoided.[40] In Germany e.g., BDU members in this context oblige to demonstrate respectable behavior in advertising and acquisition. However, even if all ethical requirements are met, the use of certain marketing instruments should be avoided. Marketing tools can be differentiated depending on their effectiveness in 'first team', 'second string' and 'clutching at straws tactics'[41]:

- According to this classification the most efficient tactics are the *first team* activities. This includes client seminars with a limited number of participants, publications in client-oriented professional journals and particularly own market research in areas interesting for potential and current clients.
- These activities are complemented by the *second string*. The term describes networking with potential recommenders, newsletters and voluntary work. These activities are definitely an effective supplement for 'first team' measures; however, they cannot substitute them under any circumstances.
- Using *clutching on straws* activities is not advisable. Particularly direct mail, cold calls, sponsoring and press advertising are less effective. Also brochures and mass seminars are less useful. The inefficiency of these methods can be explained with the so-called 'raspberry jam rule'. According to this rule marketing activities get 'thinner', the more they are spread. Due to high scatter losses they should only be used, if at all, if there are still financial and personal resources available after the 'first team' and 'second string' activities have been implemented.[42]

6.3.2 Acquisition of New Clients

In spite of the enormous significance of existing clients, constant prospect inflow is indispensable for professional service firms. In light of the strategic focus on relationship marketing, the PACE Pipeline of Walker, Ferguson and Denvir is a efficient tool to acquire new clients.[43] All aspects of the pipeline which consists of four areas, is seen as defined total market. Four possible sources for the future business success of a consulting company can be differentiated[44]:

- The overall market: identified potential clients (P1)
- Potential clients, who were already approached via marketing activities which, however do not participate in a dialogue with the consulting company (P2)
- Potential clients, with whom the consulting company has entered into negotiations. (P3)
- Existing clients (P4)

When acquiring new clients, the first challenge for a consulting company lies in the identification of potential clients. Step (a) in Fig. 6.4 outlines the selection of potential clients most suited for the consulting company's service range.

After having identified potential clients, it has to be decided in a second, so-called *prospecting* step (b), to what extent these companies are of interest as clients. The client companies rated as interesting are approached in the next step, called *promoting*. Newsletters, client seminars or networking events are suitable measures in that context. If interest on part of the client was awakened (c), the decision-makers are contacted. During the *projecting phase* a possible acquisition of the professional services is then negotiated. In case negotiations were successful, the consulting company has acquired a new client (d). After the first project this new client is among

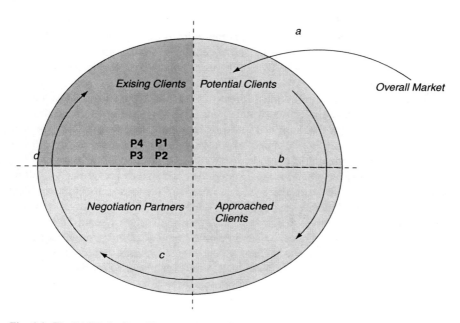

Fig. 6.4 The PACE pipeline. (Source: Adapted from Walker et al. 1998, p. 10)

the important group of existing clients. During the *protecting,* phase the task at hand is the retention of the client and thus the generation of follow-up contracts. To guarantee a constant inflow of new clients, a consulting company has to work in *all* four areas of the pipeline, since otherwise there is the risk of considerable delays between the identification of potential clients to the signing of contract.[45] The object of the acquisition of new clients thus is to shift from a broadly scattered marketing to a personal 'face-to-face' dialogue as fast as possible.[46]

Particularly networking, client seminars and publications are considered essential client acquisition tools. These marketing methods are used primarily to develop reputation and to encourage the client to make the decisive step (c), from being a potential client to becoming a prospective client. Ideally, the client approaches the consulting company and actively expresses an interest.

6.3.3 Marketing Strategies for Existing Clients

The acquisition of new clients is beyond doubt a vital task for a professional service firm. However, since between two thirds and four fifths of the turnover is generated by existing clients,[47] the project acquisition amongst existing clients which is often neglected and taken for granted,[48] assume an even greater importance. To intensively support these clients, pays off twice. On the one hand, it is easier to retain an existing client than to acquire a new one, since acquisition cost for existing clients do not accrue,[49] on the other hand the preselection can be skipped during the selection process under certain circumstances. In this case a consulting company is directly contracted, without considering other consulting firms for the project. Furthermore a long-term consulting cooperation leads to the development of a trust relation between consulting company and client.[50] The client company is then more willing to award more complex, demanding and thus more profitable projects to the consulting company.

The decisive element in the marketing with existing clients is the open ear for the requirements and satisfaction of the client. This way on the one hand the professional services can be improved and on the other hand possibilities for new consulting demand can be identified. However, similar to the acquisition of new clients a selective approach is necessary here. Junior professional, who – as a rule – have increased client contact, are most suited to detect signals for further consulting demand. Together with experienced professionals and the management the problem has to be analyzed. If there are good client relations and thus also a good chance for a follow-up contract, a solution outline should be prepared in advance, which can be presented to the client by a senior professional or partners upon request. It is however vital that a precise budget is determined for each potential follow-up contract which states how many 'nonbillable hours' can be used for the acquisition. There are four strategies to keep the amount of these hours as low as possible and to increase the probability of follow-up contract:

- At first the consulting company should go the *extra mile* in the current project, e.g., with comprehensive documentations, sophisticated presentations and detailed analyses and thus exceed the requirements of the client.
- It is also recommended to increase the *client contact* to the senior management, e.g., with regular phone calls or business lunches.
- It is of particular importance to develop a *long-term relationship* with the client. This also includes services, exceeding the project. A professional can e.g., organize seminars for employees of the client company or be of assistance with economic issues or broker the respective contacts upon request.
- In the long term a *personal relationship* should be developed in addition to the business relation. Particularly important clients e.g., can be entrusted with the private phone number or invited to spare time activities of the company.[51]

Exceeding the acquisition of follow-up contracts the trust relation and the client satisfaction furthermore leads to active recommendations to other business partners.[52] Due to the importance of personal recommendations as already discussed in the context of the selection of professionals the circle of the acquisition of new clients is completed. This is clear evidence that marketing activities for existing and new clients cannot be clearly separated. Although procedures vary, both approaches intertwine and overlap in many areas. Consistent long-term acquisition of new clients leads to an expansion of the existing clientele recommending the consulting firm to new clients, if business relations are retained accordingly.

Notes

1. See on this matter also Chap. 4 in this book.
2. See Hofbauer and Schweidler (2006), p. 90; Kindermann (2006), p. 19.
3. See Wittenreich (1966), p. 127.
4. See Wittenreich (1966), p. 128.
5. See Maister (2003), p. 114.
6. See Mitchell (1994), p. 316 et seq.
7. See Day and Barksdale Jr. (1994), p. 51.
8. See Mitchell (1994), p. 321.
9. See Day and Barksdale Jr. (1994), p. 50.
10. See Dawes et al. (1992), p. 190; Fritz and Effenberger (1996), p. 13.
11. See Kohr (2000), p. 110.
12. See Bloom (1984), p. 102.
13. See Payne and Poulfelt (1992), p. 160.
14. See Young (2005b), p. 48.
15. See Kohr (2000), p. 123; Young (2005b), p. 47.
16. See Payne and Poulfelt (1992), p. 161 et seq.
17. See Kotler and Connor (1977), p. 71.
18. See Payne and Poulfelt (1992), p. 160.
19. See Jeschke (2002), p. 243 et seq.
20. See Christopher et al. (2004), p. 5.
21. See Wittenreich (1969), p. 10, following Gummesson (1979), p. 310.
22. See Berry and Parasuraman (1992), p. 29 et seq.
23. See Hoffman and Bateson (1997), p. 43.

24. Hereby the high ratio of face-to-face interaction and the insecurity in connection with the
    acquistion is to be particularly considered; see Løwendahl (2005), p. 39.
25. See Gummesson (1979), p. 308; Kohr (2000), p. 121; van Doren et al. (1985), p. 20.
26. See Adamson (2000), p. 18.
27. See Ferguson (1996b), p. 49.
28. See Young (2005a), p. 214.
29. See Payne and Poulfelt (1992), p. 161.
30. See Christopher et al. (2004), p. 17; Young (2005a), p. 202.
31. See Christopher et al. (2004), p. 5.
32. See Grönroos (2002), p. 132 et seq.
33. See Grönroos (1982), p. 39 et seq.
34. See Christopher et al. (2004), p. IX et seq.
35. See Payne and Poulfelt (1992), p. 163.
36. See Payne and Poulfelt (1992), p. 163.
37. See Maister (2003), p. 131.
38. See Ferguson (1996a), pp. 21–22; Gummesson (1979), p. 312.
39. See Young (2005b), p. 49.
40. See Kotler and Connor (1977), p. 72.
41. See Maister (2003), p. 121 et seq.
42. See Maister (2003), p. 121 et seq.
43. See Walker et al. (1998).
44. See Walker et al. (1998), p. 7.
45. See Walker et al. (1998), p. 7 et seq.
46. See Maister (2003), p. 121.
47. See Toppin and Czerniawska (2005), p. 21.
48. See Ferguson (1996b), p. 50; Maister (2003), p. 97.
49. See Kohr (2000), p. 123; Maister (2003), p. 98.
50. See on this matter also Chap. 4 in this book.
51. See Maister (2003), p. 62 et seq.
52. See Connor (1989), p. 16.

Part III
Management of Professionals

Chapter 7
Human Resource Management in Professional Service Firms

The business of professional service firms is often described as 'people-driven'. This underlines the key role of human resources in the sector. The first chapter already outlined the decisive role of employees in professional service firms and explained why the strategic management of human resources is highly important for the success of a company.[1]

Basis for HR management in professional service firms is the understanding that highly qualified employees, the so-called professionals, have a profound impact on long-term corporate success.[2] The core service of a professional service firm – providing services in interaction with clients – is quite clearly characterized by the commitment and the skills of individual employees and/or employee teams. When trying to establish a more detailed explanation, key theoretical findings of economic science can be referred to. Of particular significance in this context is the so-called resource-based view which can be applied to human resources.[3] The central statement here is the development of long-term competitive advantages for a professional service firm, based on superior assets in the form of professionals who meet certain criteria.[4] This is based on the fact that other professional service firms are not easily able to build up the same level of professional human assets on their own.

If the argumentation of the resource-based view is developed even further, the significance of managing these professionals becomes evident. The management of professionals becomes a strategic success factor, if one assumes that use and further development of professionals largely depend on human resource management measures.[5] This does, however, not only include the activities of an institutionalized HR department, but also the promotion of junior professionals through challenging tasks, their guidance by senior managers, etc.

7.1 Objectives and Challenges

The super-ordinate objective of managing professionals can be seen in the generation of long-term competitive advantages. How can this be implemented in practice? Simply put, the objective of any human resources management in professional service firms is to ensure optimal levels of performance on part of the professionals. An optimal level of performance guarantees that all tasks the professional service firm

S. Kaiser, M.J. Ringlstetter, *Strategic Management of Professional Service Firms*,
DOI 10.1007/978-3-642-16063-9_7, © Springer-Verlag Berlin Heidelberg 2011

is confronted with are efficiently tackled. This general objective, however, has to be specified in more detail to guide management decisions. In this context it should be made clear what performance of professionals means and/or how it is brought about (1). In a second step the possibilities of optimizing performance (2) will be outlined.

7.1.1 Development of Performance

The development of professional performance is a complex phenomenon, since performance is always a result of the integration of different components. However, if these components are supposed to play a role in a target-oriented management approach, it makes sense to use simplified models. Such models are based on the assumption that professional performance is a function with three variables. It depends on

- the *skills* of the professional,
- his/her *commitment*,
- but also on organizational *framework conditions*.

While it is fairly evident that *skills* and *commitment* of professionals create performance, the term organizational *framework conditions* needs to be examined in greater detail: Organizational requirements and/or, in another step, market and client requirements are relevant, since skills and commitment originally have a mere potential character; i.e., skills and commitment can only be interlinked to form meaningful performance if they go hand in hand with organizational requirements. In other words, the performance level of professionals always has to be seen in the context of organizational requirements and thus in relation to client and market requirements.

If organizational framework conditions, however, are temporarily removed from the equation – or rather assumed to be suitable – the performance level of the human resources of a professional service firm can be represented by applying a matrix along the two dimensions of performance and commitment (see Fig. 7.1).

Both dimensions are linked multiplicatively. One isoquant accordingly displays identical performance levels. The performance level of professionals increases towards the upper right. The objective of managing professionals is to increase the performance level and/or match organizational requirements as closely as possible.

7.1.2 Performance Optimization

The performance level of professionals can be optimized in a variety of ways. To start out with, is up to human resources management to provide a suitable and sufficient number of professionals. This is ensured by *acquiring* professionals on the external work market. This – simply put – guarantees basic availability of work capacities. In order to successfully acquire suitable professionals on the external

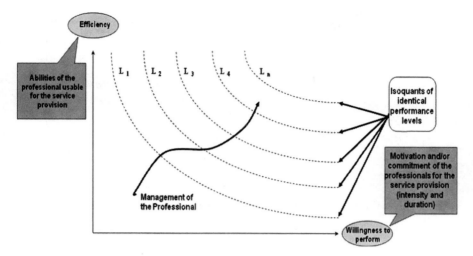

Fig. 7.1 Performance level of professionals

work market, relevant market segments have to be identified and to be tackled strategically. However, mere success in acquiring professionals does not suffice. Both performance level components, performance and commitment of professionals, have to be permanently improved. Professionals must be trained to realize performance improvements, and motivated regarding their commitment. There is more involved than *developing* the skills of individual employees, but includes generating collective performance by putting together teams where individual professionals work together synergetically. In the area of *motivation* the focus lies on motivating employees to efficiently tackle organizational requirements. In this context, suitable reward systems have to be developed. Furthermore, the loyalty of professionals, the main high performers of the company, must be retained by offering suitable career perspectives. Conversely, considerations may become necessary – especially in times of crisis – of making professionals redundant.

7.2 Performance Analysis as Informational Basis

From the management's viewpoint performance optimization of professionals can of course only succeed, if information on the actual as well as the desired performance level is available. Essential information must therefore be collected via detailed analysis of the current performance level. This also applies for a prognosis of the performance level necessary in future. The first aspect is covered by a performance evaluation (1), the latter in the course of an evaluation of requirements (2). It therefore does not suffice to merely identify general needs for action. Concrete approaches to optimize performance have to be found.

Thus first of all the performance level should be defined in terms of qualitative and quantitative aspects. In a second step, market requirements, i.e., needs of

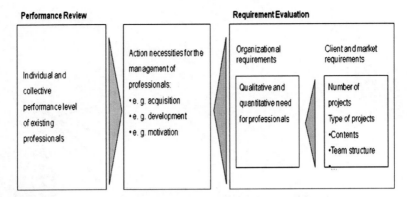

Fig. 7.2 Scheme on the derivation of action needs. (Source: Adapted from Ringlstetter et al. 2004, p. 167)

potential clients have to be predicted and to be translated in qualitative and quantitative requirements for professionals. Needs for action can be derived by contrasting the existing performance levels and predicted requirements (see Fig. 7.2).

7.2.1 Performance Evaluation

Core element of performance analysis is the evaluation of individual professionals. As a rule, this includes an evaluation of professionals across all hierarchy levels. Evaluations should be carried out regularly and systematically pursuant to comprehensive criteria, resulting from the professional service firm's understanding of the term success. Most professional service firms attempt to assess general skills of their professionals, their performance with concrete projects and in the cooperation with colleagues and employees. Big strategic consultancies evaluate their consultants, e.g., depending on their problem-solving abilities, their management and communication skills, as well as depending on their behavior in a team and towards clients.[6] Irrespective of the question whether the professional service firm is a partnership or a so called 'managed professional business', it is of special importance to assess the 'partner level' as well. Here the professional service firm's objectives can directly be transformed into individual performance criteria, such as profitability and further development of the areas of responsibility, client satisfaction, promotion of employees etc.

Evaluation processes in professional service firms take up quite some time, they are, however, indispensable. This is based on the fact that the evaluation of individual professionals is a key prerequisite for managing professionals. Only based on a performance evaluation of individual professionals can

- feedback be given on individual performance levels,
- individual, performance-oriented remuneration be determined,

- decisions on promotions be made,
- development needs be identified,
- acquisition decisions be validated.[7]

Beyond the evaluation of individual professionals, the entire pool of professionals should be evaluated as well. However, only a small number of professional service firms fulfill this requirement entirely. Two approaches are briefly outlined in the following:

- A first approach is the determination of skill areas or so-called knowledge pools within the professional service firm and the allocation of individual professionals to these fields. Most consulting firms, e.g., form targeted knowledge pools resulting both from sector requirements (e.g., consumer goods) as well as from functional requirements (e.g., marketing). This process usually includes more than the introduction of so-called company internal 'Yellow Pages' and databases since the skill-based structure of the professional service firm is determined at the same time.
- Secondly, commitment can be evaluated on an aggregated level using measures to determine the work and employee satisfaction. In the sense of the 'service profit chain'[9] the assumption is that a positive working atmosphere and the consequently related employee satisfaction generally lead to committed and motivated work.

7.2.2 Evaluation of Requirements

The analysis of existing performance levels of professionals needs to be compared with organizational requirements. At the end of the day, these result from the market, i.e., from client requirements. In terms of quantity, the number of projects to be expected is of importance. Then there is also the issue of the leverage structure of individual projects. This will provide information on how many professionals from the different hierarchical levels of the professional service firm are required.

Additionally, a qualitative and quantitative prognosis of client projects reveals how many professionals will be required in which skill areas. This is of particular importance in the case where a professional service firm cooperates with clients whose problems are characterized by significant contextual differences. Different problems require differentiated skills, and thus differently skilled professionals on part of the professional service firm. The analysis of performance levels and performance requirements thus leads to various strategies depending on the respective case. A purposeful approach for a strategy consulting company with a long-term quantitative deficit in the consumer industry is the development of professionals with the respective sector competence and the implementation of counteractions at an early stage.

7.3 Acquisition of Professionals

Even if the so-called 'lateral hires' have become common practice in the context of a slow change of management models and management structures of professional service firms, most of the acquisition efforts still target junior staff. The significance of the acquisition of high performing young professionals cannot be overestimated. It is a critical success factor for the profitability of professional service firms. In principle, the ratio between fees charged and remuneration paid is best in this scenario.[9]

Due to the growth of the professional service firm sector, the market for highly qualified professionals – even when work markets are generally relaxed – is highly competitive. While premium providers such as the Boston Consulting Group, McKinsey, Goldman Sachs, Freshfields, Bruckhaus & Deringer etc. have high acquisition capability due to their reputation, the challenges for second league players are enormous. Successful acquisition of professionals thus requires a strategic approach. In this context, relevant market segments (1) and the resulting challenges (2) must be identified. Based on this analysis, adequate acquisition strategies can be developed and implemented (3).

7.3.1 Relevant Market Segments

The first element of such a strategic approach is the determination of relevant market segments. These result from specific segmentation criteria, i.e., the desired characteristics a professional should have. Renowned professional service firms acquire their employees only from equally renowned universities and/or limit their focus to graduates among the year's 'top 10'. Other individual characteristics segmenting the overall work market for professional service firms are relevant practical and international experience, social competence or specific training contents. Due to these challenging segmentation criteria, professional service firms – as a rule – face quite competitive markets. The work market for lawyers is a case in point. While there is a general surplus of graduating lawyers, the top lawyer segment is highly competitive. This leads to top law firms paying salaries twice as high as average law firms.

7.3.2 Challenges in the Market Segments

The challenges in relevant work market segments are thus to be generally regarded as high. However, they have to be specified in more detail by examining the concrete market situation and the acquisition potential of the professional service firm.

The challenges in the relevant work market segment result on the one hand from relative market volume, i.e., from the ratio of potential professionals and the number of jobs for professionals on the market. The challenges therefore change depending on the economic situation, on the demographic development, etc., and are furthermore quite different in the individual professional service subsectors. Another aspect is the concrete intensity of competition in relevant work market segments. This is determined by the number and the high similarity of competitors, a lack of market growth or by the high specificity of market segments.

On the other hand, challenges result to a large extent from the existing 'acquisition' potential, i.e., the employer brand. This is mostly influenced by the popularity of the sector in itself, by the renown of the individual professional service firm and the individual company image. Very significant in this context are specific personages in the professional service firm sector who coin the image of a company. In the end, the employer image in a closer sense stems from a variety of individual criteria, like perceived career chances, amount and structure of remuneration, type of position, etc. Not only the objective reality, but also particularly the perception of the employer image on part of potential professionals is hereby relevant.

7.3.3 Development and Implementation of Adequate Acquisition Strategies

Some professionals service firms, first-rate strategic consulting companies amongst others, were forced to reduce de facto their requirements with regard to applicants in the currently less popular 'war for talents'[10] which has not yet been declared over, though. This reduction was born out of an acute emergency situation; in the long-term, however, it was clearly not deemed a suitable strategy. In the following, three strategies for professional service firms, likely to be successful in the relevant market segments, are outlined depending on their specific situations (see Fig. 7.3).

- *Market development strategies,* e.g., allow the development of existing or new market segments, but are very time consuming and only applicable with restrictions. An exemplary option would be the long-term expansion of market

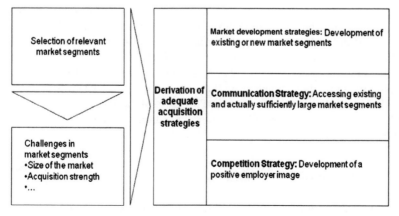

Fig. 7.3 Derivation of adequate acquisition strategies. (Source: Adapted from Ringlstetter et al. 2004, p. 171)

segments through university sector lobbying. Engineering service providers, e.g., can communicate their specific demand and influence university education through cooperations. In the context of so-called exotic programs, strategic consulting companies have already some time ago started developing new market segments and now also recruit physicians, philosophers, linguists etc. For many other professional service firms, such as corporate law firms, such exotic programs are generally not suitable.

- *Communication strategies* improve access to already existing and inherently large enough market segments. This covers the communication of an employer image in line with requirements. For an example, this communication was recently made by the Boston Consulting Group, reinforced by image campaigns. Professional service firms typically communicate an employer image characterized by challenging tasks, good development possibilities and potential earnings, team orientation and participating management style. In the long-term this only makes sense, if reality and image more or less correspond.
- *Competition strategies* are suitable to develop a positive employer image in the relevant market segments. This concretely involves the identification and fulfillment of positive employer image criteria. Following the competitive strategies on product markets, there are two levers for this purpose: First, the product 'workplace' can be designed in such high quality that it meets the requirements of potential professionals to a high extent (differentiation strategy). Secondly, in professional service firms high workloads have to be compensated by competitive remuneration so that the potential candidate perceives the workplace as 'reasonably priced' (cost leadership). Both strategies can be combined at the work market.

Of equal significance is the implementation of selected strategies. Of course, certain conditions have to be in place. On the one hand they require a relatively high willingness to pay on part of the professional service firm. It is not enough to have access to certain candidates in a market segment. Much more important is to select the right ones. To do this, extensive methods of testing but also a series of interviews are usually employed to do in-depth analysis of specific skills of candidates. In order to ensure such selection procedures, senior professionals are expected as a rule to actively participate in junior staff acquisition. This is, however, not always a matter of course, since the participation in interviews leads to less time for clients. Furthermore, individual strategies require additional efforts. If a professional service firm attempts to develop the market via a program of hiring 'exotic' candidates, this entails establishing training and advanced education seminars to train these exotic candidates in specific professional know-how.

7.4 Motivation of Professionals

Due to the HR intensity of professional service firms, motivation of professionals has particular significance: 'In a professional service firm, a less than fully motivated workforce (. . .) is a death knell'.[11] This statement is based on the so-called

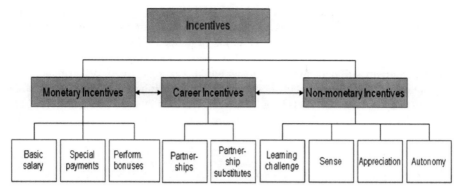

Fig. 7.4 Incentive systems for professionals. (Source: Adapted from Ringlstetter et al. 2004, p. 173)

'motivation spiral'[12] or 'service profit chain'[13]: Only highly motivated profession-als render high quality performance. This leads to client satisfaction and to market success. The resulting economic success of the professional service firm in turn guarantees the motivation of professionals through high remuneration, career oppor-tunities etc. The motivation of professionals is to be considered as equally important as the variety of ways to achieve it. Monetary (1) and immaterial (2) incentives can initially be differentiated. In individual subsectors they are applied to varying degrees. This is possible because monetary incentives can be compensated with immaterial ones. In between lies the important field of career incentives (3) (see Fig. 7.4).

7.4.1 Monetary Incentives

Monetary incentives in most professional service firms are primarily a high salary and benefits, such as privately usable company cars, laptops and mobile phones, etc. Exceptions are junior professionals in some of the 'creative' subsectors, e.g., advertising and communication agencies, or architecture firms. Furthermore, mone-tary incentives are provided by collective or individual performance bonuses. Apart from the motivational aspect, the advantages of these performance bonuses are that entrepreneurial risks can be transferred to the professionals, if remuneration payments are kept variable. Company and employee objectives are furthermore aligned as far as possible. The motivation problem can thus be reformulated so that individual professionals do not just pursue their individual, but also company interests.

A precondition for granting individual monetary incentives are, of course, func-tioning evaluation systems. These evaluation systems must be able to differentiate individual contributions to the company's performance.[14] Linked with that is, how-ever, the risk that professionals feel overly controlled. This in turn can lead to a decrease of existing intrinsic motivation. It is also important to emphasize that the main responsibility for entrepreneurial success, in the sense of entrepreneurial decisions, is often in the hands of a small circle of people, like the managing board or individual partners. It is precisely in this area that even today the allocation of monetary incentives still depends on seniority and not exclusively on performance. The advantage of this arrangement, however, is the high binding effect. Such loyalty to the company may be useful for all professionals. Since the monetary year-end bonus does not lead to a long-term retention of professionals, a separation of long- and short-term bonuses is recommended.[15]

7.4.2 Non-monetary Incentives

For non-monetary incentives to be motivationally effective, they have to meet requirements of the professionals. The requirements of the individual professionals in turn, however, depend on his or her characteristics, values etc. Immaterial incentives should thus be individualized as far as possible. Nevertheless, many experts of the professional service firm, both in practice and science, assume that professionals match requirements typical for the profession.[16] Consequently, a few generally valid statements can be made:

- Professionals expect from their companies the possibility for personal development and the chance to learn as much as possible, either in the course of formal trainings or also via appropriately challenging tasks. A core incentive with immaterial character thus is the provision of long-term coordinated development paths, combining challenging, interesting and alternating projects and formal trainings. On the other hand, there is the necessary acknowledgement for steps already achieved. Maister therefore recommends two leading ideas[17]: 'Treat them as winners' and 'Always keep the next goal out front'.
- In a second step, professionals often desire a certain degree of autonomy and self-determination in their professional work. In this case a participatory leadership culture and real involvement of younger professionals in decisions appear to be reasonable.
- Thirdly, professionals seek a meaningful occupation with high significance for clients. Executive personnel in professional service firms are responsible for the communication of this objective.

7.4.3 Career Incentives

The previously outlined monetary and immaterial incentives are superimposed by career prospects within the professional service firm. However, career prospects in individual professional service firms are – at least at first glance – diverse. A core distinction is the question whether the professional service firm is a partnership or not. In partner-based professional service firms at least, the prospect of becoming a partner is a primary incentive containing both material and immaterial elements. In light of the motivational challenges it can be assumed that a partnership system, combined with the ambition of young professionals, solves many motivation problems.[18] Of course, not all professional service firms have a structure allowing professionals to become co-owners.[19] Professional service firms without partnership structure, however, have adopted some characteristics intrinsic in partnerships.[20] Senior managers, e.g., are on the one hand members of decision-making bodies and thus have similar tasks as managing directors. The potential to increase remuneration is designed to serve as a substitute for a real partnership depending on seniority.

Furthermore the so-called performance tournaments, also known as 'up-or-out' and/or 'grow-or-go', vary only marginally between partnerships and non-partnerships. This applies in particular for the subsectors of consulting firms and recruitment agencies, however, partly also for auditing firms and investment banks. Only engineering service providers and advertising and communication agencies tend to face less tough performance tournaments. The performance tournaments are based on regular evaluation rounds, which are often subject to varying evaluation criteria depending on the respective hierarchical level.

7.5   Development of Professionals

The core challenge for any professional is the permanent further development of his or her skills, not only for the sake of performance tournaments. Skills can be developed differently and with various strategies. Figure 7.5 provides an overview

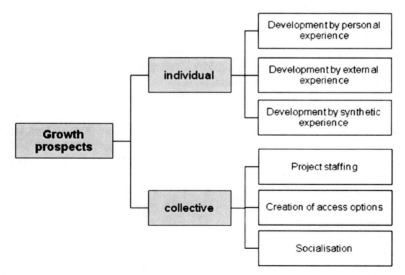

Fig. 7.5 Overview development possibilities. (Source: Adapted from Ringlstetter et al. 2004, p. 176)

of various ways and directions of performance development. In the following, the development of individual performance (1) and the development of collective performance (2) are discussed separately.

7.5.1 Development of Individual Performance

The development of professionals is subject to the problem that the objective criterion of the development, namely professional skills, cannot easily be determined. On the one hand, there is encodable knowledge to be imparted. On the other hand, professional skills have implicit character. They can only be determined by actions of professionals.[21] Examples in this context are the effective conduct of interviews, the establishment of trust among clients, the structuring of problems, etc.

Core factor in the development of skills of individual professionals is therefore learning through experience (a). This is the primary and outstanding source of skills of professionals and corresponds to a development 'on-the-job', also in real life situations.[22] Professional service firms should thus do everything in their power to systematically support professionals in gaining experience because, since these skills are not imitable, this is how the company in the end establishes a unique set of skills, suitable to generate competitive advantage in the long term. In a second step, making use of external experiences (b) in the sense of observational learning is relevant. After all, professionals do not have to make all mistakes by themselves. Accordingly, using coaching measures etc. can lead to even more efficient learning processes. Thirdly, concrete skills can be further developed with synthetic experiences (c), for example through specific seminars.

7.5.1.1 Development by Personal Experience

From a learning theory perspective it is particularly important to support learning processes based on personal experience by challenging professionals with specific tasks. Why? Only when the professional perceives a certain gap between the requirements of the current task and his or her available skills, he or she will strive to improve these skills by reflection on new potential solutions and approaches. The challenge in turn results from the degree of novelty and the level of task completion. It can thus be stated that skills are advanced via experiences which, in turn, depend on the task to be completed.[23] The speed at which tasks are changed directly influences the speed of development.

Particular impact on the development has therefore the decision which projects the professional is entrusted with,[24] which clients he or she is in contact with, which sectors and/or company functions he or she gets to know, which legal problems he or she tackles, etc. The so-called 'staffing' for projects does hence not only serve the purpose of fulfilling client requirements, it is also the core instrument in the development of professionals. To plan this kind of development, professional service firms can use so-called 'career maps' allowing a general visualization of skill areas.[25] The concrete organization also strongly influences the training of professionals as generalists or specialists. This, in turn, has considerable influence on the question whether a professional service firm is generally flexible or inflexible. The more professionals are trained to be 'generalists', the more flexibly the professional service firm can react to changes in client and market requirements.

Furthermore, it must also be taken into account that professional development can be subject to pronounced, sometimes even major changes concerning the respectively required competences. One example in this context is the transition from junior consultant status and solving operative problems to partner status and selling projects to clients.

7.5.1.2 Development by External Experience

Theoretical findings on learning point out that skills can be acquired by observing a model and integrating external experiences.[26] The integration of external experiences allows professionals to minimize expenditure of time during learning processes. The principle of integration of external experiences is on the one hand based on the mutual observation of relevant behavior patterns by professionals. On the other hand, the exchange concerning the observed behavior patterns via the medium language plays an essential role.[27]

In principle, all people the individual professional comes in contact with are possible suppliers of external experiences.[28] However, it is logical that different persons are more or less suited as role models. How suitable someone is as a role model, is influenced by various factors. Of particular importance in this context are the role model's charisma, authority and reputation.[29] Highly suitable are consequently senior managers and/or for junior staff also project managers in professional service firms. As a rule, this group receives special attention. On this basis, role models can impart experiences in the following three areas[30]:

- On the one hand the focus lies on *factual knowledge* regarding methods, sectors, clients etc.
- On the other hand *communication skills* are taught.
- Also *institutional knowledge*, i.e., knowledge concerning organizational, explicit and implicit rules, roles of individual members of the professional service firm, as well as knowledge related to company values and culture is imparted.

In addition, however, other factors – partly with higher logical priority – such as frequency and intensity of the contact are relevant. In other words, role models have to invest time to actually have model function. When looking at professional service firms, though, it turns out that this is not always the case. Analyses of the professional service firm sector show that reward systems for senior managers do not always motivate them to invest time in the development of their employees.[31] In day-to-day business, their focus is rather on client problems. It is therefore important to introduce corresponding criteria in the qualitative evaluation, in particular also in the evaluation of senior managers. The big and successful players in the professional service firm sector have long recognized that. mentoring and coaching for instance are part of the evaluation with Goldman Sachs, or 'people asset building' is one of five criteria in the determination of the remuneration with Bain.

Experience transfer on the part of senior managers has furthermore key significance for the ability of professional service firm to acquire staff on the external work market and for retention of high performers. Especially the best young professionals expect constant input and permanent feedback from their role models for their personal development.

7.5.1.3 Development by Synthetic Experience

Apart from the development through personal or external experience, skills and knowledge of professionals can also be improved via synthetic experiences. Synthetic experience is any experience gathered 'off-the-job' and not in the actual working process. This includes formal and advanced trainings, seminars, etc.

These off-the-job training measures can be implemented by external trainers or also by internal specialists and experienced professionals. They are highly important for the development support of professionals. Members of the junior staff in particular can be familiarized with methodical key tools in orientation programs. Large professional service firms set up their own training centers; McKinsey's Alpine University in Kitzbühel or the Gray Academy are only two examples. In addition to the transfer of knowledge these centers also promote topics like team-building and team spirit.

7.5.2 Development of Collective Performance

An often overlooked aspect in performance development is the combined performance of all professional staff. However, this is especially relevant in professional service firms, not least since a major part of the professional performance is provided in teams. There are very few professional service firm sectors where client problems are solved by individual persons. As a rule, in line with the idea of the professional trick,[32] several professionals are involved in the problem solution process providing complementary knowledge and skills. Which factors constitute this collective performance though? It is primarily a result of the complex interaction of skills of individual professionals based on organizational rules and structures. It can be assumed that collective performance is more than the sum of its individual skills. In fact, new problem-solving qualities develop in the process, so that it could also be described as an emergent phenomenon.[33] Such emergent phenomena are not only difficult to grasp, it is also hard to create them with targeted management approaches. Nevertheless, key mechanisms can be identified.

The core and main mechanism to create collective performance is the allocation of professionals to projects and tasks. The so-called 'project staffing' leads to the creation of collective problem-solving skills. Within project structures, individual skills are combined, communicated, and different views are exchanged. What matters overall, though, is not the complete mutual exchange of knowledge, but rather the possibility of accessing individual skills. This mechanism can also be labeled with the term of 'know-who' management. This first mechanism is supported by two additional factors:

- Permanent access to knowledge: This can be ensured in the form of documentations and knowledge databases, storing encoded knowledge. Knowledge can, however, also be accessed in a personalized way, by creating knowledge databases containing information on specialized contacts for a specific field of knowledge.
- Highly significant for the interaction of individual skills is the establishment of a common orientation with which professionals are able to comprehend the general context. The creation of common orientation patterns is achieved by socialization. Socialization processes result in professionals understanding their individual roles in the organization.[34] Closely connected to that is the corporate culture which reflects the values and standards of the professional service firm in common orientation patterns. Naturally, there are tensions between levels of socialization being too low or too high. 'Over-socialization' leads to the professional service firm becoming too rigid, preventing innovations. 'Under-socialization', on the other hand, results in a lack of adaptability and communication ability of individual professionals.

The considerations on the development of collective performance once more lead to the direct interdependence between human resources and organizational structures. In the end, the development of individual professionals and the structured combination of individual skills to solve client problems result in an organization structure relating to skill and thus to persons, which ideally meets all market and client requirements (see Fig. 7.6).

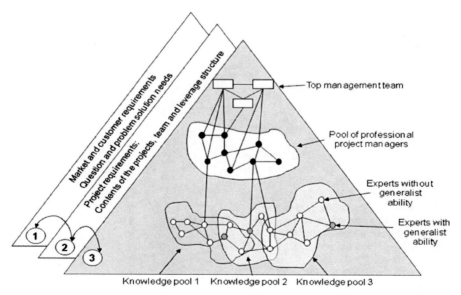

Fig. 7.6 Connections between HR structures, organizational structures and market requirements. (Source: Adopted from Weber (1996), p. 196)

Committed and efficient professionals have a major impact on the long-term success of the professional service firm. Particular attention should be paid to the management of professionals, just as much as to client requirements.

A special feature in professional service firms which so far has only been indirectly addressed is the involvement of all organization members. Human resources management is not just an HR department task, but lies in the responsibility of every individual professional on all hierarchy levels. Key factor in this context is not only the management of other professionals, but also the personal development of the individual human resource in the entrepreneurial sense.

Notes

1. See also Sect. 3.1.
2. See also Shapero (1985), p. 1.
3. See Boxall and Purcell (2000).
4. See e.g., Wright et al. (1994).
5. See in general Kaiser (2001), p. 20 et seq.
6. See Müller-Stewens et al. (1999), p. 103 et seq.
7. See Shapero (1985), p. 92 et seq.
8. See Heskett et al. (1997).
9. See Scott (2001), p. 30.
10. See Chambers et al. (1998).
11. See Maister (1997), p. 165.
12. See Maister (1997), p. 166.
13. See Heskett et al. (1997).
14. See Scott (2001), p. 119.
15. See Scott (2001).
16. See Maister (1997), p. 169; Scott (2001); Løwendahl (1992, 1997).
17. See Maister (1997), p. 170.
18. See Maister (1997), p. 163.
19. See also Chap. 12. in this book.
20. See also Chap. 14 in this book.
21. See Maister (1997), p. 155.
22. See Lorsch and Tierney (2002), p. 84.
23. See Maister (1997), p. 156.
24. See also Müller-Stewens et al. (1999), p. 101.
25. See on the career maps idea Kaiser (2001), p. 157 et seq.
26. See Bandura (1979).
27. See Schreiner (1998), p. 278.
28. See also Kaiser (2001), p. 95 et seq.
29. See regarding these terms Ringlstetter (1997), p. 154 et seq.
30. See Müller-Stewens et al. (1999), p. 101.
31. See Lorsch and Tierney (2002), p. 75; Maister (1997), p. 157.
32. See Tordoir (1995), p. 21.
33. See Willke (1996), p. 144.
34. See Schirmer (1992).

Chapter 8
Professional Service Firms as High Performance Work Systems

The previous chapter focused on individual human resources management instruments in professional service firms. The next chapter now takes things one step further and discusses possible advantages of a systematic combination of individual HR measures in the sense of an integrative approach in comparison to a random application of individually designed personnel measures. This view is based on the finding that the coordination of individual HR measures in the sense of a consistent concentration increases the success of personnel management.[1] The so-called *high performance work system* approach takes this insight into account by emphasizing the systematic concentration of personnel measures with the purpose to enhance entrepreneurial performance.

In the following, a short overview on the development of the idea of 'high performance work systems' shall be provided (8.1). Based on the presentation of basic principles, individual components (8.2) and their respective interdependencies are (8.3) discussed, followed by an assessment of the relevance for the PSF sector (8.4).

8.1 The Idea of High Performance Work Systems

Since the discovery of the employee as a source of sustainable competitive advantage, human resources management is becoming increasingly important in scientific consideration.[2] Since the mid-1990s in particular, the effects of human resources management on company success have been of special interest, both for scientific and for practical application.[3] Therefore, the employees of a company are the main source of sustainable competitive advantage and ensure outstanding overall entrepreneurial performance.[4] Companies following a management approach and thus enabling high employee performance are called 'high performance work systems'. Synonyms are terms such as 'high involvement organizations' or 'high commitment organizations'. This integrative approach provides a comprehensive view of individual corporate staff measures, which are systematically coordinated. Of specific interest in this context are the reciprocal interdependencies of individual

Co-author: Simon Woll

S. Kaiser, M.J. Ringlstetter, *Strategic Management of Professional Service Firms*,
DOI 10.1007/978-3-642-16063-9_8, © Springer-Verlag Berlin Heidelberg 2011

measures and their effects on the performance of employees and thus, at the end of the day, on the overall entrepreneurial performance. In professional service firms, performance is almost exclusively provided by employees. At this point it already becomes quite clear how closely high performance work systems are connected to a direct increase of performance.

There are many reasons for the growing expansion of high performance work systems in recent times. Changes in the competitive environment due to increasing internationalization and technological development serve as determining factors. Connected with that is a shift in focus away from pricing aspects to quality and/or differentiation aspects of products and services.[5] At this point it becomes clear that strategic considerations of this kind can have effects reaching as far down as the individual employee level.

By today's standards, high performance work systems are almost considered normal in organizations. HR departments who see their responsibilities – to put it succinctly – not only in the administrative organization of advanced training measures by external providers but in the strategic management of human resources, stress their holistic, coordinated approach when implementing HR measures. Often, however, company reality is quite different. Especially in the introductory phase of high performance work systems, many problems occur which can lead to failure and/or early termination of the implementation on part of the organization.

High performance work systems are considered to be an expression of a shift in management paradigm. The trend is to move away from a traditionally bureaucratic management style with extensive control mechanisms towards an approach characterized by open communication and joint decision-making processes providing more employee integration.[6] In contrast to traditional work systems, where employees develop expert skills without gaining knowledge due to the constant repetition of routine task, high performance work systems focus on the innovation potential and the human capital of employees. Due to competitive dynamics, it is not only individual maximization of productivity which leads to competitive advantages. Recently, criteria like compliance with high quality standards, client orientation, consumer friendliness and constant development of innovative products have become crucial elements.[7] If at this point one again considers the characteristics of the PSF sector, these new challenges can be identified as core elements of the sector.

Therefore, high performance work systems can be seen in the context of 'knowledge work' or 'intellectual capital' which stand for a changed interest in employees as a source of competitive advantages.[8] This particularly applies to professional service firms since apart from employees there are, as a rule, only little alternative resources available.

By implementing a host of HR practices in companies, the basis for high performance work systems is laid. Of specific significance is the relationship between individual practices, which are subject to a cause-and-effect-chain. This includes 'empowerment' in the sense of an increased involvement of employees in decision-making processes, their improved commitment and the resulting higher performance.

8.2 Elements of a High Performance Work System

When taking a closer look at the individual elements of a high performance work system the question arises, how broad the definition of the approach has to be. At this point this book refers to Guest's model (see Fig. 8.1)[9] which is specifically characterized by the comprehensive identification of results, essential for evaluating the human factor and its influence on human resources management.[10] From the normative point of view, human resources management allows an integration of behavioral theories and clearly defines the connection between HR practices and performance. For this purpose, MacDuffie's *expectancy theory*, which is the implicit basis of the model, can be used.[11] It illustrates the relationship between motivation and performance and/or processes which allow high individual performance. High individual performance therefore results from high motivation in connection with the availability of necessary skills and adequate positioning of employees, including a certain understanding of role on his or her part. In a next step, the desired effects can be allocated to the individual HR management practices. Careful selection of candidates during the recruitment process and high investments in training measures can be used to ensure specific skills. To achieve high motivation, comprehensive employee involvement and performance-oriented remuneration are suitable amongst other things. Practices focused on the design of tasks, as well as communication and feedback, promote a corresponding perception and flexibility on part of the employees.

The model connects the factors of external context and strategy with the achievement of high performance, however, it identifies the core HRM task in developing practices leading to high commitment, quality and flexibility on part of the employees. If human resources management is able to achieve these three results, a change in behavior and consequently an increase in performance are likely.

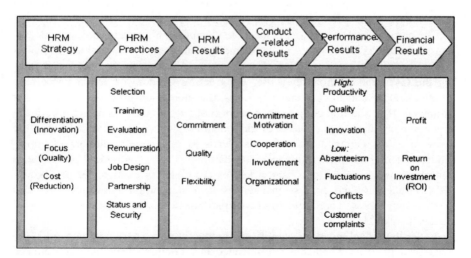

Fig. 8.1 Elements of a high performance work system. (Source: Adapted from Guest (1997))

In order to understand the development of high performance, it is essential to measure the result influenced by human resources management.[12] Here, results related to behavior, performance and financial aspects can be differentiated. This is a first indicator of the complexity of the term performance and complications of performance measurement.

When trying to get an overview of the literature on the topic of high performance work systems, it soon becomes clear that HR functions related to employee development, training, involvement, empowerment, information transfer, as well as reward systems are most often identified as high performance work system elements.[13] A team is formed via the HRM tasks of selection, development, retention and motivation which is intended to achieve outstanding results in competition.[14] The fact that HRM tasks in professional service firms are different to those in other branches was already discussed in the previous chapter. Empirically gathered results show that the same HR measures can have different effects on different target groups.[15] Therefore, it seems to be appropriate to specifically expand HR measures in light of the target group to be addressed. In case of professional service firms, professionals are associated with a particularly high value for the innovation and value-creation process. Kor and Leblebici effectively express the significance of professionals in PSF, by calling the role of professionals 'the crown jewel of knowledge-producing entities'.[16] Professional service firms support strict profession-related standards and thereby promote the homogeneous identity of professionals with an organization. This has to be considered when designing target group-specific HR measures.

In addition, studies have shown that there is a positive relation between self-managed teams and company performance indicators. In a broad understanding, self-managed teams are thus also regarded as high performance work system elements.[17] Team work is routine in professional service firms. It is difficult to imagine the work process without it. This is another argument for the use of high performance work systems in the PSF sector.

The participation of employees is a core element in high performance work systems. In industrial companies the involvement of employees in operational decisions is already a first possibility to increase autonomy and control of employees regarding the tasks and methods they use. By granting freedom of action concerning communication and the exchange of ideas, the innovation process can be further promoted. If in addition cooperations in form of autonomous teams are introduced in a company, the range of tasks of individual employees can be expanded in the sense of a 'job enlargement'. This also leads to an increased number of opportunities for individual performance contributions.[18] These individual performance contributions are on the one hand a key career planning element for professionals. On the other hand, professional service firms depend on innovations provided by their employees. Therefore, employee participation holds vital potential for all parties involved.

As for individual measures, quality and productivity in a participating work organization depend on whether it is embedded in a comprehensive and coordinated bundle of measures.

These measures are meant to ensure on the one hand that employees are capable of making the right decisions, and that on the other hand the respective incentives are provided to make them. In literature many possibilities of creating reward systems in professional service firms can be found.[19] In this context the decisive factor is the 'fit' of existing situation, individual requirements and suitable incentives. Only when the 'fit' is adequate can the desired performance be achieved after activating motivation. Which form this can take in individual professional service firms has already been briefly outlined in the previous chapter.[20]

8.2.1 Performance

Performance is the key target figure in high performance work systems; however, it is a multifaceted phenomenon. In his model, Guest points out the broad understanding and/or the ambiguity of the term performance.[21] The definition of the term depends to a considerable extent on the targets and/or results to be achieved. Performance is, e.g., reflected ex-post in the profits generated or the revenue of past business years.

Performance furthermore also includes a future-oriented component. This allows the derivation of future-oriented implications from measured performance values.

In professional service firms, professionals often determine by themselves which aspects the performance definition contains, particularly due to their shareholding in the company in the partner model. Apart from the aspects already mentioned, performance in professional service firms is also based on a value-creating perspective related to the *input-process-output* chain.[22] Simply put, problems of the client and the knowledge provided by the employees of a professional service firm are called *input factors*, while solutions are the *process factors* and the final concept and/or its implementation represent the *output factors* in this service-oriented value creation chain. A comparison of input and output may lead to conclusions about the efficiency of the intermediary process.

Furthermore, a distinction can be made between strategic performance aspects, focused on results related to work productivity, innovation, quality, efficiency and flexibility, and more social performance aspects stressing legitimacy and fairness.[23] Both performance aspects are equally important in professional service firms.

Business performance thus is a multi-dimensional construct. When discussing the relationship between HRM and performance this fact has to be taken into account.[24]

8.3 From High Performance Work Systems to Employee Performance

The individual employee stands between the high performance work system and performance as objective at the end of a functional chain. To guarantee access to the 'black box' which employees represent, the effects of high performance work systems on the staff have to be considered. As regards the previously mentioned participating work organizations, studies have shown that they often coincide with a working relationship based on trust. Correlations between intrinsic motivation and trust, as well as commitment and work satisfaction, can be ascribed to this.[25]

High performance work systems are understood as multi-dimensional constructs since the parameters to be affected, i.e., motivation (1) and commitment (2) are also multi-dimensional constructs, as outlined in the following.

8.3.1 Motivation

One key to multi-dimensionality is the differentiation between *intrinsic* and *extrinsic motivation*. *Intrinsic motivation* means that the motivation to fulfill a task lies in the fulfillment of the task itself.[26] Deci and Ryan point out that the development and retention of *intrinsic motivation* is generally connected to the perception of autonomy, assigned competence and personal attention ('relatedness').[27] This means in turn that external control, disapproval and social isolation attenuate *intrinsic motivation*.

Extrinsic motivation is motivation which springs from outside rewards instead of from the task itself. *Extrinsic motivation* can result both from the hope for reward and the fear of punishment. In the PSF sector the most common rewards supposed to generate *extrinsic motivation* are financial bonuses, career and development opportunities or the increase of power and status.

Intrinsic and *extrinsic motivation* are in turn interconnected in a complex system. The higher the *intrinsic motivation*, the lower is the need of a person for additional extrinsic incentives. Conversely, extrinsic incentives can result in *intrinsic motivation* being suppressed (suppression effect). If the employee is dissatisfied with the task itself, he or she is also likely to be dissatisfied with work conditions in general. The following mechanisms are the reasons for a suppression effect between *intrinsic* and *extrinsic motivation*[28]:

- *Limited self-determination*: The individual perceives an external intervention as a limitation of its options for action. A sense of external control of the personal work situation arises.
- *Lower self-regard*: The reward is perceived as sign that the already existing intrinsic motivation is not seen or valued.
- *Reduced means of expression*: Intrinsic motivation is a way to express oneself. It is superimposed by extrinsic rewards and consequently reduced.
- *Excessive motivation*: If it were possible to influence the individual by external interventions, the person would feel overly motivated in case of pre-existing intrinsic motivation. If the extrinsic incentive cannot be ignored, intrinsic motivation is reduced as compensatory measure.

External interventions suppress *intrinsic motivation* when they are not perceived as reward or acknowledgement, but instead as external control. *Intrinsic motivation*

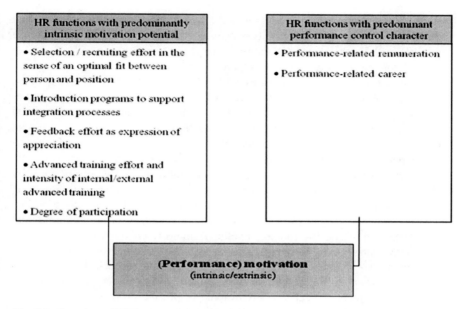

Fig. 8.2 Overview of HR functions with different impact on the achievement motivation

is all the higher, the closer and more personal the work relation, the more stimulating the respective position, the higher the level of self-determination in the work organization and the closer the connection of a reward to a specific performance is. In these cases there is an increased risk of suppression effects caused by a reward.[29]

With regard to the high performance work systems one can assume that elements like further training, information and participation, as well as flexible work conditions – as a rule – have above all an intrinsic motivational effect. Feedback systems are more likely to have intrinsic effects when they have a more informative character; however, they have extrinsic effects and thus at the same time endanger the *intrinsic motivation* when they are perceived as control interventions. As a general rule it can be assumed that performance-related variable remuneration systems have predominantly extrinsic effects on the performance motivation.

With regard to the type of motivation activated by individual HR functions, one can differentiate between functions with a predominantly *intrinsic motivation potential* and functions with distinctive *control character* in relation to the measurable performance of the employee (see Fig. 8.2):

8.3.2 Commitment

Under the construct of the high performance work system, measures suited to ensure staff commitment can be subsumes.[30] In this context it is often assumed that commitment is a one-dimensional construct. This assumption, however, neglects the findings of empirical commitment research, which suggest a multi-dimensional approach. One thus differentiates between *normative, affective* and *calculative* commitment.[31] Furthermore, different effects of commitment, i.e., *identification, increased efficiency* and *retention* are regarded separately.[32]

A study outlined why staff measures have different effects on the often examined success variables of service quality, fluctuation rate or productivity. The (normative) willingness for increased efficiency is particularly connected to organizational performance standards and career opportunities as well as to the relationship with colleagues. In turn, the (affective) identification with the organization is rather based on the experience of fairness and loyalty in the management relationship.[33]

Another option to differentiate between commitment forms is provided by Wallace's study on the influence factors of the structural working environment on the commitment of professionals.[34] She distinguishes between *organization-related* and *profession-related commitment*. These rather independent forms of commitment are characterized by specific personnel policy framework conditions.

If a professional works in an organization with distinct profession-typical structures, which also includes human resources management aspects, his *profession-related commitment* is higher than the commitment of a professional in a position which does not meet typical standards of the respective profession. Apart from career chances and reward systems, *organization-related commitment* also depends on the perceived autonomy of the professional. This aspect should also be considered in the concrete organization of projects. If an employee of a professional service firm is fully responsible for a project and if he is granted project-specific freedom of action, this will positively influence his *organizational commitment*. Training measures which impart company-specific skills and have no relevance in other companies also positively influence *organizational commitment*. The previously outlined work motivation, i.e., the value an individual attributes to his or her work, is furthermore an important factor influencing *professional commitment*.[35] The usually high workload in the PSF sector has to match these conditions. Only where these values correspond, can employees maintain consistent work motivation in the long term.

The above considerations suggest that high performance work systems can be seen as constructs with multi-dimensional interdependencies. It can also be stated that a strategic approach in human resources management, as represented by high performance work systems, is an important factor when trying to define the term performance. Studies have found that the use of high performance work systems leads to a win-win situation both for the professional service firm and for professionals.[36]

8.4 Professional Service Firms as Field of Application of High Performance Work Systems

The potential and possibilities of using high performance work systems in professional service firms are briefly summarized below. The factor knowledge has a dual role in professional service firms as it provides considerable input for service processes and, at the same time, is also the elementary product of these companies. Professional service firms thus offer their clients intangible problem solutions and use the knowledge of their employees in the process.[37]

Since employees of a professional service firm are considered to be carriers of the resource knowledge they have to be given particular attention in light of the generation of sustainable competitive advantage. This leads to the almost necessary consequence of using high performance work systems in professional service firms to a greater extent. It is therefore surprising that so far only few studies have explicitly examined the relations between personnel management and economic success of professional service firms.[38] One possible explanation is that professional service firms are a rather new research area. This chapter therefore intends to contribute to the often postulated attention on the context of high performance work systems by placing them in the context of professional service firms.[39] According to Boxall (2003), high performance work systems so far were created in the context of the production industry. On this basis, direct implications for HR strategies in the service sector were derived under consideration of market characteristics and competitive dynamics. He sees the PSF sector as the 'natural' framework for high performance work systems. In a study Boxall (2003) found out that the 'fit' between competitive strategies and HR strategies in the service sector is even bigger than in the production sector, where the development of high performance work systems is deemed to have originated.[40]

The previous considerations lead to the conclusion that high performance work systems are an effective and profitable approach for professional service firms.

In the beginning, the focus on service aspects based on competitive dynamics was listed as one reason for the prevalence of high performance work systems. Professional service firms are in this context a natural 'habitat' of high performance work systems, since they inherently embody an existential service aspect.

In the context of high performance work systems, the professional is seen as a decisive factor, by bundling HR measures under consideration of their effects on motivation and commitment of employees. This approach has acknowledged the complexity of interdependence between HR measures and performance. In addition, it can be stated that the clarification of a connection between performance and individual HR measures is difficult, if not impossible. Due to the multi-dimensional character of high performance work systems, however, this does not come as a surprise.

Arguments of a target group-specific focus of HR measures caused by profession-typical characteristics and the high significance of the fit between company and HR strategy in the service sector also reflect the potential of high performance work systems in the PSF sector.

Notwithstanding all the excitement, it should not be forgotten that research on high performance work systems still has a very long way to go. At this time, both science and practice face a row of tasks and questions yet to be solved. How can correlations between individual measures be measured? Which performance indicators are important in such a measurement? How can high performance work system be organized cost-efficiently? What role does the employee perspective play in that context? Furthermore the question remains open, if and how high performance work systems can/should be organized target group-specifically.[41] Studies on the target group-specific focus of HR measures and their efficiency, as well as aspects of participatory work and task organization, can be elements of future scientific research.

The claim that high performance work systems are relevant for a broad range of economic sectors and should therefore be available has also yet to be confirmed by empirical studies in various sectors and the subsequent combination of results.[42] The potential of high performance work systems in this respect was outlined in the present chapter, and the theoretical basis for empirical studies in the context of the PSF sector was established.

Notes

1. See Ichniowski et al. (1997); MacDuffie (1995).
2. See Huselid (1995); Wright et al. (2001).
3. See Gmür (2003).
4. See Kerr et al. (2007).
5. See Whitefield and Poole (1997).
6. See MacDuffie (1995).
7. See Bailey (2004).
8. See Becker and Huselid (1998).
9. See Guest (1997). For further models see for example Becker et al. (1997), Appelbaum et al. (2000).
10. See Guest (1997), p. 269.
11. See MacDuffie (1995).
12. See Guest (1997), p. 269.
13. See Boselie et al. (2003).
14. See Kerr et al. (2007).
15. See Hartog Den and Verburg (2004).
16. Kor and Leblebici (2005), p. 980.
17. See Chaston (1998); Way (2002).
18. See Bailey (2004).
19. See Baschab and Piot (2005), p. 217et seq.
20. See also Chap. 7 in this book.
21. See Guest (1997), p. 270.
22. See Fitzgerald et al. (1994).
23. See Paauwe and Boselie (2005).
24. See Way (2002).
25. See Bailey (2004).
26. See Deci and Ryan (1985).
27. See Deci and Ryan (2000).
28. See Frey (1997), p. 23et seq.
29. See Frey (1997), p. 32et seq.
30. See Arthur (1994); Huselid (1995); MacDuffie (1995).
31. See Allen and Meyer (1990).
32. See Cook and Wall (1980); Benkhoff (1997).
33. See Benkhoff (1997).
34. See Wallace (1995).
35. See Wallace (1995).

36. See Bailey (2004).
37. See Ditillo (2004); see on this matter also Chap. 5 in this book.
38. See e.g., Hitt et al. (2001); Sherer (1995).
39. See Hartog Den and Verburg (2004).
40. See Boxall (2003).
41. See Hartog Den and Verburg (2004).
42. See Boxall (2003).

Chapter 9
Work-Life Balance in Professional Service Firms

The compatibility of work and private life – in short, work-life balance – undergoes an increase in personnel political significance also in professional service firms; the topic is even seen as 'the name of the game'.[1] Professional service firms demand enormous working hours, highest flexibility and constant employee motivation from their employees. Since the respective services are often provided directly at the client's, company consultants, e.g., spend a considerable part of their working time away from their places of residence. The activities of professionals are furthermore characterized by extremely high work intensity. More than 60 hours per week are rather the rule than the exception.[2] A further complication is the high responsibility of most of the employees in professional service firms and the resulting stress and performances pressure. Such a job profile, characterized by high workloads on the one hand, but attractive tasks and above-average remuneration on the other, primarily attracts young, career-oriented and flexible applicants. However, after a few years of 'full throttle performance', many professionals pursue a professional career outside professional service firms, since work requirements become increasingly incompatible with the personal lifestyles and private changes such as marriage, starting a family, etc. The recruitment of qualified university graduates in parallel is an increasing challenge since the balance between job and spare time/private life is highly important for many, and attractive salaries and a fast career are no longer considered sufficiently high incentives.[3] In particular in the last years a shift towards extraprofessional objectives has been identifiable in the value orientation of university graduates.[4]

In consequence, many professional service firms have to deal with high fluctuation and difficult conditions in the context of personnel retention and acquisition. The loss of employees means loss of critical resources for professional service firms, since knowledge, relational competence and reputation are often closely connected to the employees themselves.[5] A further consideration is that consulting firms are often not attractive as employers for women. The low quota of women in professional service firms, particularly in consulting firms, often below 20%, contributes to the fact that specifically female competences is hardly used in daily business,

Co-authors: Cornelia Reindl and Martin L. Stolz

S. Kaiser, M.J. Ringlstetter, *Strategic Management of Professional Service Firms*,
DOI 10.1007/978-3-642-16063-9_9, © Springer-Verlag Berlin Heidelberg 2011

and that women are thus more likely to feel discouraged by the 'male-dominated culture' in consulting organizations.

Professional service firms therefore face the challenge of considering a balance between vocational requirements and the realization of personal life plans, both for their employees and for their potential junior staff. After basic considerations of the term 'work-life balance' from a scientific and practical perspective, factors influencing the compatibility of the life areas and positive individual and organizational outcomes are outlined below. In conclusion it will be discussed, how professional service firms can improve the work-life balance of their employees using suitable measures.

9.1 Ideas About the Balance of Work and Life

To be able to generate work-life balance initiatives in professional service firms, it is necessary to have a clear idea about the topic of work-life balance. In spite of numerous scientific studies and publications on the topic, consensus on its exact definition has so far not yet been reached.[6] One explanation for this is certainly the interdisciplinary character of this research area. Apart from disciplines like psychology and pedagogics, also economics[7] and other disciplines[8] have been interested in questions of the compatibility of work and private life for the past decade or so. Different approaches and perspectives have thus lead to a diversity of terms, which makes it difficult to form an overview: work-life conflict, work-life facilitation, life domain balance, work-life integration, work-life interference.[9] Two basic trends can be identified here: the *conflict perspective* and the *enrichment perspective*:

- The *conflict perspective* assumes that conflicts can arise between the various roles an individual has in his or her life (e.g., work and partnership/family life). Greenhaus and Beutell (1985) define the conflict between work and family as follows:

  > [work-family conflict is] a form of interrole conflict in that the role pressures from the work and family domains are mutually incompatible in some respect. That is, participation in the work (family) role is made more difficult by virtue of participation in the family (work) role.' (Greenhaus and Beutell 1985, p. 77)

- At the beginning of work-life research, the roles of work and family were at the centre of discussion. However, with the increasing differentiation of CVs, this perspective was expanded to 'non-work' roles, i.e., family, partnership, spare time and association activities, etc. and not least to the aspect time for oneself.[10] From a *conflict perspective* the term work-life balance thus stands for a minimum interference between work and other life areas.

- The *enrichment perspective* is based on the assumption of a positive interaction of different life roles. Following the trend of a positive psychology,[11] the conflict perspective was expanded and positive interdependencies between work and other life roles were added. This perspective[12] examines positive contributions of and relations between different life roles. In one role, for instance, skills can be acquired or emotions can develop, which positively influence other roles (positive spillover) and thus enrich those. [13]

The term *work-life balance* unites the *conflict perspective* and the *enrichment perspective* insofar that a person experiences a successful work-life balance in the form of the lowest possible work-life conflict and a maximum of mutually enriching interaction of roles. In most cases, however, work-life balance refers to a general role orientation[14] where the potential for conflicts between roles is as low as possible[15] and where resources like time, energy and involvement are allocated evenly to the various roles, or are at least perceived as adequate.[16] In a simplified way, work-life balance can be seen as the satisfaction with the space which work, family, partnership and other roles takes up in the life of a person. The 50:50 ratio, which is implied by the term balance, must be seen critically, since a perfect balance is neither realistic nor necessarily desired by individuals. Scientists therefore often talk about 'life balance'[17] or 'work-life integration'.[18] The term work-life balance, however, has prevailed in science and practice and remains the most common description for the compatibility of work and other life areas.

9.2 Factors Influencing Work-Life Balance

Various factors affect the work-life balance of a professional adversely or positively. For a start, the social and temporal framework conditions of different life areas play a role; to a large extent, e.g., work-structural modalities (1). Personality factors, attitudes and individual values are also significant (2).

9.2.1 The Life Cycle as Framework for WLB Measures

Often role conflicts are caused by so-called 'critical' events, i.e., special important stages of life, or decisive points which radically change one or several life areas. Such critical events are traditionally the start of a family (marriage, birth of children) or the illness/care of a relative. Studies, for example, show that married people/people with children use work-life balance initiatives much more often than singles or people without children.[19] In addition, compared with male employees it is mostly women who use initiatives to improve compatibility of role requirements.[20] Organizational WLB measures should therefore be individually adapted to the life cycle of an employee. Smith and Gardner (2007) showed that employees use different initiatives in different life phases. Younger employees predominantly use initiatives from which they personally profit (health programs, sabbaticals, etc.). Older employees increasingly use supporting services (parental leave, childcare, the care of relatives, etc.), helping them to organize the care of children and relatives.[21]

In everyday vocational life, however, it can be stated that some employees can better cope with critical events than others. Often there are simple explanations, such as a supportive partner or family taking care of the children, or other support. Other explanations might be individual characteristics, attitudes and individual values of a person.

9.2.2 Personality Traits, Attitude, Values

According to science, a personality trait is a (in the medium or long-term) stable, internal (non- situational) factor, which makes the behavior of a person consistent and distinguishable from other people's behavior. Personality traits explain why individuals react differently to different situations and requirements. Studies showed that personality traits also affect the perception of the personal work-life balance, which in turn determines sensitivity for WLB measures. Studies, for example, have found that people with high negative affectivity, i.e., a tendency to negative emotions and low self-esteem, tend to have a low work and life satisfaction level.[22] Negative affectivity as personality trait thus influences the assessment of the respective work and life situation and therefore also affects the perception of the work-life balance. Increased stress at work or in the private life of a person can in this context contribute in particular to a limited work-life balance.[23] Some studies also suggest different contexts of the so-called 'big five' personality traits (extraversion, neuroticism, openness for new experiences, agreeableness and conscientiousness) with work-life balance perception. Neuroticism (similar to negative affectivity) often coincides with increased conflict perception between work and other areas of life.[24] Extraverted individuals, on the other hand, might perceive some situations as less stressful due to their positive attitude towards life. People with high agreeableness seek support from colleagues or friends more actively[25] and thus also reach a work-life balance more easily.

Apart from personality traits, attitudes and value orientations towards family and work (role perception, career orientation, etc.) play an important role. A company consultant with an extremely high level of career orientation and perhaps an additionally high commitment towards his employer, for example, might consider a work-life balance not desirable at all.

9.3 Promotion of the Work-Life Balance of Professionals

Companies have a broad range of possibilities allowing their employees to achieve compatibility between work and their private life. A large part of such initiatives begin with the factor time, i.e., various models of flexible working hours, telework, etc. or leaves (parental leave, sabbatical). Other measures include direct services like childcare information centers or company-internal kindergartens. In the end, the objective of the companies is an increase in productivity of the respective professional and a better working climate, as well as the lowering of absenteeism, stress-related health problems (e.g., burnout) and avoidance of high staff fluctuation.[26] Sutton and Noe (2005, p. 153) list recruitment and retention of employees as well as the reduction of work stress and performance improvement as reasons for HR departments to implement work-life balance measures. Related to this is surely the reputation of an organization as being employee- and family-friendly.[27]

9.3.1 WLB Measures for 'Unaffected' or 'Affected' People?

The influence of life situations and personality traits on the perception of inter-role conflicts leads to considerations that WLB measures should be aligned to them.

Measures to promote the compatibility of work and private life can be categorized in compensatory and real work-life balance measures. Compensatory measures primarily address the symptoms of work-life conflicts – often at short notice – with stress management, regeneration and similar measures. Real work-life balance measures actually attempt to diminish the underlying inter-role conflict by, for example, reducing working hours or by making them more flexible. Looking at the life cycle roles and critical events for the individual work-life balance reveals that not all employees require work-life measures, and particularly not at the same time. In this sense professionals could be categorized regarding their need or, to put it simply, as 'affected' and 'unaffected'. Both positions are influenced by the individual life cycle, the respective life situation and also by personality traits and attitudes:

- 'Affected' people could be, for example, company consultants, who have been working in the sector for several years, are now about to start a family and, due to their own situation and the work situation of the partner, require measures suitable to achieve compatibility of the role as company consultant and the role as mother or father. If the situation is aggravated by the respective personality traits of the consultant, for example, because he or she is particularly stress prone, the already outlined inter-role conflicts can be stimulated. Compensatory measures in these cases are often just 'a drop in the ocean' and underline the necessity of real individualized work-life balance measures.
- 'Unaffected' people on the other hand are characterized by a strong focus on professional life. A university graduate in his first year in a consulting company, who has focused his life primarily on the topic 'work', could be listed as an example in that context (Fig. 9.1).

Employees labeled as 'unaffected' principally have no or rather low demand for WLB measures, since the compatibility of work and private life is not highly important for this group. The provision of compensatory measures for this group is a waste of company resources. Real work-life balance measures even result in the company foregoing willingly the employee's manpower.

This means for the professional service firms that the success of WLB measures particularly depends on the individualization level. Prior to the introduction of measures, companies must make themselves knowledgeable of who belongs to the group of 'affected' people. Based on this finding, it should be investigated which measures are most suited and how these measures can be provided to efficiently generate an

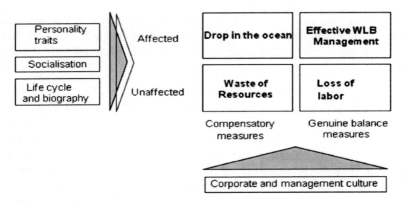

Fig. 9.1 Categorization of WLB measures

appropriate cost-benefit ratio for the individual and the organization. After all, it is the individualization of WLB measures which, due to increased complexity, lead to increased coordination expenditure.

9.3.2 Categories of Work-Life Balance Measures

To implement an individualization of WLB measures, professional service firms ideally have a broad range of possibilities to react to compatibility problems between work and family. In the past, various attempts have been made to categorize WLB measures. Thompson et al. (2006, p. 284), for example. differentiate time-related, informational and financial strategies, as well as direct services. *Time-related strategies* are flexible work time models and leave phases, such as parental leave or sabbaticals.[28] In addition, flexible working time models (working hours account, flextime, telework, etc.) and work reduction models (part-time jobs, 35 hour week, etc.) can be differentiated. Particularly in highly qualified professions it is often perceived as problematic, both by employees and employers, to create part-time positions. Here all parties involved should reconsider their point of view, e.g., by adapting project teams in consulting firms in accordance with the work-life balance profiles of consultants. *Informational strategies* concentrate on informing and consulting employees, for example, in the form of individual work-life balance consulting, but also in the form of targeted events and seminars on the topics of stress management, regeneration methods, etc.[29] Zedeck and Mosier (1990, p. 245) see this simple strategy as the most cost-efficient option for companies. *Financial strategies* focus on different types of support measures, from company-internal insurances, to family and child bonuses.[30] In a broader context, leave and reemployment options as well can be added to the finance-based strategies, since such measures indirectly lead to financial protection.[31] *Direct services*, i.e., services directly offered by the company, can take different forms and can include on-site child day-care facilities, holiday programs for children, homework supervision, elderly care facilities and company-owned fitness studios.[32] Such initiatives are also often called flanking measures.

Despite well-researched and also proven positive effects of WLB measures, scientists agree that the focus on compatibility of work and private life of employees also has to become part of corporate culture and its respective values.[33] Harrington and James (2006) propose in this context a change management concept to reconcile individual wishes and requirements with the corporate culture. The main feature of this change program is the 'Standards of Excellence Index (SEI)' (p. 672) which concerns management aspects, as well as organizational strategy, infrastructure, communication and measurement, commitment and relationship building. This comprehensive change strategy is a step towards integrating WLB measures into the organization's culture and towards a work-life balance culture of individuality, instead of a system of 'exceptions' to generate high company performance in the long-term. In addition, the support of partners and project managers in the line is a key prerequisite for the implementation successful WLB initiatives.

9.4 Positive Impacts of a Good Work-Life Balance

Numerous studies and reviews have meanwhile shown that providing WLB measures is not just corporate philanthropy.[34] Work-life balance measures have positive effects both on the company and on the employees. Against the background of numerous studies and in general it turned out that the influence of work-life balance instruments on company success can only be represented in complex cause-effect relationships (see Fig. 9.2).

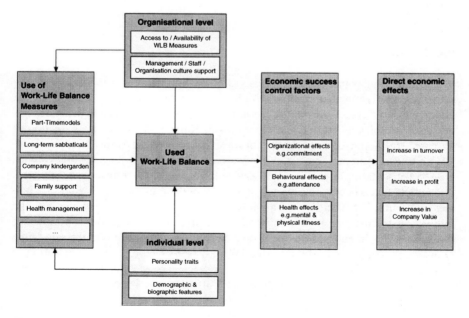

Fig. 9.2 Impact of work-life-balance instruments on the company success

9.4.1 Attitudinal Effects

Some scientific studies were able to show that work-life balance measures change the attitudes of employees. Some investigations have confirmed that the commitment, i.e., the level of identification of an employee with his company, can be increased by family-friendly measures.[35] It was even proven that the introduction of family-friendly measures positively influences the commitment of employee groups which, due to their family status, (currently) have no need of such measures.[36] Lyness and Thompson (1997) examined three different forms of employee commitment. The study showed a positive context on the work-family conflict with calculated commitment, no context with normative commitment and a negative context with affective commitment.[37] The last result is particularly important in view of the emotional relationship of an employee with his company and is probably the most important form of commitment. It thus makes sense to promote the affective employee commitment through adequate work-life balance measures.

The individually perceived work-life balance therefore positively affects the employee's attitude towards the professional service firm and thus also the fluctuation of professionals. The motivation to change to other companies decreases when work and private life are compatible,[38] for example with the help of childcare support. Job satisfaction can also be positively influenced by fewer conflicts between work and private life. Several meta-analyses[39] confirm the negative context of job satisfaction with work-life conflict, i.e., the fewer conflicts there are between life roles (i.e., the higher the work-life balance), the more satisfied employees are with their work. Similar results can be found for the general satisfaction with life.[40] However, there are also some studies, which fail to prove the mentioned or similar effects.

9.4.2 Behavioral Effects

When examining behavioral effects caused by the introduction of work-life-balance measures, this altogether results in rather uneven findings. The example of the effects of absenteeism shows that the influence of work-life balance measures has not been completely determined. Giardini and Kabst (2008) found a reduction of absenteeism in consequence of the introduction of family-friendly measures (on-site child-care, parental leave, flexible working hours, help with resuming careers, etc.).[41] Particularly for professional service firms, which often face high employee fluctuation, this aspect is an essential argument for the introduction of work-life balance measures. WLB initiatives can thus be an effective means to increase both the motivation and the long-term commitment of employees and to positively influence the innovation climate and the innovative capability of companies at the same time (Kaiser and Ringlstetter 2005). Further WLB aspects like, e.g., the preservation of employee qualification and the avoidance of absenteeism in companies (Badura and Vetter 2004), can furthermore also positively affect innovative capability. However, the mentioned research findings on behavioral effects of work-life balance measures cannot be considered final, since there are studies showing no or opposite effects. An implicit problem of behavioral effects might lie in the factor measurability, since many of these studies are based on self-reported questionnaires and not on experimental data. This is compounded by the complexity of the work-life balance concept and its influencing factors. After all, there surely are also some employees seeking compensation in work for their stressful private lives. This would certainly not lead to increased absenteeism, but even so it can be seen in a work-life balance context.

9.4.3   Effects on Health and Well-Being

More significant results, on the other hand, are provided by studies examining health effects caused by work-life balance measures. Flexible working hours are considered an essential control lever in that context. Although they cannot be clearly attributed to attitudinal effects, it was possible to show positive effects of flexible working hours for the physical well-being.[42] It is also possible to highlight stress-reducing effects of work-life balance measures.[43] These results are backed by the general meta-analytical finding that an extremely high number of working hours negatively correlates with the health of the employee.[44]

9.4.4   Economic Effects

The closely calculating controllers of individual companies, however, are more interested in the question whether work-life balance instruments – in addition to the achievable internal targets – directly affect economic success.[45] There are not many studies focusing on these economic effects, since company success is subject to a complex cause-and-effects system. A clear attribution of work-life balance measures therefore seems problematic, mainly due to methodical reasons. Frone et al. (1997) showed a significant context between work-life balance and the performance of an employee. However, their data are based on self assessments, which might be influenced by various determinants (mood, life/work satisfaction, etc.). Such results thus have to be critically reflected. Proven direct effects related to company success and based on the introduction of work-life balance measures should therefore be regarded skeptically. Often an existing work-life balance indirectly affects company success in the form of economic variables (see above).

For company practice and HR management it is therefore advisable to focus on the effects of work-life-balance measures, and in particular on the effects of family-friendly measures on the level of economic aspects of success. For it is generally known and uncontested that health and attitudinal effects like, e.g., commitment, job satisfaction, etc., contribute significantly to the success of a company.

It must be said, however, that work-life balance measures have not only positive effects. Employees without families in particular might feel disadvantaged in the short- or the long-term when family-friendly work-life balance measures are introduced and remain the only company-related work-life balance efforts. This aspect has only been considered recently by science and practice, for example in the examination of a 'singles-friendly work culture'.[46]

At the end of the day, the practical implementation of work-life balance measures is not always successful in individual cases. Particularly the corporate culture and the actual moral concepts have to be adapted in light of a 'work-life balance'. Achievable effects demonstrate their potential for company success already today. However, consideration of the compatibility of work and private life really has to find its way into company values and culture, so that the topic of work-life balance is more than just a 'buzzword' in the staff policy of professional service firms.

Notes

1. See Ostendorp (2007), p. 187.
2. See Brett and Stroh (2003), p. 67 et seq.; Litrico and Lee (2008), p. 998.
3. See Kaiser (2004); Krieger (09 Jun. 2007).
4. See Nederstigt (2005).
5. See Ringlstetter et al. (2004), p. 12.
6. See Jones et al. (2006), p. 2; Eikhof et al. (2007), p. 325ff; Morris and Madsen (2007), p. 439 et seq.
7. See Drago and Golden (2006), p. 267 et seq.; Kossek and Friede (2006), p. 611 et seq.
8. Medizin: See Badura and Vetter (2004).
9. See Jones et al. (2006), p. 2; Morris and Madsen (2007), p. 439 et seq.; Schobert (2007), p. 22.
10. See Friedman and Greenhaus (2000), p. 55; Gröpel and Kuhl (2006), p. 54 et seq.; Casper et al. (2007), p. 478 et seq.
11. According to Seligman and Csikszentmihalyi (2000) positive psychology is the study on 'strength and virtue' (p. 7), e.g., with the focus on prevention and positive emotions/cognitions instead of illnesses and their treatment.
12. See Rothbard and Dumas (2006), p. 19.
13. See Frone (2003), p. 143 et seq.
14. See Marks and MacDermid (1996), p. 421.
15. See Clark (2000), p. 747.
16. See Kirchmeyer (2000), p. 79.
17. See Gröpel and Kuhl (2006), p. 56.
18. See Jones et al. (2006), p. 292.
19. See Frone and Yardley (1996), p. 351 et seq.
20. See Smith and Gardner (2007), p. 3; Allen (2001), p. 423; Thompson et al. (1999), p. 408.
21. See also Allen (2001), p. 423.
22. See Carlson (1999), p. 241; Frone et al. (1997).
23. See Stoeva et al. (2002), p. 3 et seq.; Schneewind and Kupsch (2007), p. 155 et seq.
24. See Rantanen et al. (2005).
25. See Penley and Tomaka (2002), p. 1215 et seq.; Wierda-Boer et al. (2009), p. 8.
26. See deGraat (2007), p. 232.
27. See Lee et al. (2002), p. 209 et seq.
28. A sabbatical is a phase of 1–12 months, allowing the employee to stop working for a longer period while still being employed with a normal or reduced salary; see also Carr and Li-Ping Tang (2005), p. 160 et seq.
29. See Thompson et al. (2006), p. 284.
30. See Thompson et al. (2006), p. 285.
31. See Harrington and James (2006), p. 672; Zedeck and Mosier (1990), p. 248.

32. See Thompson et al. (2006), p. 284.
33. See Burke (2006); Dikkers et al. (2007); Thompson and Prottas (2005).
34. See Dex (1999); Perry-Smith and Blum (2000); Beauregard and Henry (2009); Connor et al. (1999); Halpern (2005); Baltes et al. (1999).
35. See Hammer et al. (2003), p. 425 et seq.; Boyar et al. (2005), p. 919 et seq.
36. See Smith and Gardner (2007), p. 8 et seq.
37. Organizational commitment is the degree of identification with an organization. Organizational commitment consists of affective (emotional; desire to stay with the company), calculated (remaining with the company based on a cost benefit analysis) und the normative commitment (remaining with the company based on standards and values); see Allen and Meyer (1990); Gauger (2000); Meyer and Allen (1991).
38. See Greenhaus et al. (1997); Lyness and Thompson (1997); Netemeyer et al. (1996).
39. See Allen et al. (2000).
40. See Adams et al. (1996); Bedeian et al. (1988).
41. See Goff et al. (1990); Halpern (2005); Hammer et al. (2003) for the respective studies.
42. See for example Frone et al. (1997); Grawitch et al. (2007); Halpern (2005) for findings on effects of supporting initiatives in light of health issues of employees.
43. See Yasbek (2004); Aryee et al. (2005); Grant-Vallone and Donaldson (2001); Anderson et al. (2002).
44. See Baltes et al. (1999).
45. See Thiehoff (2004), p. 409 et seq.
46. Casper et al. (2007) are among the first researchers comparing the perception of the work-life balance support on part of the organization of single employees and employees with families.

Chapter 10
The Alumni Network

Alumni networks are a key success factor for professional service firms. They are particularly relevant in the consulting field, but also play a vital role in other sectors. Alumni act as key suppliers of resources crucial for the success of professional service firms: client relations and knowledge.[1]

The term alumnus originally comes from the Roman military. Alumni (singular: alumnus; Latin for: 'pupil', of alere, 'raise', 'support') were injured and retired soldiers who were supported by the ancient Roman Empire for free. Analogously, the equivalent concept of the alma mater became established. Meanwhile, the term alumni is used for former students and graduates, as well as for former and retired employees in the English and increasingly also in the German language area. These people often count among the circle of people supporting their former alma mater. Often this support is rendered via institutionalized 'alumni networks' running their own marketing departments for acquiring former students. The simple relationship between organization and former employees is then replaced by the idea of networking for generating mutual benefits.

The implementation of alumni networks – as a social network for the management of former employees – has significant implications for the success of professional service firms. The value chain of HR management is expanded by the chain link of alumni. This means in practice that networks and platforms are created to provide social settings for the development of (former) employees and the positive evolution of the company itself. The basis of solid and sustainable networking with alumni is a process of give and take of the network participants. Two groups of participants can be differentiated in alumni networks of professional service firms:

- On the one hand is the professional service firm in its role as alma mater, including its active professionals.
- On the other hand are the former employees with their social relationships as informal sources and networks.

Co-author: Adrian Bründl. Additional thanks to Stefanie Kroth, who provided essential input to this chapter.

S. Kaiser, M.J. Ringlstetter, *Strategic Management of Professional Service Firms*, DOI 10.1007/978-3-642-16063-9_10, © Springer-Verlag Berlin Heidelberg 2011

Both sides have the intention in common to develop and advance promising networking potentials. This incentive structure for alumni is based on networking. Furthermore, access to company knowledge, job offers, free or subsidized trainings and invitations to events and social get-togethers is provided. With this opening to the outside world, professional service firms gain the restructuring potential of the alumni for their own enterprise. The professional service firm's efforts are rewarded with an improved corporate image with alumni acting as job returnees, business disseminators, bearers of knowledge and ambassadors. Alumni are furthermore not only ambassadors of the corporate image, but in exceptional cases also provide valuable potential as returnees. Via their outplacement, alumni of professional service firms help getting to know and understand competitors, or to expand relevant market segments and to establish professional services. Alumni consequently also assist in the development of active professionals following the principle 'learning through external experience'.

10.1 Origins of Alumni Networks in Professional Service Firms

Professional service firms with their high employee fluctuation depend more than others on relationship management as an alternative to classic knowledge management. This applies especially for professional service firms which due to their up-or-out systems are deemed companies with a particularly high fluctuation rate. An increasing pursuit of alumni as alternative success potential can be observed in consequence. This is documented in practice by an increasing number of professional service firms which have already installed an alumni network.

The origins of alumni networks, however, date back as far as the 20's of the last century. Only occasionally were networks in professional service firms established in the last decade. This development is inevitable, since professional service firms, and predominantly management consultancies, are systems which are mainly driven by relationships, based on employee contacts. The objectives of the implementation of such alumni networks are manifold. A general target is to bring together satisfied and loyal former professionals and create a cross-sector network reaching all the way into client companies. These networks are meant to bring about both the discussion of new business ideas and the development and expansion of the personal networks of the alumni. The aim is to maintain (lifetime) contact between professional service firm and alumni. This solidarity results in a lifelong support cycle. Alumni can perform different roles in this context and act as mentors, external advisors, clients, ambassadors or friends. Apart from the benefits for the professional service firms, the network also provides added value for the alumni. In addition to strengthening the mutual relationships, the network is also able to promote business contacts between alumni. Due to such objectives alumni networks have become an important pillar for the marketing efforts of professional service firms.

10.2 Organization and Size of Alumni Networks

When considering the organization of alumni networks, member-related character-istics are particularly relevant. The networks consist of former professionals who voluntarily participate in the system. Some networks impose minimum membership requirements, so that not all former employees are necessarily part of the network. As a rule, it is irrelevant for the alumni status and network membership whether retirement from the professional service firm was voluntary or whether the employ-ment was terminated. With regard to access to the alumni network of management consultancies, different options can be observed in practice: In some all members have access, in others accessibility is limited. In the latter cases, active employees could for example have only access to job databases while alumni are able to access all data. Interns generally cannot access the network. With respect to the composi-tion of alumni networks in various sectors it can be observed that not all alumni join potential clients; some also join competing professional service firms.

Often the respective sector competences of professional service firms are reflected in the distribution of alumni across sectors. However, consulting profes-sionals hardly ever change across sectors, but instead change rather to upper or lower value chain levels. In case of an organization depending on positions, all hierarchical levels are represented in alumni networks. About one third of consulting com-pany alumni fill executive or management positions after a change of jobs, where in turn decisions on the consulting need and selection of professionals are made. Consequently, a deliberate positioning of alumni in strategically important positions can be assumed in the industry. This suggests that professional service firms often are a stepping stone for further functional management positions with big companies or for a business management position in a medium-size company.[2] Apart from the specific sector distribution, one can generally assume a homogeneous organization of members in alumni networks of professional service firms.

Due to their different regional focus, the alumni networks of management con-sultancies differ in terms of size. A significant comparison of the valuation of alumni networks can therefore only be made on the basis of the ratio of former and active professionals.

10.3 Key Elements and Selectivity

Depending on their objective, alumni networks of professional service firms often have some typical features. Among the core elements of such networks is the internet as a primary platform. Alumni directories are installed on the web site – respectively in password-protected areas – of the professional service firms, listing all participating alumni. In addition, success stories of former employees or rele-vant press releases are presented. The alumni area generally serves as a channel for exchange of ideas and to disseminate knowledge.[3] Sometimes the alumni are even able to manage their pension funds online. With its manifold performance possibil-ities the internet is predestined to develop an effective and extensive network using limited resources.[4] By providing a career platform and job offers, the internet portal, like the network in general, supports the career development of alumni.[5] On career pages alumni can obtain information on companies hiring, or have the option to publish their CVs or place job search ads.[6] As another key element, regular events are held in the form of personal meetings.[7] These provide both the alumni and the professional service firms with the possibility to establish and maintain contacts for vocational and business development. Other elements are the distribution of newly published books and studies or electronic newsletters.

Trust must be regarded the constituting element of networks, especially of alumni networks,[8] since it is the factor decisively contributing to the improvement of communication on part of the alumni.[9] When considering the resource intensity in addition to the key contents it becomes obvious that a selective approach[10] by of tailoring of activities makes sense. Selectivity can apply to the selection of network elements as such, or also to the alumni. A selective approach is for example suitable when choosing the respective elements for information material or in case of invitations for certain events. Apart from the allocation to a specific sector, selectivity in terms of alumni can also be distinguished depending on regions, companies, or hierarchies. The personal network of the alumnus is also used as a segmentation criterion.[11] The professional's decision to join a new company has particular significance. Within the sector, alumni in the industry are deemed more valuable than alumni in competing consultancies, since alumni networks are often based on the idea of development of new business relations.

10.4 Relevance of Alumni Networks as Success Factor

Alumni as former human resources do not directly affect the corporate success of a professional service firm; they are rather to be seen as 'condition of the possibility' to generate future success and are thus consequently deemed potentials to be developed.[12] This idea of potentials, however, plays a part in various forms. The four most prominent potentials are represented in Fig. 10.1. The relevance of alumni

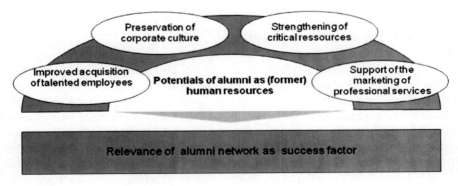

Fig. 10.1 Potentials of alumni as (former) human resources

networks as success factor is initially based both on the potential of the alumni to acquire talented employees (1) and on the promotion of the corporate culture (2). In addition, the networks can strengthen the critical resources of professional service firms (3) and thus specifically support the marketing of services (4).

10.4.1 Improvement of Acquisition of Talented Employees

Talented employees are crucial for the success of a professional service firm. The resulting 'war for talents'[13] makes the acquisition of talented employees a sensitive task. Since an alumni network provides the option to resort to references and recommendations within the networks,[14] this can also improve acquisition efforts.[15]

First, alumni can indirectly support acquisition activities by providing an example for a successful career. With the careers of their alumni, professional service firms therefore draw attention to the prospects of success for the time after employment with them. In case of individual professional service firms it can be observed that the possibility of contacting former employees and the availability of a large network[16] as 'insider information source' are advertised in job and internship ads.[17] This indirect support can lead to savings with recruiting efforts and during the resource-intensive personnel selection.

In a second step, these references also provide the opportunity of the employment of alumni from another professional service firm in the form of 'lateral hires'[18] or by 're-hiring' from industry companies.[19] In case of 'lateral hires', possible savings can be generated by avoiding headhunter costs; with 're-hiring', integration costs for professionals can be reduced. According to a study, recruitment costs for comebackers are significantly lower than in regular acquisition processes; besides, the 'boomerangs' are often more productive and happier due to their conscious decision.[20]

10.4.2 Survival of the Corporate Culture

Apart from human resources themselves, the actual corporate culture can provide competitive advantages for professional service firms and thus represent a critical part of their strategic identity. The term corporate culture describes the influence of cultural aspects within organizations. It is a fixed motto as well as a psychological contract between the professionals and the company and represents one of the most significant separation criteria of professional service firms.

The maintenance and cultivation of the respective corporate culture should therefore have main priority. In this context, alumni networks can advance to become a strategic component of the survival of the culture. A unique and strong corporate culture contributes substantially to 'commitment maximizing' and the team-building of professionals. Especially the ambivalent public image of professional service firms and the deliberate decision for working in a professional service firm decisively shape junior staff members, who often join a professional service firm directly after graduation.[21] Solidarity often reaches as far as everyday life, which additionally strengthens the culture. There are often significant differences in the cultures of individual professional service firms.[22] Apart from the internal sealing-off of a company, corporate culture with a tightly knit alumni network also provides external delimitation from competitors.[23] This can lead to the advantage of avoiding 'lateral hires' due to a lack of cultural conformity. In industrial companies the survival of the 'one-firm culture' is guaranteed by targeted outplacement of alumni.[24] The 'lifelong rose-colored consultant's view' conditioned by the intensity of consulting work and the commitment of the alumni can facilitate client work. Alumni consequently contribute professional service firm culture to other professional service firms as well as in industrial companies and acts as targeted contacts. From a competition point of view this non-monetary value also contributes to the success of a professional service firm and provides therefore another potential element of alumni for future success.

10.4.3 Strengthening of Critical Resources

Dependence of professional service firms on a few key resources makes their handling a critical strategic task. The dependence on resources can be deliberately improved by social networks.[25] Networks themselves emerge from relations between people, and professional service firms lacking tangible products depend on them. Alumni networks also help strengthening critical resources of professional service firms such as knowledge, social competence as well as reputation. With regard to knowledge alumni networks, similar to social networks, can have general impacts on the knowledge management of professional service firms by influencing knowledge generation and sharing as well as the increase of knowledge.[26] The possibility of discussing new consulting ideas with alumni is a vital source of information for such networks. Due to their involvement in various sectors, alumni help to generate sector knowledge[27] by sharing their practical knowledge in the consulting process. This back channel additionally promotes the sharing of knowledge. Alumni can furthermore contribute to an increase in knowledge as information processors[28] which can be a decisive competitive advantage for the professional service firm.[29] Furthermore, networks can strengthen and shape relationships. This consolidation of relations causes a strengthening of social competence in a consultant.[30] Moreover, alumni networks can improve reputation.[31] Although alumni are no longer active members of the company, they can increase its reputation as (external) representatives.[32] This is ensured with references on which basis insecurity regarding the service can be reduced. In conclusion it can be stated that alumni networks have the potential to strengthen critical resources of a professional service firm, which in turn might affect the (future) success of the company.

10.4.4 Support of Marketing of Services

Human capital is significant for corporate success of professional service firms, which is based on the sales of its services. Alumni networks can also support marketing efforts. The development of relationships, as core element in networks, shows the connections to the relationship marketing, respectively indirect marketing sector.[33] The alumnus, as contact person in an industrial company, gains significance if he or she can decide on the possible need for external services and is able to use his or her influence in selecting the professional service firm.[34] In case of such a marketing perspective, alumni are valuable marketing resources.[35] They can support the marketing of their former employers by communicating competences. This can involve personal contacts and references[36] on part of the alumni.[37] Alumni thus act as disseminators, ambassadors and commissioners in many different ways.[38] Contact development between professional and clients and thus the marketing of services, is therefore based on the existence and use of a comprehensive (alumni) network.[39] Active marketing is promoted in particular through various alumni events which provide business opportunities for professional service firms, for clients and for the alumni. The contact and the development of contracts between client and professional service firm can be implemented based on personal relationships in the style of an interactive marketing approach and the idea of networking[40]. Therefore, professional service firms have the chance to obtain information on needs for external services via their alumni networks earlier than the competitors and to take appropriate steps. In conclusion, the connection to the alumni does not generate direct profits; however, it improves the capabilities to generate new business relations and to maintain existing relationships.[41] Since the marketing of services is indispensable for success, alumni can also improve the 'conditions of possibilities' for future success.

10.5 Implications for the Management of Professional Service Firms

Social networks can generally contribute to sustainable company success.[42] When considering the manifold success potential of alumni networks for professional service firms,[43] this leads to the requirement of strategic management of these networks.

The management of professionals becomes a strategic success factor if one assumes that the use and advanced development of professionals depend significantly on human resources management measures.[44]

Based on the strategic implementation of human resources management (HRM), a strategic connection of the management of former human resources also seems beneficial, due to the essential role of (former) employees in professional service firms.[45] As a first step, it is thus useful to create organizational framework conditions (1). In a second step, alumni management can be strategically implemented (2) by connecting it to the HRM (3).

10.5.1 Creation of Organizational Framework Conditions

To start out with, organizational framework conditions defining the relationship management with the alumni must be created to strategically implement the alumni policies. These can be summarized with planning, organizational and control aspects and can furthermore include suitable technologies as well as implementation in the corporate culture. The first objective is careful planning of the management of alumni networks. This process commences with the verbalization of goals and certain guidelines, and extends to the decision on the organization and selectivity of the respective contents.[46] Planning should include an adequate budget of resources, available for long-term.[47]

The implementation of alumni management in the organizational structure comprehends the two elements of organization and execution. In this context different handling approaches are possible. One option is the establishment of a department or the employment of an alumni manager as cross-linking approach. To guarantee functioning of the communication, the entire professional service firm including its respective departments must be involved. Apart from planning and organization it is also important to control the added value to evaluate the efficiency of the alumni management.[48] But then, measurability of added value of relationships such as quantification of immaterial assets is generally one of the key challenges for professional service firms.

Moreover, for the control of alumni networks the use of suitable technologies supporting the network's creation and preservation is also necessary.[49] Since the internet provides a central platform, the technology for management and administration of the alumni networks should also be internet-based. Such technologies are often cost-efficient and ensure data completeness and topicality. This also facilitates a selective and targeted approach. To guarantee optimal functioning of alumni policy it is furthermore recommended to integrate it in the corporate culture.[50] Cultural implementation of the management of alumni networks often arises inevitably, since the network itself is inherent in the system and is part of the corporate culture of the professional service firm. Lastly, organizational framework conditions facilitate the strategic implementation of alumni management which can be taken care of in connection with HRM.

10.5.2 Linking Alumni Network Management with Human Resources Management (HRM)

Organizational framework conditions are the basis for successful implementation of alumni networks. Due to the fact that alumni are (former) human resources of professional service firms, the connection to HRM is self-evident.[51] The relevant components like expert forums, newsletter dispatch, advanced training measures, provision of incentives and social events are daily practice and, for the implementation of an alumni management, have to be combined and centralized. The contribution to corporate success of a professional service firm by maintaining lifelong relations to the alumni is supported by the organization of alumni management following the 'principle of lifelong affiliation'.[52,53]

The lifelong HRM support cycle is based on the (vocational) life cycle of professionals.[54] In this context alumni management, with its creation and preservation of relations to former employees with alumni status, is an additional task field

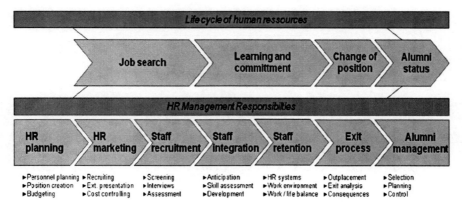

Fig. 10.2 Implementation of alumni management in HRM

in the original life cycle. This additional phase in the HR cycle and its relevance to the (vocational) life cycle of professionals is underlined in Fig. 10.2.

10.5.3 Strategic Focus of HRM on the Management of Alumni Networks

Due to their dependence on human capital, management consultancies should tread new paths to remain competitive with their HRM. In future, strategic recruitment aspects will become more and more important. Personnel marketing, recruitment and assessment should be centralized.[55] Talent Relationship Management (TRM) is one concept to deal with the topic alumni.

TRM as a strategic concept is a personnel policy measure based on the ideas of customer relationship management. The focus is on active development of long-term relationships with talents who are considered sustainable and valuable assets by companies throughout their whole vocational life cycle. Due to their high fluctuation of human resources and their appeal as employers, management consultancies, law firms and auditing firms in particular have large pools of former employees and applicants.

From a strategic and operative perspective it is therefore logical to create a talent pool[56] consisting of candidates who currently can either not be offered suitable positions, or candidates, and in particular alumni, who are currently not available for the company. The pool provides an overview of all existing and potential personnel resources and is part of the company strategy (see Fig. 10.3).

The development of long-term relationships is attempted by targeted measures in tune with the preferences of the respective candidates. Typical measures can be: regular telephone contacts, gifts, newsletters, invitations to company events, corporate magazines, i.e., the concentration on active, cooperative and communicative means.

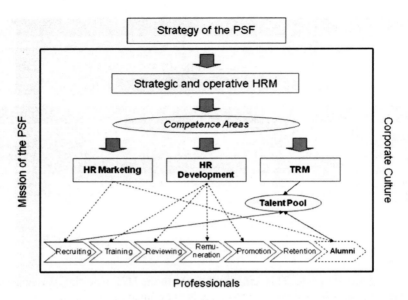

Fig. 10.3   Holistic implementation of talent relationship management in the company strategy

The introduction of TRM should not fizzle out as a unique event; it should rather be ensured that all pillars support this strategic component. Of particular significance therefore is the retirement process of professionals. When professionals leave, it is mandatory not to lose their loyalty, particularly in the case of professionals having been made redundant. The phases of establishing friendly relations and redefinition can otherwise not be ensured, and all efforts for managing the former employees would be in vain. Altogether, the strategic connection between the management of alumni networks and HRM provides possibilities to maintain (lifelong) relationships with alumni which in turn can impact future success.

10.6   Development Tendencies of Alumni Networks in Professional Service Firms

In the increasing competition among professional service firms, active marketing strategies become more and more important. The 'golf club principle' is not declining in significance: Business is easier with people one already knows. Alumni networks thus become an integral part of the recruitment strategy of consultancies. But the concept can easily be applied to the entire PSF sector. Altogether, such networks are of general significance for knowledge-based companies, like professional service firms, where learning experience is relevant.

The advantages of implementing an alumni network lie on the one hand in the marketing of services. The cultivation of an image as problem solver is strengthened on basis of special information and the derivation of direct consulting needs.

Active professionals can obtain acquisition-relevant information of service needs not only from their own companies, but also from competitor, supplier and client companies. On the other hand, alumni networks directly affect the recruitment and participation philosophy. Hiring decisions are based on informal contacts. The participation option enables professionals to learn and network. The target group of HR recruitment and planning is expanded to external performance carriers, including re-recruiting via the talent pool. Alumni networks furthermore also strengthen social competence. In light of these potentials, alumni networks will become increasingly important for professional service firms in the future. As regards the motivation to actively participate in the network, incentives to improve commitment in the classical sense cannot be of any interest for the alumni, since they are no longer employed by the company. Alumni should rather be specifically motivated to actively participate in the network.

In some professional service firms and industrial companies, however, another implementation strategy can be observed. Here, commercial and open platforms with low inhibition thresholds are used to distribute content and podcasts. Useful in implementing such networks are platforms like Xing, Facebook, LinkedIN, and Select Minds, which are used to install portals with restricted access. These platforms are independent from the development of corporate culture in the companies. However, such alumni areas are often networks in the sense of 'friendship groups' with a high degree of autonomy, loose connections and without superordinate objective of all members. One advantage in this context, however, can be the bridging function to other networks. Problematic issues for both alumni-strategies still are the associated technical and competitive security risks when sharing intellectual property. At this point, both the IT and management sectors will face high requirements also in the future.

Notes

1. See on this matter also Chaps. 4 and 5 in this book.
2. See Breipohl (2004), p. 116.
3. See Wells (28 Jun. 2005), p. 16.
4. See Anders (2002), p. 17.
5. See in general about the role of the Internet as career platform DeFillippi et al. (2003).
6. See Anders (2002), p. 17.
7. See Nohria and Eccles (1994), p. 303 et seq.
8. See Fey (2005), p. 12.
9. See Wagner (2004), p. 77 et seq.
10. See Harding (1990), p. 44. Harding postulates ten rules for better networking in professional service firms, one of which covers the selective approach.
11. See Barabási (2003), p. 71.
12. See as to thinking in potentials Kirsch (1990), p. 356 et seq. as well as Ringlstetter and Kniehl (1995), p. 155 et seq., and the literature indicated there. The individual potential of an alumnus becomes at an aggregate level the potential of the entire alumni network.
13. See BDU (2005), p. 15 as well about the war for human capital Müller-Stewens et al. (1999), p. 98 et seq.
14. See Granovetter (1973).

15. See Fernandez and Castilla (2001), p. 85 et seq.; Marsden (2001).
16. See The Boston Consulting Group (2005), p. 11.
17. See Lorsch and Tierney (2002).
18. See Ringlstetter and Bürger (2004), p. 290 et seq.
19. In the case of re-hiring, alumnis return to their original firm.
20. See Sertoglu and Berkowitch (2002b), p. 20.
21. See Müller-Stewens et al. (1999), p. 98 et seq. about recruitment in professional service firms
22. See also on sealing off from competitors Höselbarth (2000), p. 213 et seq.
23. See also on cultural agreement Müller-Stewens (1999), p. 48 et seq.
24. See Maister (2003) p. 308 et seq.
25. See Mizruchi and Galaskiewicz (1994), p. 245 et seq.; Nahapiet and Ghoshal (2002), p. 682. This can happen when they open up access to resources and, at the same time, represent a valuable resource in themselves.
26. See Inkpen and Tsang (2005), p. 150; Sveiby and Lloyd (1990), p. 61; Burt (1992), p. 13 et seq.
27. See Sertoglu and Berkowitch (2002b), p. 20 et seq.
28. See on the topic of boundary spanners Aldrich (1979) as well as on the theory of weak ties Granovetter (1973). A key precondition for the flow of information lies in the creation and use of network positions.
29. See Rottloff (2004), p. 24 et seq.
30. The relationship between consultant and client must be identified by mutual trust; see Fink and Knoblach (2004), p. 88. Consulting is to a high extent a matter of trust; see Höselbarth (2000), p. 219.
31. See on the increase of reputation Bürger (2004), p. 157; Sertoglu and Berkowitch (2002a), p. 8; as well as Zabala et al. (2005); Bamberger (1998), p. 243 et seq.
32. See Wells (28 Jun. 2005), p. 16 as well on the function of the (alumni as) boundary spanner Aldrich (1979), p. 248 et seq.
33. In the sense of indirect marketing, a large part of long-term interactions generally takes place by relations at a high level in the hierarchy. In consulting, these negotiations often take place between senior professionals and decision makers on part of the client, such as executive boards or managing directors; see Bürger (2004), p. 152.
34. See Lorsch and Tierney (2002), p. 89
35. See Iyer (1998); Iyer et al. (2000).
36. See Bamberger (1998), p. 253.
37. See Schade (1996), p. 108 et seq.
38. See on the role of employees as disseminators for enabling and recommending new business contacts Glückler (2001), p. 24.
39. See e.g. Schade (1996), p. 105.
40. See Kohr (2000), p. 178 et seq. as well as Becker and Schade (1995), p. 338 et seq.
41. Social capital creates opportunities to generate income with financial capital (by investing in relations with the alumni) and human capital (as the alumni him/herself); see Pennings and Lee (2002), p. 53.
42. See Mizruchi and Galaskiewicz (1994), p. 239 et seq.
43. This addresses in the first place practical management implications. In parallel, more attention should be paid to alumni networks in theoretical analysis, as they could represent a source of value increase through social networks and the building up of social capital.
44. Ringlstetter et al. (2004), p. 163 et seq.
45. See on HRM as cornerstones in the strategy of professional service firms Baer and Stoll (1999), p. 200 et seq.; see also Chap. 7 in this book.
46. This should be affected in coordination with other organization targets. In addition it would be useful to have the support of top management for the initiative and decisions as well as including seniors as contact partners.

47. See Coleman (1990), p. 91. The budget should be planned for long term to allow for the necessary continuity in the development of social relationships.
48. See Sertoglu and Berkowitch (2002b), p. 20. Costs depend on the size and configuration of the network, as they will increase with the size of the network; see Nahapiet and Ghoshal (2002), p. 691.
49. See Lesser (2000b), p. 13 et seq. Especially when building up social capital, appropriate technologies are indispensable.
50. See Iyer and Day (1998), p. 26.
51. See on the subject of alumni as *Part of the Value-Adding Chain* in HR of professional service firms Müller-Stewens et al. (1999), p. 87 et seq. as well as on the life cycle of a professional, p. 98 et seq. The value-adding cycle of professionals recalls a life-long model and is equal to a continuum starting with the acquisition and ending with the maintenance of the relationship with the former professionals; see Lorsch and Tierney (2002), p. 88 et seq.
52. See Reischauer and Schlesinger (2005), p. 91.
53. See concerning employee policies von Booz Allen & Hamilton as well as to the following Höselbarth (2000), p. 216 et seq.
54. See concerning the concept of life cycle of human resources Ringlstetter and Kniehl (1995), p. 151 et seq.; Kaiser (2001), p. 3 as well as on the value-adding cycle of professionals Lorsch and Tierney (2002), p. 88 et seq. See also on HRM in professional service firms Kaiser (2004).
55. See Richter and Stähler (2003).
56. See Jäger and Jäger (2004).

Part IV
Management of Strategic Development

Chapter 11
Strategic Development of Professional Service Firms

For professional service firms, above average company growth and the highly competitive business environment represent central challenges for strategic development. With the reorganization of the sector, these challenges caused by excess capacities and price pressure gain additional importance. To continue working successfully against this background, specific development strategies are necessary which must be supported by correlating organization architecture. For the development of professional service firms, three strategic options are presented: diversification, internationalization and strengthening of the core businesses (11.1). Implementation of these development strategies can on the whole only be effected by internal reorganization (11.2), through acquisitions (11.3) or cooperation (11.4).[1]

11.1 Generic Options for Strategic Development

The market for professional services is characterized, at least since the beginning of the 1990ies, by above average company growth, but also by higher competitiveness (1).[2] Against this background, there are three strategic options open for the strategic development of professional service firms: diversification, internationalization and concentration on the core business (2).

11.1.1 Growth and the Competitive Situation in the PSF Sector

The organization structures of professional service firms can ideal-typically be represented – independent of the concrete hierarchy levels – as a so-called professional pyramid based on three levels: the seniors and/or partners, the managers and the junior staff members (Fig. 11.1).[3]

As a career path, however, the topmost level of this pyramid is only open to the very best professionals. The career path system in numerous professional service firms, which are mostly in the consulting sector, is characterized by the concept of 'up-or-out'. 'Up-or-out' defines a career path model where employees are either

Co-author: Bernd Bürger

S. Kaiser, M.J. Ringlstetter, *Strategic Management of Professional Service Firms*,
DOI 10.1007/978-3-642-16063-9_11, © Springer-Verlag Berlin Heidelberg 2011

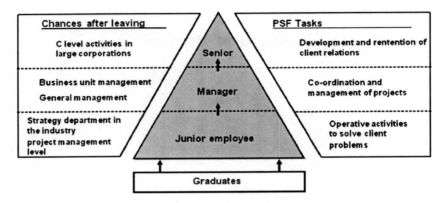

Fig. 11.1 Levels of the professional pyramid with their corresponding areas of responsibility

promoted (up) or laid off (out) after predefined time periods. This is to ensure the excellence of the employees at all career levels. This personnel strategy was implemented for the first time around 1950 in the consulting firm McKinsey. The basic idea behind this was that separation from professionals should be done quickly in order to facilitate a new start. A positive side effect for professional service firms is, however, that during the selection and hiring phase the professional's qualification for management responsibilities later on, is of no immediate concern. This part of the selection processes is happening 'on the job'.

Whether it is 'up' or 'out' is predominantly decided by controlling and reporting systems informing company management as comprehensively as possible on the added value contribution (impact) of individual professionals. The majority of consulting projects comprehends activities and work steps known from previous projects which only need to be modified to suit any specific client. By involving experienced managers and seniors in the project teams, synergies are generated from which results the added value of the projects for customers and clients. An optimized structure of the project teams is thus the precondition for an effective and economical activity of the consulting firm. This can only be guaranteed as long as there is a correlation between employees at the junior, manager, and senior levels of the company. On the one hand, junior professionals who have not yet been promoted represent an insufficient investment value for professional service firms. On the other hand, many professionals decide consciously against 'up' within the professional service firm and leave, not because of a lack of perspectives, but to pursue other options. In this context, the mostly very steep learning and experience curve counts as a career catalyst for professionals at the medium level of the professional service firm. The professionals get to know numerous companies and, more to the point, the senior management of the clients as well. Furthermore, constant movement in the personnel structure and the naturally high fluctuation rate is a decisive precondition for the effective working of the business model of a professional service firm. However, in countries with strong employees' rights, this principle can be communicated in its pure form only with certain restrictions, and is limited by the ongoing 'war-for-talents' and, more and more often, individually agreed career plans with professionals. In summary, it should be noted that the 'up-or-out'-system typical for this sector must not solely be understood as a brutal selection process, but for various reasons also as a growth pressure factor for the development of professional service firms.

The work load in professional service firms is very high, even for junior professionals. To be able to recruit new employees in spite of that, career promises play a big role. The possibility of long-term development and of ultimate inclusion in the circle of partners plays a central role in motivational criteria. At the same time, career aspirations are encouraged by the 'up-or-out' system. Professionals wanting to remain in the company are only able to do so through continuing development in connection with the corresponding career moves. But if their career promises are honored, the number of partners at the top career level must increase at the same time. As partners acquire an interest in the profits of the company – often as shareholders – enlarging the circle of partners must be accompanied by an increase of company profits. The original partners will most likely not agree to sharing their part of the profits, but will rather aim at generating an increase. Under these conditions, professional service firms must generate huge growth in order to satisfy the requirements of their professionals and maintain the relationship between senior and junior professionals.[4]

In parallel to this development, market penetration in the individual service segments increases. The number of professional services providers increases, while established firms are growing organically at the same time and are widening the spectrum of their services. The auditor KPMG, for example, has long since widened the range of its core business and is additionally active, along with other large auditing firms, in the areas of insurance, management consultancy, financial services and legal advice. This type of converging movement can be observed in various PSF subsectors[5] and leads to a highly competitive situation.[6] To exist long-term in this environment, professional service firms conceive and develop specific competitive advantages, in order to differentiate themselves from their competition. Client relationships and the company knowledge base are crucial for long-term success.

In 2001 and 2002 the challenges of strategic development increased. Above average company growth and increasing demand for professional services in den 1990ies ended with a drastic drop of demand caused by the economic downturn. Following a recovery phase and increased growth in subsequent years, demand dropped again dramatically in 2008 in the wake of the subprime crisis. Professional service firms which previously had built up massive capacities were facing a completely different market environment. The buyers of professional services became more cost conscious, and in view of that, many projects were either cancelled or postponed, the high remunerations of the professionals were put in question. The resulting development and adaptation of the remuneration systems is described in Chap. 2. In professional service firms, this process caused a sales and/or price problem. Many consulting firms lost consulting contracts, while the number of companies going public, reduced to a mere minimum, particularly with regard to investment banks but also true for numerous law firms and communication agencies, became critical. Auditors and tax advisors were not faced with a reduced number of incoming orders, but rather with increased price pressure. Since professional service firms typically try to improve their capacities by all means and not lay off any professionals, this increased competition additionally.[7]

11.1.2 Strategic Development Options for Professional Service Firms

Against the background of the aforementioned challenges three development strategies can be pursued which represent at the same time orientation along the line of client requirements and optimized use of company resources (see Fig. 11.2)[8]:

- *Diversification:* Extension of business activities to include new professional services,
- *Internationalization:* Extension of business activities to new countries,
- *Strengthening of the Core Business:* concentration on already existing activities with the aim of intensifying them.

The *diversification strategy* covers the extension of the current service spectrum. New services related to the core business are offered to the clients. The *diversification strategy* meets the client's desire for service from a 'one-stop shop' without any interfaces to lower their transaction costs.[9] From the perspective of the company such diversification in the context of a 'client leverage' aims at selling the newly created services to as many clients as possible with whom they have already existing business relations. One can distinguish between *horizontal* diversification,

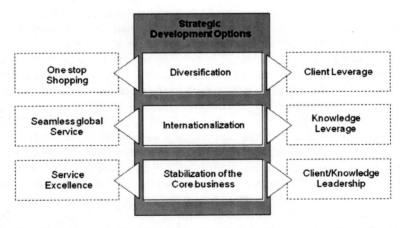

Fig. 11.2 Possibilities of strategic development of professional service firms. (Source: see Ringlstetter and Bürger 2003, p. 121)

whereby new markets are gained through new services, and *vertical* diversification, whereby the depth of services is extended. Where a professional service firm succeeds in selling their clients a variety of services at the same time, company turnover can be increased via 'cross selling'. For this reason, auditing firms in the early 1990ies extended their portfolio to include the more lucrative services of consulting and corporate finance.[10] Next to the possible turnover increase, considerations about limiting business risk could speak for a client leverage strategy. Diversification allows furthermore improving competitiveness in those cases where existing strengths can be transferred. As described in the previous section, professional service firms are highly dependent on the business situations of their clients. By widening their service range, negative repercussions of an 'ailing' sector on the total turnover can be limited or, in some cases, even compensated.[11] However, new critical criteria result from this *diversification strategy* for the business of professional service firms. Investment banks, for example, are obligated to maintain confidentiality areas to prevent insider trading. These so-called 'Chinese walls' functioning as information barriers are aimed at sealing off information from a specific area or a department, with the aim of not letting sensitive information leak into other groups or departments, in order to avoid conflict of interest. This concerns mainly analysis and trade departments. In corporate law firms, 'Chinese walls' may be found to avoid conflict of interest where one partner area handles a transaction and is separated from another area with opposite interests.

In nearly all PSF subsectors the leading companies have *internationalized* since the 1980ies at the latest.[12] In 2002, engineering service provider and auditing firms were already quite advanced in the process of extending their activities geographically, followed by consulting firms, and later on by the large corporate law firms.[13] Increased competition in the various professional service segments forces companies to improve their portfolio and adapt to client wishes. By *internationalization,* professional service firms can offer their clients a so-called 'seamless global service', i.e., the possibility to work with the same provider on a worldwide basis.[14] Besides, the extension of national services is often a precondition for long-term company success. A special challenge in this context is, on the one hand, the coordination of activities in different countries while maintaining a certain quality standard and, on the other hand, adapting the portfolio to local requirements and cultural specifics.[15] *Standardization* means that services are streamlined transnationally and are partially placed as brand services, while in a *differentiation strategy* services are locally adapted to the individual country. The advantage of standardization lies in the fact that by globalization of the services cost degression effects can be realized. But there is no doubt whatsoever that total *standardization* and/or *differentiation* makes no sense, and that the optimal degree of standardization or differentiation is a decisive factor. By internationalizing, an already existing knowledge base and problem solving capacities are generally made available to a broader range of clients. The potential of the organizational knowledge base can be optimally exploited by this 'knowledge leverage'. Besides improving turnover, the cooperation with new clients enriches the existing knowledge base with new client knowledge.[16]

Independent of pursuing these two strategies, professional service firms should continually strive for *strengthening their core businesses* for two reasons:

- For many professional service firms, such as the so-called 'Big 4' – the four largest auditing firms –, the diversification and internationalization potential is already fully exploited due to their worldwide country offices and their already existing broad range of services.
- Even where this potential is not fully exploited, new business areas or country offices are no substitute for their core business, which is subject to extreme competitive pressure and needs additional strengthening.

The aim is to improve quality, i.e., 'service excellence', in the market, and to distinguish the firm with regard to competence and client relationship from the competition and/or to attain 'client/knowledge leadership'.

Complex, knowledge-intensive services have ideal-typically short life cycles. To be able to give best performance, a continuous innovation process is therefore necessary.[17] Focusing on specific core areas can contribute to excelling the organizational know-how both of the clients and the competition. Strengthening the core businesses can here be effected by *focusing on a functional competence area* or on a *specific sector*.[18]

- *Focusing on a functional competence area* must be based on an edge over the know-how in this service area. Large corporate law firms are usually opting for this strategy and concentrate on specific areas in law.
- *Sector specialization* is based on the idea that the variances in the competitive situation of different economic segments are of greater significance than pure methods know-how. In this case, the aim of professional service firms must be to know more about the rules and 'key players' of the respective sector than their clients.

11.2 Organic Development

The different options of development can be effected internally by the organization, both via recruitment of university graduates and by so-called 'lateral hires', i.e., headhunting experienced professionals from other companies (1). With increasing growth, however, the complexity of the service provision increases as well, and requires adaptation to the organizational structures (2).

11.2.1 Internal Growth Opportunities

Companies like the Boston Consulting Group or McKinsey have brought about the enormous growth of the last few years mainly through internal resources. The existing client base and the service spectrum of the professional service firm then

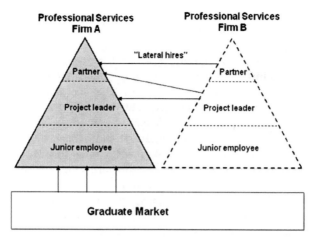

Fig. 11.3 Organic growth through lateral hires and recruitment of university graduates by professional service firms. (Source: Adapted from Ringlstetter et al. 2004, p. 290)

form the starting point for further development. Relationships with important clients can then be deepened and widened, and the service spectrum can be developed through an internal innovations process. Such 'organic growth' typically generates higher 'cash return' than acquisitions[19] and can therefore be an interesting option, even when the development speed is lower. However, this growth option is limited by the number of professionals, to be more exact: by the respective billing capacity of the company. In order to grow anyway, the capacity restriction can be overcome in two ways (see Fig. 11.3):

- Increased activity on the market for university graduates or MBA programs, in order to find newcomers for the firm.
- Growing involvement in 'lateral hiring', i.e., headhunting of professionals with work experience from other companies.

Increased activity on the market for graduates means that growth at the higher levels of the hierarchy is happening at the same time. In order to process client orders as usual, the leverage,[20] i.e., the numeric relationship between individual levels of the hierarchy, must remain the same. That means that recruitment at the lowest level of the hierarchy must generate promotion at the upper career levels. A relatively low leverage of 1:6:6 can, e.g., be found in strategy consulting and means ideal-typically that for each partner there are six project managers, and for each project manager there are six junior employees. This means that when the number of junior employees increases, it is automatically defined how many employees at the next higher and/or topmost career level should be promoted. Conversely, it also means that for each junior employee promoted to the level of project manager six new employees must be recruited for the company. For strong growth there are substantial recruitment requirements.

Particularly in times where the market for human resources was fiercely fought over by traditional corporations, up-and-coming e-commerce companies and growth focused professional service firms at the same time, new ways had to be found to cover the growing need of employees. Consulting firms like McKinsey or The Boston Consulting Group succeeded in opening up new human resources markets through so-called 'foreigner programs'. Apart from the classic MBA graduates, other graduates in mathematics. electronics, law or theology were interviewed more and more often to win them over as employees. For maintaining the quality level of employees, substantial resources, both financial and human, had to be invested in the successful selection and integration of suitable professionals.

Recruiting graduates gave professional service firms the opportunity to acquaint employees gradually with the company, to 'form' and successfully integrate them. Socializing an employee fully to the company culture is best done at an early development stage.[21] For client relations, this kind of socializing is of enormous import in the long run. By cooperation with a specific professional service firm, clients get used to the respective culture of the company and link their respective expectations to the professionals.

The described development is restricted by the fact that planning is difficult and, in particular in the case of partnerships, by often below average capitalization. The recruitment of university graduates provides the professional service firm neither new clients nor new knowledge in the short term, but is, on the other hand, linked to an enormous expenditure. Thus, investment in new employees poses a risk and is often neglected, particularly by companies with weak capitalization. This situation results in a typical 'chicken and egg problem': without an adequate number of employees no new clients can be acquired, but at the same time no new employees should be recruited as long as no new client orders are in sight.

Instead of recruiting graduates, *lateral hires* focus on experienced professionals who have already climbed a few career steps. These can either come directly from competing firms or from other companies and institutions. For professional service firms, *lateral hires* offer two substantial advantages:

- The acquisition of so-called 'Rainmaker s', i.e., professionals mostly at the partner level, who have already gathered experience in a specific business area and have a good network of client relations available, can bring the professional service firm direct turnover increase, either by the new employees contributing to extending the client base or by bringing experience and a reputation in a new business area.[22]
- In particular for the realization of diversification and internationalization, professionals must bring with them certain mobility. They must be ready to work long-term in new target market countries or to leave their traditional business area. Certain barriers to mobility applying to existing employees can be bypassed through *lateral hires*.

With corporate law firms in specific, *lateral hires* are often used to realize diversification or internationalization and to increase service excellence. The legal regulations in this sector are strongly characterized on a national basis, and many countries limit the accreditation for lawyers still to their own nationals or link them to strict conditions.[23] Efforts in internationalization by organic growth are therefore often limited to *lateral hires*. Among law firms a 'gentleman agreement' existed for a long time, which interdicted recruiting lawyers from a competing firm,[24] but this agreement erodes increasingly, and *lateral hires* serve more and more often to satisfy the human resources requirements.[25] This procedure can become problematic when there are strong cultural differences between the acquiring professional service firm and the new employees. An experienced professional cannot be socialized easily, and so the danger persists, that problems arise in the cooperation with the new colleagues, but also with long-term clients, which have become used to certain routines. In addition, these lateral hires reduce the promotion opportunities of the other professionals, and this could lead to negative motivation effects.

11.2.2 Structural Challenges of Internal Implementation

When implementing the strategies internally, structural challenges arise through the growth of the company. The described development can result in higher complexity at various levels[26]:

- By increasing the number of employees on the one hand and extending the client base on the other, multipersonality is increased as well. Higher complexity is given not only by the higher number of people, but also by the associated performance fluctuations of the employees, which can be brought about by the difference in qualifications or characters.
- By extending the activities to new business fields, the number of subservices delivered is increased. Such an increase of individual tasks leads to increased complexity.
- Diversification and internationalization, however, also cause increased heterogeneity of the subservices. On the one hand, the individual services can *per se* be quite different from each other. The services provided by leading accounting firms covering auditing, legal services, corporate finance, tax and other consulting services, e.g., is quite heterogeneous. On the other hand, extending business activities to new countries can increase heterogeneity by country-specific characteristics such as language, market conditions or the legal system.

Such an increase in complexity requires a stronger structural differentiation.[27] This means, that smaller, specialized company units must be formed either on basis of geography, by founding different subsidiaries, or at functional level, through the development of different business areas or 'practice groups'. In this case, founding regional subsidiaries for the sake of internationalization is the most costly solution, but it allows implementing a unified quality standard as well as a centralized company policy. Less advantageous is the long period of time it takes to establish this company. A combined approach has led in many professional service firms to the development of matrix structures, i.e., to a segmentation of corporate units not only by one, but by several structural dimensions.[28]

Such differentiation alone does, however, not do justice to the requirements of the client and can lead to inefficiencies. Clients working in different countries or in different business fields with the same companies, expect the same quality and spectrum of services and a specific corporate culture prevailing everywhere. It is therefore necessary to undertake steps towards full integration of the individual company units, irrespective of their specialization and autonomy, to a corporate whole. Company-wide events, job rotation between different offices or IT systems can play an important role in this respect.

11.3 External Development Through Acquisitions

Next to internal implementation within the company, well capitalized professional service firms can choose external development through acquisitions and mergers. This requires paying attention to professional and corporate regulations (1). The new knowledge and the acquired client relations can be used optimally only after successful integration of the acquired company. Person-specific objections against the merger can endanger the integration process and must therefore be reduced as far as possible (2).

11.3.1 Opportunities and Limits of Management Acquisitions

Internationalization or diversification can be effected by buying or merging with professional service firms which are active either in different countries or in other business areas. Even companies in the same country and/or business areas could be interesting candidates if they have a well-defined clientele or a specific knowledge base increasing the company's service excellence. This form of inorganic growth or internationalization can be effected faster than internal growth and is distinguished by management control of the respective company. As a company, Werbeholding WPP has experienced an enormous growth process in the last 18 years by undergoing numerous acquisitions. The example of WPP demonstrates one of the key advantages of acquisitions compared to 'lateral hires': They make it possible to 'buy' not only person-related but also company-related reputations. All subsidiaries of WPP continue acting under their own strong brand names.

When acquiring professional service firms, attention must be paid to corporate as well as professional regulations of the companies in question:

- There still are numerous professional service firms organized as partnerships which are owned by their partners. This limits the takeover chances, since consensus of the partners, particularly in joint partnerships,[29] is legally required as defined in the company agreement. Takeovers against the wishes of a partner are therefore not possible in most cases. But even with public companies hostile takeovers bear a risk as they can have negative effects on employee motivation, particularly in view of their company loyalty. An incremental takeover in the form of shareholding in the company can reduce these negative effects.[30]

- Even more far reaching than corporate regulations can be the limitations to shareholding imposed by professional norms which legally require for many liberal professions to form legal partnerships in which shares – whether the majority or all – can only be held by members of the same profession.[31] This limits severely any extension of the service spectrum in the context of a diversification strategy. In addition, professional norms in many countries restrict the circle of shareholders to persons accredited in accordance with the respective national laws, and thus render share acquisition by professionals from other countries more difficult.[32] This puts a limit to the opportunities of internationalization.

Financing the purchasing price for professional service firms that are not publicly owned can pose problems in three different aspects. First, it is often not possible to use own shares as acquisition currency; second, their own equity base is limited since in many cases taking on investing shareholders without the required professional accreditation is prohibited; and third, the possibilities of outside financing are limited due to a lack of collateral assets. I should be noted, however, that in the case of corporate law firms organized as partnerships mergers do not require much capital, as there is no more required than a re-formation.

11.3.2 Integration Challenges

Acquisitions aim at tapping into new strategically valuable resources without having to grow them internally. This is relatively unproblematic in the case of brand names and reputable elements not linked to specific people. Codified know-how in databases, manuals or in patents can be transferred to the new firm without any particular difficulties.[33] In contrast, where strategic resources are linked to a person, know-how demerger and person-related relationship assets are rendered more difficult, particularly where employees have a negative attitude towards the cooperation.

What is problematic is that 'The mere occurrence of an acquisition is a sure predictor of a myriad of people-related problems, especially for members of the acquired firm.'[34] Person-specific problems can lead to stress, tensions, fear, financial insecurity, dissatisfaction, reduced productivity or fluctuation and can thus have a negative effect on the business situation of a professional service firm. Two main reasons have been identified – fear of 'exploitation' and fear of 'contamination' – why professionals reject the cooperation in the context of an acquisition[35]:

- Fear of exploitation exists in those cases where professionals rate their own know-how higher than that of their new colleagues. For this reason they do not see this cooperation as advantageous.

- Fear of contamination by integrating 'foreign' services appears when professionals rate their 'image' higher than that of their new colleagues. They foresee danger to the value inherent in their image, which for them is getting reduced by the cooperation.

The greater the difference between the two companies, and the more the professionals reject the cooperation, the more likely it is that certain employees leave the firm. As happened in the takeover of the investment bank Bankers Trust by the Deutsche Bank, experienced professionals not only take crucial company know-how and 'their' clients with them when they leave the company, but also their most trusted employees. But even the migration of young employees can be detrimental for the company. They have not yet acquired an extensive company-specific know-how and may not yet have built up their own client network, but they often generate the highest profit margins in the professional service firm. Luckily, not all employees face takeovers with a negative attitude. Some recognize die opportunities for higher earning by the cooperation or for future development, and they encourage the integration process.[36]

As a result of this, there are two main challenges for the managers of the integration:

- The acquisition object should be selected such that strategically as well as from the organizational point of view the two companies fit together, or at least can be made to fit.[37]
- Even if they view the changes with apprehension, the employees should be won over to sharing their know-how and client relations with the new colleagues.[38] The possibilities of management are here restricted to creating the appropriate framework conditions for facilitating the integration process.

The fact that integration can be carried out successfully despite initial reservations is demonstrated by the merger between the two corporate law firms Freshfields (UK) and Bruckhaus Westrick Heller Lober (Germany). Worries that the merger would result in an English-dominated takeover led to only two thirds of the Bruckhaus partners agreeing to the deal in April 2000. Lengthy negotiations led to a compromise guaranteeing the partners in both law firms considerable influence in the management of the new company. People in doubt could thus be won over, and the merger in August 2000 is now considered to be one of the most successful cooperations in the field of corporate law firms.[39]

11.4 External Development Through Cooperations

A second option for external company development available to professional service firms are cooperations which help them improve their competitiveness. A cooperation can be effected with other professional service firms as well as with other companies (1). For cooperations to be successful and stable in the long run, a number of preconditions must be fulfilled (2).

11.4.1 Networks as Specific Form of Cooperation

For professional service firms, acquisitions and organization-internal developments are restricted by laws as well as by the prevalent form of partnerships. cooperation with professional service firms or other companies can be a good option to overcome such barriers. cooperation furthermore provides advantages without having to enter a financial risk or overstretch management possibilities.[40]

In networks, the typical form of cooperation, at least two legally discrete and economically autonomous parties – be they individuals, groups or companies – are working closely together. The relations between the parties are less close than in an ideal-typical hierarchy, but closer than in an ideal-typical market.[41] Inter-organizational networks enable the implementation of a concentration, internationalization or diversification strategy without having to extend the resource base of one's own firm.

The following two groups in particular are potential partners for cooperation (see Fig. 11.4):

- Networks with professional service firms that form no direct competition
- Networks with other companies and/or organizations

Professional service firms that are no direct competition may offer a different service spectrum or be represented in other geographic areas. In the context of a 'co-specialization' the parties can thus each bring unique competences into the cooperation.[42] Ideal-typically each of the network partners discloses its existing client contacts as well as its service spectrum for exploitation within the network. This gives each participant of the network the option of providing to their own

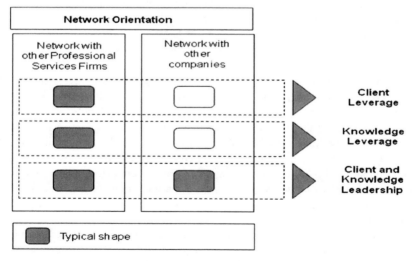

Fig. 11.4 Possible networking options and cooperation objectives. (Source: Adapted from Ringlstetter et al. 2004, p. 299)

clients 'one-stop shopping' and 'seamless global service'. At the same time, each one can improve its service quality by the reciprocal learning process. This increases at the same time client satisfaction and the turnover of the participants.

If, however, there is too much overlapping in the competence areas of the service spectrum or geographic presence, there is a danger that the network partners try over time to obtain leverage not within the network but exclusively for their own company. Cooperation with other companies or organizations can be used as well, especially for improving service quality.

One way to cooperate is through expert networks.[43] Next to professional service firms which may be specialized in other service areas, this can include other companies or institutions such as universities. A large number of professional service firms uses such networks to exchange ideas and experiences by accessing the specialized knowledge of the partners and so effecting knowledge transfer between the companies.[44]

11.4.2 Requirements for a Successful Cooperation

Independent of the intent with which the cooperation was formed and of who are the partners in the cooperation, the advantage of a successful and long-term stable cooperation must be evident for all participants. For example, it must be ensured that client leverage is not done unilaterally, but that all participant companies will cross-sell across the network. Clear rules, such as for commissions, can be a starting point. To realize internationalization, diversification or strengthening the core businesses within the network, cooperation partners must fulfill different requirements[45]:

- *Intent*: The transfer of knowledge and relationship capital is the declared intent.
- *Transparency:* The readiness to give the partner insight into one's own knowledge and clients base is given.
- *Receptivity:* The companies involved are adaptive.

Joint market efforts do not only lead to competitive advantage, but also create reciprocal dependencies by using the resources available within the network which can restrict activities.[46] Individual companies in the network can exploit these dependencies and start extending their own activities to use cross-selling advantages solely for themselves. In addition there is the danger that by way of cooperation company-specific and competition-critical know-how is transferred from company.[47] Since not every component of the cooperation can possibly be defined, the relationship between the network partners must be based on trust. The respective company reputation then represents a sort of guarantee for the service and cooperation quality.

Even though networks between professional service firms are a common occurrence they are often viewed critically. The stability and advantageousness of diversification and internationalization networks between companies is questioned in particular. Turnover increase via cross-selling may be the declared intent of inter-organizational partnerships, but often it is not or only to a less than satisfactory extent fulfilled. Scott views inter-organizational cooperation exclusively as intermediary to a subsequent acquisition.[48]

Above average growth and a highly competitive environment represent for the strategic development of professional service firms increasingly important challenges. In view of this, professional service firms have three strategic development options available to them: strengthening the core business, internationalization, and diversification. Selecting the right strategy can contribute to improving use of the key resources of know-how and social competence (client leverage, knowledge leverage, client/knowledge leadership), and at the same time to meeting client requirements (one-stop shopping, seamless global service, service excellence). When implementing the selected strategy, specific legal, cultural and organizational characteristics of professional service firms have to be considered.

Notes

1. See Ringlstetter and Morner (2000), p. 1481.
2. See Müller-Stewens et al. (1999), p. 24et seq.
3. See Maister (1982), p. 17.
4. See Maister (1982), p. 22.
5. See Scott (2001), p. 16 et seq.
6. See Müller-Stewens et al. (1999), p. 30.
7. See Scott (2001), p. 26.
8. See also Ringlstetter and Bürger (2003) for subsequent comments.
9. See Müller-Stewens et al. (1999), p. 28.
10. See Koza and Lewin (1999), p. 643.
11. See Scott (2001), p. 38.
12. See Müller-Stewens et al. (1999), p. 30; Brown et al. (1996), p. 66.
13. See Gray et al. (2001), p. 4.
14. See Müller-Stewens et al. (1999), p. 27 et seq.
15. See Post (1996), p. 86.
16. See Bouncken (2001), p. 205.
17. See Strambach (1995), p. 102.
18. See Scott (2001), p. 42.
19. See Scott (2001), p. 46.
20. The leverage factor depends on the offered services. For leverage, see also Maister (1982).
21. See Shah and Kraatz (15–17 August 2002), p. 9.
22. The topic of lateral hires was described in particular for law firms. See Shah and Kraatz (15–17 Aug. 2002), p. 10; Galanter and Palay (1990), p. 750; Weisbord (1990), p. 44.
23. See Spar (1997), p. 11.
24. See Shah and Kraatz (15–17 August 2002), p. 9. The agreement referred to was originally concluded between the big New Yorker law firms and extended later on as a general „gentlemanly practice of the profession".
25. See Shah and Kraatz (15–17 August 2002), p. 4.
26. See for subsequent complexity dimensions Benkenstein and Güthoff (1996), p. 1500 et seq. Other dimensions referred to were duration of service provision and individuality of service.
27. See Gray et al. (2001), p. 9 et. seq.
28. See Müller-Stewens and Lechner (2003), p. 449.
29. See Rose and Glorius-Rose C. (1995), p. 41 et seq.
30. See Scott (2001), p. 44.

31. See Rose and Glorius-Rose C. (1995), p. 39. The active ability of buying shares in law firms, auditing and tax advising companies is in Germany limited only to companies owned entirely by members of these professions. See Castan (1997), p. 225.

32. For example, accounting firms in countries within the European Union (EU) for the most part are obligated to have a majority of executives and a majority of shareholders having the professional qualification of annual auditor according to national law. See Lenz and Schmidt (1999), p. 119. For law firms there are also severe restrictions in numerous countries. See Spar (1997), p. 11.

33. See Bouncken (2001), p. 221. This does not lead to conclusions concerning the subsequent internalisation of knowledge by employees.

34. See Greenwood et al. (1994), p. 239 et seq.

35. For subsequent considerations, see the results of the empirical study in Empson (2001b), p. 857 et seq. and Empson (2000), p. 43 et seq.

36. See Empson (2000), p. 43.

37. See Greenwood et al. (1994), p. 250.

38. See Empson (2000), p. 40.

39. See o.v. (04 Jan. 2002).

40. See Scott (2001), p. 45.

41. See Sydow (1995), p. 629.

42. See Tidd and Izumimoto (2002), p. 140; Koza and Lewin (1999), p. 639.

43. See Peterson (2001), p. 61.

44. See Strambach (1995), p. 160.

45. See Hamel (1991), p. 89 et seq.; Hamel identified three factors facilitating learning in alliances.

46. See Sydow (1992), p. 420; Weber (1996), p. 111.

47. See Scott (2001), p. 45.

48. See Scott (2001), p. 44.

Chapter 12
Networking as a Strategy for Small and Medium Professional Service Firms

Next to the big representative ones, more and more small and medium professional service firms characterize the way the sector appears. In the past they have not been given much attention, since in the end it was only the large professional service firms that had the decisive control of developments in the sector. In the meantime, this situation has changed such that the number of smaller and medium professional service firms has increased considerably. This can be ascribed, e.g., to spin-offs and increased demand from smaller and medium companies with a limited budget for professional services. In this book we would like to compensate for this omission by addressing the strategic growth possibilities for small and medium professional service firms, in particular with focus on the networking of added value processes and use of social capital.

12.1 The Basic Problem

Growth is an important strategic target of the PSF sector. To reach this target professional service firms can resort to a host of growth strategies.[1] The impact of these professional service firms depends on their size and financial setup. In particular the concentration on core business is strategically relevant, since in many PSF sectors the potential for diversification, e.g., is quite limited. On the one hand, diversification of products is often limited by law, particularly with regard to auditing firms, tax consultants and lawyers. In the respective professional regulations it is clearly defined in which areas services may be offered. On the other hand, in many sectors the potential for internationalization has largely been exhausted. This is particularly true for the auditing sector.[2]

Furthermore, the prevailing human resources situation can be a limiting factor for growth when professional service firms, for reasons of their size or financial means, are not able to position themselves adequately on the important markets for human resources.[3]

Co-authors: Tim Kampe and Simon Woll

S. Kaiser, M.J. Ringlstetter, *Strategic Management of Professional Service Firms*, DOI 10.1007/978-3-642-16063-9_12, © Springer-Verlag Berlin Heidelberg 2011

In addition, growth creates other, particularly structure- and management-related challenges for professional service firms, since the complexity of the organization altogether increases.[4]

The possibilities of external growth are limited for small and medium professional service firms. Thus, opportunities for growth through acquisition are generally only an option for well-capitalized professional service firms. The possibility of growth by mergers often represents loss of power for professional service firms run by their owners.

Due to their structural specifics, the often locally or regionally operating small and medium professional service firms are thus subjected to the well-defined limitations of organic and external growth.

Added to this are client requirements, such as for *one-stop shopping* or *seamless (global) service*. One-stop shopping implies a comprehensive and fully integrated service portfolio from one and the same company. Seamless (global) service describes the worldwide, integrated and – as regards service and quality standards – consistent service with only few interfaces.

One possibility of meeting meet these client requirements and still remain in business, in spite of the concentration processes on the part of the service providers, is the provision of complex services within value-adding networks of a number of professional service firms. Today, value-adding networks can be seen in almost all PSF subsectors, as demonstrated by various examples outlined in the observations below.

Providing complex services in value-adding networks makes it possible, also for small and medium professional service firms, to pursue different development strategies in parallel. Each of the network partners contributes originally its own core business and/or core competence to the network and can thus achieve high service quality (Service Excellence). By providing complementary skills and services, it is furthermore possible to provide One Stop Shopping as well, as one or more complex services can be offered to the client within the association. Depending on the geographic location of the local network partners, it is even possible to offer Seamless (Global) Services.

12.2 Value-Adding Networks, Social Capital and Professional Service Firms

Value-adding networks are normally a result of intended cooperation between companies. It is the goal of such cooperations to add value by way of intelligently linking individual value-adding activities and processes.[5] This linking of activities and processes can be described more precisely as the linking of material and immaterial resources of both individual and of collective agents. In the end, it is the individual activities of agents drawing on resources, upon which value-adding activities are based. Recent research in the domain of business administration organization, sees such a perspective on the cross-linking of value-adding activities increasingly as related to the concept of social capital. Social capital can be understood as the aggregate of resources that can be mobilized by a network of social relations. This is why the social relations of agents and the significance of networks along with their structure are the focus of scientific interest.

12.2.1 Social Capital – A Critical Network Perspective

The starting points of all value-adding networks are the social relations of the agents involved. It is these social relations, known since the early 1990s under the catch-phrase of 'social capital', which have become the focus of research on business administration organization.[6] For quite a long time, organization research on social capital assumed relatively uncritically that social connections and associated net-work structures served the economic success of a company.[7] The generally accepted assumption that networks of social agents provide access to resources, and thus are to be regarded without exception as positive and valuable, is by today's stan-dards obsolete. Social capital should rather be evaluated in view of the specific context factors and aims,[8] which, however, increases the complexity of straightfor-ward assumptions. In addition, the concept of social capital represents a so-called 'umbrella concept'.[9] The great variety of perspectives allows analysis of diverse phenomenon from the viewpoint of social capital, but this makes the results less distinct.[10]

12.2.2 Seminal Statements

In analyses of social capital, the structural characteristics of the social network rep-resent the key elements. They can be analyzed, e.g., with regard to the strength of social connections or the density and integrity of a social network.

As a general rule, the differentiation between friends and acquaintances is still accepted as the dividing line between strong and weak ties among people.[11] How to interpret weak or strong ties with regard to their social capital depends very strongly on the situation. Weak ties are considered to be an advantage wherever increased distribution of information is the aim, or where more information is to be received.[12] Close or strong ties, on the other hand, reduce the breadth of received information but may, under certain circumstances, increase its potential for use.[13] Furthermore, strong ties provide a higher potential for control and sanctions com-pared to weak ties.[14] Whether weak or strong ties are considered positive or negative depends therefore on the respective situation.[15]

The density and closeness of social networks provide similar scope for interpreta-tion, as core areas of network theory.[16] On the one hand, dense and closed networks in particular (mostly in combination with strong ties) can be considered as social capital, since within them it is possible, by way of trust and sanctions, to coordinate and secure the exchange of resources.[17] On the other hand, so-called bridges over structural holes can represent particularly valuable social capital, as via the connec-tion of two networks by this bridge both owners of the connection obtain so-called

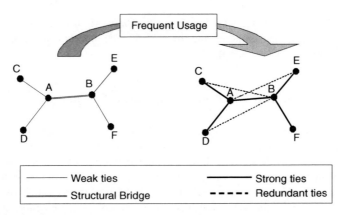

Fig. 12.1 Representation of structural characteristics in a social network. (Source: adapted from Perry-Smith and Shalley 2003, p. 93)

'brokerage rights'.[18] This is exemplified on the left page in Fig. 12.1 in the connection between partners A and B. The information advantage obtained thus shows in faster access to a larger information quantity. In addition, the associated control advantage provides thus the opportunity to distribute or retain specific information and thereby influence opinions and, ultimately, decisions.[19]

It is furthermore strongly assumed that trust, identity and solidarity play a decisive role in social networks.

Whether the capital of social networks can be used successfully by professional service firms depends, last but not least, on the qualities and properties of the professionals, groups and organizations linked in social networks. The success of a cooperation may be influenced considerably by, e.g., status differences between the two partners or the reputation of a partner. This aspect of quality, beyond the structural characteristics of the social capital, is implied in quite a number of studies and was even documented by a few analyses.[20] Some references can be found in Wegener (1987) that (1) the strength of the tie between two people loses in importance when the status difference between the two people decreases, and (2) that for the success of a cooperation the reputation of the other partner is particularly relevant. Qualitative properties of the individual or collective agents seem thus to have a decisive influence on the successful use of social capital.

Furthermore, with regard to social capital being used successfully by professional service firms, attention must be paid to the fact that social capital changes in the course of and by being used. Using weak ties repeatedly renders them strong by definition. The degree to which knowledge transferred via individual, weak ties is new thus decreases over time automatically. Structural bridges to other networks are reinforced by new ties whenever they are activated. The importance that role brokers play with regard to these bridges thus decreases over time.

Apart from the positive aspects mentioned, there are also negative effects of social capital for professional service firms.[21] In banking, e.g., an existing strong network of links can limit the flexibility for business relations with other banks and thus the forming of new network links.[22] The role of brokers mentioned already in connection with positive aspects can also be interpreted as a bottleneck in the social and information structure of a network.[23] Apart from that, an existing social network cannot per se guarantee that the use will benefit professional service firms.[24] This requires additional incentive systems that could motivate the professional to using his social network for the benefit of the company.[25]

The consequences which these theoretical reflections have on the specific configuration of value-adding networks for small and medium professional service firms will be addressed below.

12.3   Configuration of Value-Adding Networks for Small and Medium Professional Service Firms

Today, value-adding networks can be found in almost all PSF subsectors.[26] They enable small and medium professional service firms to realize, in spite of their often restricted resources, the development options mentioned above. To achieve this, each professional service firm within the value-adding network adds its core competences and can thus achieve focusing on the core business (Service Excellence). At the same time, all participants in the network can diversify into the dimensions outlined below by way of the examples:

- *Diversification according to services:* by introducing complementary services and/or competences, the participants in a value-adding network are able to offer their clients a complex service portfolio, something the individual professional service firms could not have provided. An example would be the purchase of a company (or part of) by a client. This complex transaction would be difficult to achieve by any smaller professional service firms. In a value-adding network consisting of auditors, tax consultants and lawyers, the client can be provided with the entire service as a 'one-stop shop'. The due diligence required for the purchase is carried out by the auditing firm, the law firm gives legal support in the course of the complex transaction and the tax advisor can arrange for the transaction to be optimized tax-wise with the other network participants. The client thus is provided with the desired one-stop shop.
- *Diversification according to regions/countries:* Small and medium professional service firms are often active within specific regional and/or national markets, not only because of limited resources but – with the exception of consulting companies – due to the respective national legal restrictions within which corporate law firms, auditing firms and tax consultants above all must act. The respective national legal systems – especially German tax laws – have reached dimensions which would overtax small professional service firms, particularly in the context of trans-national projects, and present almost insurmountable hurdles. One possibility to provide the client with 'Seamless (Global) Service' could then be effected by merging with professional service firms of the same subsector into a trans-national value-adding network. This opportunity was seized early on by

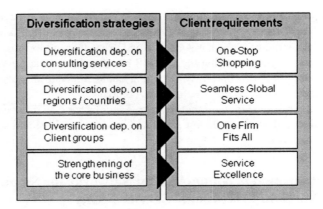

Diversification strategies	Client requirements
Diversification dep. on consulting services	One-Stop Shopping
Diversification dep. on regions / countries	Seamless Global Service
Diversification dep. on Client groups	One Firm Fits All
Strengthening of the core business	Service Excellence

Fig. 12.2 Strategic development options of professional services firms

small and medium auditing firms in Germany which could thus secure auditing foreign subsidiaries of their clients.

• *Diversification according to client groups:* Here the participants bring their functional knowledge, but also their client know-how into the value-adding network. This kind of diversification could also be effected along the line of client groups, e.g., jointly providing services to the public sector: An IT consultant having specialized successfully on the implementation of document management systems, but so far without any experience with the specifics of the public sector, could provide his service within a value-adding network. Networking with a professional experienced in the public sector in the field of process consulting could provide the solution. To the client it would have the feel of comprehensive service from one and the same provider along the lines of 'One Firm Fits All'.

Figure 12.2 summarizes the strategic development options by diversification schematically. Another question is how value-adding networks between small and medium professional service firms should be structured when pursuing one of the above mentioned strategies? The answer to this question is here given from the perspective of an individual professional service firm participating in a value-adding network. A point to be taken into consideration is that the individual aims of individual network partners may very well collide with the collective aim of a value-adding network.

12.3.1 Structural Aspects of Value-Adding Networks

As mentioned before, questioning the structural aspects of value-adding networks addresses the *strength* of the ties, the *density* of the network, the existence of *structural holes* and/or *bridges* as well as the use of appropriate *coordination media*.

- The first question around the configuration is about the *strength of the ties* between network partners. Is the joint added value characterized by frequent and intensive interaction (strong ties) or rather by sporadic exchange (weak ties)? Normally it is uncontested that the beginning of a diversification strategy via value-adding networks is effected through weak ties. First access to new knowledge, so far not provided services, etc. is possible via weak, not yet fully characterized social links.[27] In the course of time and the joint added value, these ties are strengthened through communication and interaction. This reduces the cost of transaction, i.e., the costs of agreeing before the joint added value and coordination in the course of joint activities. By no means is this to imply that a complete transfer of implicit and explicit knowledge should take place due to the development of strong ties. It is more interesting for individual professional service firms to concentrate on their own core services and, at the same time, strive for mutual co-evolution or specialization of the individual partners within the value-adding network. In the end this means that individual professional service firms should create relations with multiple partners and/or should add new value-adding partners after certain time periods, so as not to build up a rigid network structure.[28]

- Similar arguments can be made with regard to the *optimal density* of a value-adding network between professional service firms. The density of a value-adding network is represented by the share of joint value-adding activities within the theoretically total of possible links between the participating professional service firms. The advantage of a high density value-adding network is (1) that the network can better present a unique face to clients and that thus the quality of the joint services (One-Stop Shopping) can be communicated more easily; (2) it can be assumed that due to the manifold dependencies, the added value of the network can more easily be calibrated as a whole. Conversely, it is dense social networks which are more readily isolated from new knowledge. From the perspective of individual professional service firms, a very dense network makes it more difficult to enter into relations with new value-adding partners, since many other ties would be affected at the same time.

- It may be of special interest for a professional service firm to fill *structural holes* in networks as so-called brokers, i.e., to be the person providing contacts to new knowledge and services for any third parties. A precondition for that would be obtaining a position of status or power by having unique knowledge, a reputation and providing high quality services. The tie of the structural bridge should be mature and thus strong. Via strong ties, relations between third parties can be brokered to one's own advantage. For the development of structural bridges in the people-driven business of professional service firms, personal relationships formed outside of the working environment (e.g., when playing golf) should generally be of particular relevance. As it were, bridging structural holes can also serve as a business model. In the area of 'interim management', there are professional service firms which concentrate on bringing together individuals or groups of self-employed interim managers connected within a loose network with temporary value-adding networks for specific client projects against remuneration and/or financial participation

With regard to the structural configuration of a value-adding network between professional service firms the question arises, in which way the structures should be supported by appropriate *coordination media*, such as. trust or contracts. One should assume that in new and weak relations this is predominantly effected with complex contracts and sanctions, due to the uncertainty with regard to the services of the value-adding partner, while in long established and strong value-adding relations the coordination is supported by reciprocal trust and identity.

12.3.2 Aspects Beyond Structure

Next to the structural configuration of value-adding networks, other contextual and dynamic aspects must be considered. What about the *quality of the network partners*? Who is *really benefiting from the social capital* in a network? And which *dynamic modifications* can appear in a network? These questions are dealt with in the following paragraphs.

- An important question is with whom, from the perspective of the professional service firm, value-adding activities should be entered into. Here, the *quality of the potential value-adding partners* is the focus of consideration.[29] One can distinguish between the aspect of content and the aspect of level. The former refers to the type of services and/or core competences of the value-adding partners. depending on the selected diversification strategy, the competences should be complementary or identical to the focal professional service firm. If the partners of the value-adding network aim at offering a complex service such as, e.g., M&A consultancy, then it is necessary that each partner brings its unique competence into the value-adding network. Only by intelligent linking of complementary value-adding functions and/or processes is there in this case an added value for the client and the participants of the network. This situation is reversed in the case where diversification is intended by regions/countries in the network. Here one must pay attention to having the appropriate competence, so that one can provide the client congruent services in different geographical locations along the lines of Seamless (Global) Service. The aspect of level in the quality of the partner addresses the quality of the value-added activities generated by the network partners. The quality level of the network partners should at least be equally good or better for the cooperation to generate added value from the perspective of the focal professional service firm.[30] From the perspective of the focal professional service firm no social capital is generated when strong ties and dense networks are being formed with professional service firms which do not fit with regard to content and quality standards with one's own enterprise. Structural bridges to incompetent partners also generate no social capital. Insofar the quality of the (potential) network participants plays an immanently important role in the configuration of value-adding networks. In this context it is problematic that the quality level in particular cannot be thoroughly assessed before entering into a partnership. The following criteria may serve the focal professional service firm as starting points for assessment. Assessing the quality level can be done a priori by looking at the reputation of the potential partner as a sort of quality surrogate.[31] In the course of the cooperation, the reputation of a partner can be used as a pawn by the focal professional service firm, and opportunistic conduct of the partner can be communicated accordingly on the market and/or within the sector.[32] Furthermore, in many PSF subsectors there exist precautionary arrangements meant to guarantee a minimum of quality. For example, there is the legally required peer review for certified accountants as well as quality requirements put up by professional associations such as the International Federation of Accountants (IFAC). But in the end, all this can only reduce the insecurity to a certain measure. The focal professional service firm should therefore retain to a certain extent the ability or readiness to separate again from the partnership.

- In connection with the (aimed at) building up of social capital, the question must be addressed who the *real beneficiary* of this social capital is and/or can be. as described above, social capital can also have negative consequences when one of the partners in the value-adding network resorts to opportunistic conduct and, e.g., withdraws relevant knowledge or (human) resources from the focal professional service firm. Apart from that, there can also be negative consequences within the observed professional service firm. In the end, the social capital is based on the relations of individual agents. Now, if one of the individual professionals acts as, e.g., a bridge within the value-adding network, this professional plays a critical role for the professional service firm. If this agent leaves the company, the network can collapse in the worst case, if the corresponding knowledge and relations are leaving the network with the agent.[33] The professional service firm is here tasked to give the professionals appropriate incentives to use the social capital such that it benefits the focal professional service firm and, secondly, to ensure, if possible, that this social capital cannot be used after leaving the professional service firm. In this context one should consider in particular putting fixed non-compete clauses in the work agreements which would prohibit business contacts to a client for a certain term after leaving the professional service firm.

- Using the social capital will naturally lead over time to changing it, i.e., it undergoes a *dynamic development*. As mentioned before, one must assume that over time the relations between the network partners will solidify, i.e., weak ties will turn into strong ones. This is a welcome development insofar as that over time trust built up and transaction costs could be lowered. Through co-specialization of the network partners, the participants each can reach Service Excellence. On the other hand, one must keep in mind that strong ties and co-specialization can lead to clearly characterized rigidities and thus result in loss of flexibility. In the end, this could even lead to negative overcompensation of the saved transaction costs. Where structural holes exist, one can assume that with the ongoing development of the cooperation in the value-adding network additional ties and thus bridges will form.[34] This implies as well, that over time the professional service firm serving as a bridge will lose its 'brokerage rights', i.e., its information and control advantage.[35] This professional service firm will therefore try to hold on to its especially valuable social capital and to limit as far as possible the direct interaction of the other network participants, i.e., their social capital. A solution to this dilemma from the perspective of the other network participants could be found by establishing a 'neutral' agency as a bridge. As an example serve the above-mentioned value-adding networks of small and medium auditing firms: In the network 'HLB international' the structural holes between national networks are bridged by the respective national offices, which are being financed by all national members.

In summary it can be said that value-adding networks may quite well represent a useful option for diversification of the business while concentrating at the same time on one's own core services. By drawing on the concept of social capital it becomes clear, however, that there are numerous controls in the configuration of value-adding networks which are highly significant, especially in view of the long-term success of a value-adding network. As a result, any professional service firm must meet the challenge and, within the context of specific strategic aims, master various conflicting priorities – such as, e.g., between lowering the transaction costs and developing rigid structures.

Notes

1. For strategies, see also Chap. 11 of this book.
2. See Brown and Cooper (1996), p. 66.
3. See also Chap. 7 of this book.
4. See Ringlstetter and Bürger (2004), p. 293 et seq.
5. See Ringlstetter et al. (2004).
6. See Adler and Kwon (2002).
7. See Nahapiet and Ghoshal (1998). Respectives studies analysed, e.g., the positive effects of social capital on the exchange of resources in inter-organisational co-operations, strategic alliances and loose network associations (Gulati and Higgins (2003); Koka and Prescott (2002); Walker and Kogut (1997)). The focus of network-oriented social capital studies is naturally relatively wide, as the overall statement that social capital provides access to resources implies an improved access to all possible resources, such as people, capital or know-how (e.g., Inkpen and Tsang (2005)). A prominent subsector is given by studies dealing with the success of regional clusters, resp. the success of companies within such regional clusters (Cohen and Fields (1999); Johannisson (1995); Powell et al. (2002); Westlund and Bolton (2003)).
8. See e.g., Burt (1997); Gulati and Higgins (2003).
9. See Kaiser (2007), p. 132.
10. See Hirsch and Levin (1999), p. 200 et seq.; Astley (1985), p. 501.
11. See Granovetter (1973), p. 1368 et seq.
12. See Granovetter (1974), p. 93.
13. See Carpenter et al. (2003), p. 414 et seq.
14. See Bian (1997); Carpenter et al. (2003); Jansen and Weber (2004).
15. See Burt (1997); Gulati and Higgins (2003); Hansen (1999); Tsai (2000).
16. See in general Jansen (2003).
17. See Coleman (1988), p. 103.

18. See Burt (1992).
19. See Gargiulo and Benassi (2000), p. 184.
20. See Nahapiet and Ghoshal (1998).
21. See Gargiulo and Benassi (2000).
22. See Baker (1990); Ebers (2003), p. 6.
23. See Cross and Parker (2004), p. 69 et seq.
24. See Blyler and Coff (2003); Leana and Buren (1999), p. 546; Moran (2005).
25. See also Chap. 7 of this book.
26. See Friese (1998), p. 302; Jones et al. (1998). Other studies cover, e. g., investment banks (Podolny 1993, 1994), management consulting (Aharoni 1997b), engineering services (Aharoni 1993b).
27. See Granovetter (1974), p. 93.
28. See Ebers (2003); Wegener (1987).
29. See Bruhn (2000) for a seminal introduction to quality aspects in services.
30. See Jones et al. (1998), p. 402 et seq.
31. See from a client perspective Bürger (2005), p. 50 et seq.
32. See Büschken (1999), p. 3 et seq.
33. See also Greenwood and Empson (2003), p. 916; Seabright et al. (1992), p. 127.
34. See Burt (1992).
35. See Gargiulo and Benassi (2000), p. 184.

Chapter 13
Surviving Crises – Crisis Management

13.1 Growth Crises in the PSF Sector

In the past, professional service firms were highly profitable and were able to achieve high growth rates. Currently, however, many of these companies are in crisis. The current market situation does not lend itself to reaching growth rates as before, and that even though professional service firms are by definition obligated to permanent growth, due to the career promises they made to their employees. But if they were to honor these career promises, their profitability would be destroyed as a consequence. Customers more and more experienced with consulting services, increased specialization in industries and themes, and the transition of small national shops into worldwide corporations have modified the consulting firm sector. In recent years, growth has mostly come from developing new themes within existing client relations.

For most professional service firms, growth targets pose a great challenge. This is due to market developments in recent years. During the boom years, companies have sharply increased their capacities by hiring resources, and some of them have grown more than was necessary. In a few cases this even led to a watering down of quality when the hiring criteria were significantly lowered.

The growth of entire sub-sectors of professional service firms, such as investment banks, law firms and PR agencies, is furthermore negatively affected by the reduction in IPOs on the market as well as by the reduced number of M&As, i.e., the consequences of the economic downturn. Added to this is the fact that clients of professional service firms have become more cost- and therefore price-conscious, so that the high remunerations of professionals are being put in question.

This results in the fact that those professional service firms which do not grow anymore have less leverage in motivating their professionals by career promises, and therefore lose acquisition potential in the human resources market.

Co-authors: Bernd Bürger and Adrian Bründl

S. Kaiser, M.J. Ringlstetter, *Strategic Management of Professional Service Firms*,
DOI 10.1007/978-3-642-16063-9_13, © Springer-Verlag Berlin Heidelberg 2011

13.2 Strategic Options

There are, however, possibilities of weathering the times of growth crises by choosing and using the right strategic options. To develop these options, which are systematically outlined below, it is important to understand the typical management model of professional service firms and their principles of organizational structure. These include constitutive features such as, i.e., achievement tournaments between employees, important with regard to the career promises made and to the resulting permanent growth pressure, as well as an organization mainly based on projects. Using these constitutive features, it is possible to outline success-promising strategies for finding ways out of the crisis: Achievement tournaments can be adapted in various ways (1) or the organization can be restructured either horizontally (2) or vertically (3) to meet client requirements while assuring profitability at the same time. It must be kept in mind, however, that following any one of these strategy options will lead to achieving different goals. Adapting achievement tournaments, e.g., is just a way to weather a growth crisis for a short period of time. Vertical structuring, on the other hand, means far-reaching modification of the business model, as outlined below.

13.2.1 Adapting the Tournament

When the market situation in a phase of economic weakness has deteriorated to a point where the internal growth pressure cannot be absorbed by an adequate number of projects, the profitability of the company is in danger. The number of employees at all career levels continues growing without their being used to capacity. This brings forth a negative divergence between increasing human resource costs and turnover.

To avoid this kind of divergence while maintaining the given leverage structure, achievement tournaments as a main feature of the career system can be modified (see Fig. 13.1).[1] The aim here is to bridge a growth crisis by short-term reaction. In practice it is *frequency*, *severity* and *admission* of new participants in such achievement tournaments which can be tweaked to reduce growth pressure:

- Lower *frequency* prolongs the time span a professional remains at a specific career level.
- Apart from such time delay, the *severity* of the achievement tournament can be increased by restricting the promotion quota. The chances of coming out as the winner of a tournament are thus reduced.
- At the same time, a *limitation of the admission* to company-internal tournaments will also lead to avoiding this negative divergence. Activities in the human resources market will be reduced. This may apply to university graduates as well as to lateral hires, i.e., professionals headhunted from, e.g., other professional service firms.

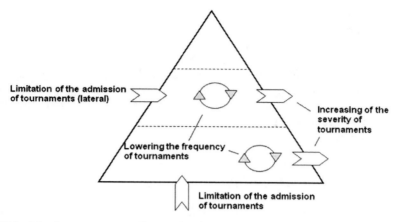

Fig. 13.1 Adapting tournaments. (Source: Author, partly adapted from Ringlstetter and Bürger 2003, p. 121)

Mention was already made of how important the challenges of an up-or-out career system are for motivating professionals or as a criterion for the choice of future employer.[2] Modifying the rules for achievement tournaments will naturally also have an effect on the incentive structure. Negative influences on the motivation of professionals must be factored in, all the more so when communication of the necessity for such rule changes is not successful. There is furthermore the danger of losing acquisition potential on the job market. In spite of these limitations, modifying the achievement tournaments will remain the key means for short-term reaction to growth crises.

13.2.2 Horizontal Structuring

Another option for maintaining the leverage ratio in spite of changed market conditions lies in the modification of horizontal structuring. What this means is that by re-grouping human resources, the existing knowledge pools will be enlarged or reduced and/or new types of knowledge pools are being developed. This must be done not only with the modified requirements of the market and/or clients in mind, but must also and specifically be in keeping with the existing leverage ratio.

Such market- or client-oriented restructuring means more than just steady allocation of professionals to specific projects, as it entails a shift in content focus. This process is occasionally referred to as *patching strategy* and has proven to be especially successful in industrial enterprises.[3] Successful professional service firms are using this strategy as well. To profit from the e-business boom, strategy consultants, such as McKinsey & Company and the Boston Consulting Group, focused on carrying out studies in this field. In times of economic crisis, however, they re-directed their focus back on restructuring projects and cost reduction programs.

For restructuring horizontally, some requirements must be met. In the first place, *employees* must be willing and capable of dealing with projects of a new content type. In other words, the human resources of the company must show a certain functional flexibility.[4] The professional service firm is thus permanently required to decide whether their professionals should be trained as *specialists* or as *generalists*. Extensive specialization brings with it a certain structural inertia and limits horizontal restructuring.[5] In addition, there are two more important preconditions which must be considered. In the first place, new growth-promising *markets* must be identified in which the professional service firm can be active after the respective 'patching'. Secondly, the professional service firm needs a sufficient measure of *innovation power*.

13.2.3 *Vertical Restructuring*

Where horizontal structuring is not an option, companies can only resort to vertical restructuring. In vertical restructuring, a modification in the leverage ratio is permitted to happen in professional service firms, thus that new project types can be handled. Such a step will become necessary when no strong, profitable growth is to be expected for the core area in future, and focusing on new growth-promising areas by horizontal restructuring also doesn't seem feasible. If both negative conditions apply, the profitability of a professional service firm can only be secured via long-term vertical restructuring.

Two basic options lend themselves for modifying existing leverage ratios (see Fig. 13.2). For one thing, professional service firms can try completely restructuring

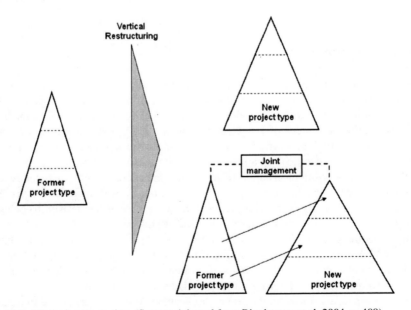

Fig. 13.2   Vertical restructuring. (Source: Adapted from Ringlstetter et al. 2004, p. 409)

the former project area, build up a new leverage structure long-term, and thus distance themselves from the former way of working. For another, it is possible to build up a second area of activity in parallel to the existing business, and to thus diversify with regard to project types. This has been done, e.g., by strategy consultants additionally engaged in IT consulting.

By modification of the achievement tournaments, activities in the traditional field of business can be reduced in parallel to working in and developing the new field of business with its different leverage ratio. Professionals from existing project types could be offered a transfer to this new project business.

This type of restructuring is usefully supported by external company development options. Mergers are a option, or lateral hires, i.e., headhunting partners and other professionals from other professional service firms. Both make it possible to obtain expertise and the associated reputation for the new project types, and to generate client relationships.[6]

Vertical restructuring is admittedly time-consuming and should therefore be considered only as long-term strategic option. It can only be considered a way out of a growth crisis when the market does yield new growth-promising business fields. Vertical restructuring is furthermore particularly risky in the sense that if the restructuring fails, the motivation of the employees, the reputation of the company and the trust of the clients in the professionalism of the work can be damaged.

13.3 Company Areas Relevant for Crisis Management

The services market developed so quickly in the last decade that professional service firms not only offer strategic consulting to the executives of a company but also implement decisions more and more often. This leads to a stronger integration of the professionals in the every-day work of their clients. It must be said, however, that this development often led to selling success concepts in a rollout process multiple times to large companies. The classic development of consulting themes went from growth-related issues during the boom years via efficiency issues during economic downturns back to growth issues when the economy recovered.

The first performance test for established professional service firms arose at the end of the 1990s with the start of the New Economy. Classic professional service firms not only lacked concepts for the key goods of the New Economy, but also service competence for the newly developing management structures of companies. Very quickly start-up consulting firms tried to fill this gap and thus push the established professional service firms into a defensive position with their client-specific approaches, driven by their entrepreneurial mentality. To counter this development, classic professional service firms needed basic restructuring with new strategic aims. This required high flexibility, since the core strategy of these companies had long remained unchanged in a simple format, often since the company had been founded.

In times of crisis, professional service firms face a paucity of business projects, both quantitatively as well as qualitatively. These challenges accompany rapidly changing markets, client preferences and products. Business models, value-adding chains and organizations are very quickly being put in question or even becoming obsolete. With their knowledge and know-how, professionals hold the future of a company in their hands.

Moreover, increased criticism of professional service firms and professionals attacks one of the most important competitive factors of the sector: reputation. This is all the more damaging since the sector must face up to criticism, that by their concepts and strategies they were at least partially responsible for the crisis. Before this background and the current economic situation the question arises what future there is, and what strategies there are, for a sector which in the 1990s had double digit annual growth rates and for which the trend had always been upward. One thing seems clear, however, that today there is no straight way forward like back in the boom times.

Strategies for the management of professional service firms in times of economic crisis can be identified for diverse areas. The human resources of a professional service firm are one area often affected by crises. Certain measures allow here to save costs at short term, while laying the foundation for a long-term competitive advantage from a strategic perspective (1). Another area are specific sales measures (2). A third topic which should play an important role, especially in times of crisis, is the question of compliance (3).

13.3.1 Personnel Measures

Ever since the experiences made with reactive and non-strategic human resources measures, at the time when the New Economy bubble burst in 2000/2001, it seems clear that the follow-up costs incurred by short-term personnel reductions often are higher than the intended savings, particularly when there are plans of re-staffing the competitive positions after the crisis. The mere announcement of lay-offs damages the firm's reputation and dampens the motivation of the professionals. The consequences of their radical course were felt by the professional service firms directly after the crisis. By early 2004, the worst set-backs of the crisis were overcome and the sector began to recover gradually. During the phase of intensive recruitment certain projects could not be realized because of insufficient staffing with professionals. This problem was the result of reactive personnel reductions not based on strategic targets.

In the wake of these cuts, considerable costs were incurred. While planning and implementation of measures can cause considerable direct costs, there are up to 40% indirect costs on top for adverts, induction and development of new employees after a phase of personnel consolidation. The young professionals rejected at the time are now not available at the executive level. But for the management of professional service firms it is particularly true that there is always a time after the crisis. The danger of intensifying long-term problems, such as the demographic shift and the 'War for Talents' by short-term and reactive action, should always be factored into the crisis management. And still, there are professional service firms reducing costs again in the current economic crisis which started in 2007. This covers material and travel costs in the first place, but also individual personnel cuts. For the most part, however, a future- and demand-orientated personnel strategy can be discerned. Efforts are made to keep key personnel within the company by trying to use them in different positions rather than letting them go when there are not enough projects. This approach might include intelligent offers for further training in subject-oriented, career or personal areas interesting for the professionals, as well as trying to motivate and qualify them for new tasks. In addition, anti-cyclical investment policies in human resources lend themselves for increased personnel development and for recruiting available High Potentials and partners under advantageous conditions.

13.3.2 Special Sales Measures During Times of Crisis

For companies, economic crisis spells less demand, an under-capacity work load, decreasing turnover and profits as well as volatile raw materials prices. The competition is more aggressive with price deductions, sales are experiencing loss of trust when implementing new market strategies, prices threaten to collapse. The macroeconomic data have a direct effect on consumer behavior. There is less demand, and price-consciousness rises. Consumers hold back and wait, they postpone purchase decisions for diverse goods and professional services. During a crisis, professional service firms must therefore move away from dealing equally with diverse client segments, but use aggressive or at least active sales strategies and push-methods instead. Only those companies who, in difficult times, seek active contact with their (potential) clients can maintain a positive profile in the competition, and can use the changing consumer preferences for their own benefit, while their competition resorts only to reducing material costs and travel budgets.

Next to the traditional form of *acquisition through existing contacts*, companies must resort in times of crisis to the option of *cold calls* for winning new clients in the context of direct sales. *Cold calls* are first contacts with potential clients with which no previous business relation exist, and it is done such that the addressed company receives an unexpected and unplanned-for contact call. Only people in executive positions will be addressed, and in this age of the internet their names can be found on websites and in publications. Even if one assumes that the potential commercial client has a basic interest in being addressed, there is always the danger that the call is experienced as somewhat pestering.

Here, the acquisition potential of the caller is the determining factor for delimiting competitive relations, since professional services can only be seen as heterogeneous when the potential clients and buyers have subject- or time-related, personal or local preferences. To reach this unique selling point and to minimize scattering losses in the calls, available professionals must, in times of crisis, be used for meticulously planning and preparing the process of *cold calls*. This requires detailed expert knowledge including statistics and media information as well as modern marketing and sales methods. Important is here in particular the individual fine-tuning of the service offer and the exact identification of potential clients, where the consulting requirement can be traced at least to media reports or similar sources. Addressing the wrong client or addressing the right client at the wrong time brings with it the danger of losing the status of equal business partner and to create the impression, damaging for the reputation, that the company has nothing better to do.

A more individual approach is possible when *pitching* in the context of tenders from potential clients. The *pitch* is a kind of customer-organized sales talk, where professional service firms present and offer their services and concept outline in competition with other consultants, and has the character of a tender. This very character allows minimizing scattering losses, as the client's problem is already known when preparing the *pitch*. For the creation of a concept draft it is, however, necessary to bind resources to a high extent, the cost of which is lost in case the order could not be secured due to poor performance with the *pitch* or an incompatible concept outline. Another problem can arise when the concept outline was positively received; the potential client adopts the ideas of the professional service firm but develops or realizes them through another consulting firm without paying the firm who conceived them. To safeguard against this, it is recommended to conclude a *pitch agreement* which regulates the obligation of the client not to further develop or realize the presented concept with any other but the professional service firm which pitched it. A *pitch agreement* is free of charge for both sides, but the client may feel that opportunistic intentions are being alleged. When setting prices for the offered professional services, the professional service firms always moves within the magic triangle of its own calculation, the calculations of its competitors and the visible use for the customer. Charging direct expenses may lead clients to compare apples with oranges. Senior consultant, e.g., often do their work more efficiently and bring higher savings and more use, or the concept scope of various professional service firms may vary strongly. But the client often sees only the considerable differences in hourly rates or the bottom line. To avoid any direct price comparison and to demonstrate entrepreneurial abilities in times of crisis, one could offer client-related fixed prices. In summary, one should remember that passive sales strategies are incompatible with the proactive mastermind image of the sector, while active strategies are always in danger of achieving the opposite of what was intended and must thus be carefully dosed. But they are the ones which provide the potential basis for a successful partnership.

13.3.3 Compliance Measures

Especially in times of economic crisis, professionals become more willing to disregard internal rules and regulations in order to reinforce their own position. These so-called *compliance violations* are being watched quite attentively in times of crisis, since the authorities, the exchange supervisory authority and the public are more than usual sensitized and set great value on correct behavior by companies. People receiving a large part of their remunerations from profit-related bonus payments will possibly want to secure these with unauthorized methods. The consequences are painful fines, loss of reputation or even legitimacy of the professional service firm. Incentives should therefore be considered and checked very carefully to see whether the targets defined in the years of steady growth are still realistic. One internal measure to report *compliance violations* by the professional themselves is, e.g., setting up a separate phone line which is often referred to as *whistleblower hotline*. But apart from such problems, a crisis can also be seen as a chance to correct previous mistakes and to create a new basis for a healthy future of the company. It is the viewpoint which decides whether a crisis is seen as a threat to the survival of the company or as a chance for growth. In the end, what counts in a crisis, are expertise and speed in taking up the chances of the new market and to realize them with the right kind of strategy in a value-adding manner.

Notes

1. See Malos and Campion (2000), Fig. 1.
2. See also Sect. 7.4 in this book.
3. See Eisenhardt and Brown (1999).
4. See general Atkinson (1984).
5. See Løwendahl et al. (2001).
6. See Weisbord (1990).

Chapter 14
Archetype Change Towards Management

The networking of professional service firms, outlined in Chap. 12, is a current trend linked to the deregulation of the sector, but also quite generally to an increasing focus on economic success for the companies and growth strategies. This trend towards more business-oriented thinking, discerned by many managers and scientists, is referred to with the term *archetype change*[1] in PSF research, and is currently being discussed specifically with regard to law firms and auditing firms.

The key concept of the archetype approach can be summarized in a few simple words: Organizations acting within similar settings and which compete against each other form, for efficiency reasons, similar structures and management systems. This is ascribed to a shared interpreting scheme[2] which usually encompasses the predominant perception on what an enterprise should do, how it should do it and in which way this should be rated. This is how organizational structures and systems generate and develop in line with the currently valid interpreting scheme.

Change in the PSF-sector, which is necessary to ensure that business models remain efficient and competitive, will therefore have to be accompanied by modification of the interpreting schemes of professionals. Furthermore, measures that currently are considered suitable may be considered unsuitable in the future. In other words, modification of the interpreting schemes brings about change in the structures and systems (see Fig. 14.1).

To begin with, the dimensions of archetypes are presented below (14.1). In line with the different dimensions there emerge two prominent archetypes which are under discussion for professional service firms: the so-called P^2 form and the Managed Professional Business (14.2). In conclusion, some ideas are suggested pertaining to the question whether a change of archetype is happening in the PSF sector at all (14.3).

14.1 Dimensions of Archetypes

In PSF research, quite a number of dimensions are taken into consideration for describing archetypes of a professional service firm.[3] These are *structures*, *systems* and *interpreting schemes*.

S. Kaiser, M.J. Ringlstetter, *Strategic Management of Professional Service Firms*,
DOI 10.1007/978-3-642-16063-9_14, © Springer-Verlag Berlin Heidelberg 2011

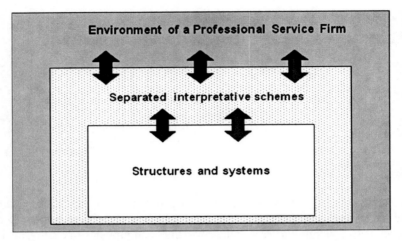

Fig. 14.1 Reciprocal effect of the environment and the shared interpreting schemes on the structures and systems of the PSF sector

Professional service firms form organizational structures in order to gain competitive advantage through specialization. Since these specialized activities and sub-units must be re-integrated by a mechanism, provisions must be made for implementing this integration. The *structure* is thus an expression of the degree of differentiation and integration: Primary distinguishing characteristics are:

- Number of sub-units
- Number of formal checks between executives.

Systems serve for controlling a company. One must differentiate between strategic, financial, market-oriented and operative control.
Strategic control is characterized by:

- a mission statement
- written, long-term, strategic plans
- an officially responsibly person for the development of the company
- long-term recruitment plans.

The category of market-oriented and financial control is identified by characteristics such as:

- responsibility of the hierarchy levels for their financial performance
- defined processes for quote generation
- polling of customer satisfaction
- a person responsible for marketing
- a formal marketing plan.

The category of operative control consists of characteristics such as:

- number of criteria for performance evaluation
- percentage of profit-related share of the total remuneration
- number of criteria for a promotion
- intensity of the formally used quality control
- extent of investments in IT.

The *interpreting scheme* comprehends the values, ideas and principles of the agents. It finds its expression in categories such as governance, profession and efficiency. Interesting in the category of governance are ideas, values and principles with regard to good stewardship of a professional service firm. Appropriate characteristics are:

- property and control in one entity
- leadership by partners
- equality between partners
- profit distribution among partners.

The second category contains those ideas, values and principles a lawyer represents in his professional work. This covers characteristics as:

- importance of professional knowledge
- control of professional work
- indivisibility of responsibility
- flat hierarchies
- type of relationships with clients.

The last category covers the field of efficiency. The efficiency category can be described by characteristics like:

- efficiency of processes
- familiarity with competitors
- degree of competitive behavior
- consequent operative cost management
- deliberate cost management.

14.2 P² and the Managed Professional Business

The *Professional Partnership (P²)* differs by the type and extent of control exercised (control dimensions) based on the specifics of the primary task (the profession) and the resulting governance and owner structure of other already existing approaches.

From the point of view of the management systems prevailing in the P^2 form, three forms of controls can be described[4]:

- *Strategic control:* The P^2 allows only weak or medium strategic control, with objective analysis having a low rating, and a consensus culture having a high rating.
- *Market-oriented and financial control:* This type of control concentrates on a precise definition of financial targets, with a relatively tolerant approach toward accountability in terms of how the aims were achieved. In such cases, short-term orientation is explicit and the long-term orientation is implicit.
- *Operational control:* The extent of involvement in operative control proves to be relatively low in P^2. The focus of involvement lies in professional standards and high service quality.

In essence, the P^2 form promotes professional satisfaction and maintains and develops professional standards. At the same time it is less effective with regard to market penetration as far as finding new clients and established aspects of financial results are concerned.

Two reasons are given as to why this form of organization emerges, but the academic debate lacks path dependencies[5] and general considerations of dependency on other factors, such as the size and age of the organization, or its relationship with markets and the competition.

In many cases, P^2 is also the most efficient type of organization of professional work.[6] It may therefore be assumed that efficiency is rated relatively highly by the parties involved in such an organization.

Another archetype is the *Managed Professional Business (MPB)*, which appears most often in big international auditing firms and which must be seen, as far as the formation of structures and systems is concerned, as being diametrically opposed to P^2. This archetype underlines the aspects of economic focus in professional service firms. The differences from the P^2 form are illustrated in Fig. 14.2 below.

Changing from P^2 to MPB can be carried out on a continuum both in its structure and its system, but the change requires substantial modification of the interpretative schema. The two archetypes do not therefore constitute extremes of a continuum but ideal forms within two clearly differentiable clusters. The arguments can also be extended to other influencing factors. For example, the change could be ascribed to a modification in size or the market environment, but a movement from P^2 to MPB in particular requires a change of values, ideas and conceptions.

14.3 Change of Archetype – Yes or No?

To obtain a more differentiated view of the theory of archetypes in the context of professional services, the questions concerning the existence of an archetype change, the form of this change and the extent of its empirical relevance must be considered.

			P²-Form	MPB-Form
Interpretive Scheme			**Governance** Fusion of ownership & control Representative democracy Managerial tasks among owners Local office center of commitment **Primary task** Professional knowledge Peer control Work responsibility Strong links with clients Minimum hierarchy	**Effectiveness / efficiency** Management Client service Competition Marketing and growth strategies Rationalization Productivity
Systems	*Strategic Control* *Financial & Market Control* *Operational Control*	Rationality Interaction Targets Tolerance Orientation Involvement Focus Centralization	Low analytical emphasis Consensus decision making Precise financial targets High Short term Low Professional standards & quality Decentralized	Moderate analytical emphasis More directive decision-making Precise targets Low Short & long term orientation Medium Standards, quality, planning, marketing More centralization
Structure	*Differentiation* *Integration*	Specialization Criteria for Specialization Useof integrative devices Use of rules & procedures	Low Personal interest Low Generally low	Medium Functional difference Medium, cross-functional teams More rules generally

Fig. 14.2   Characteristics of PSF archetypes partnership (P²) and managed professional business (MPB). (Source: adapted from Hinings et al. 1999, p. 134)

This leads to the conclusion that in some areas (mainly in areas of marketing, such as the key function for marketing and quality control), changes towards higher professionalization of management tasks in the organization can indeed be observed, whereas other areas (mainly strategic, e.g., personal relationships between partners and clients, a consensus culture between partners[7]) show a high measure of continuity. At this stage, however, the argument of a change of archetype is not fully underpinned by current research results. Corporate law firms, for example, have already adapted a few management practices, but have not yet succeeded in fully shedding all aspects of the P² form. The key elements of the interpretative scheme, in particular, have not yet been fully modified.[8]

One fundamental criticism of the way archetype approaches have been received is that initial empirical results are being generalized rather uncritically. In the context of the theory of archetypes, it is often assumed that concepts which have developed within law firms and auditors in North America can be applied to other sectors[9] and countries.[10,11] However, there are various reasons for doubting this. First of all, professions in every country have historically developed national characteristics which differ considerably.[12] Secondly, professions and the organization of professional work depend largely on individual, country-specific legal situations, existing professional rules and regulations, as well as administrative hierarchies (at sectoral and national level).[13] Moreover, the reasons for change (consolidation, commodification, increasing efficiency, international orientation etc.) and change processes in different sectors and countries are not identical.[14] In some sectors, such as auditing, a radical transformation can be observed, whereas in other sectors, such as architecture, traditional structures remain quite robust.[15] The linear image of change in the theory of archetypes which regards any restructuring of management as a movement from one archetype to another should indeed be called into question.[16]

In summary it can be said that an archetype is no more than the ideal-typical representation of a cluster of organizations. Some authors postulate an archetype change in the organization of professional work, away from the traditional P^2 form and towards professionalized Managed Professional Business. But this admittedly very catchy concept has been strongly and repeatedly criticized, even from within the approach. For small and specialized professional service firms in particular, intentions focusing on more management practices should be challenged. A traditional partnership in such cases may yet prove to be the right solution.

Notes

1. See Greenwood and Hinings (1988, 1993); Greenwood et al. (1990); Hinings et al. (1999); Cooper et al. (1996); Pinnington and Morris (1996, 2002, 2003); Morris and Pinnington (1999); Brock et al. (1999); Ranson et al. (1980).
2. See Greenwood and Hinings (1988), p. 293.
3. See Hinings et al. (1999); Cooper et al. (1996); Pinnington and Morris (1996, 2002, 2003); Morris and Pinnington (1999).
4. See Hill (1988), p. 403 et seq.; Miller (1987), p. 7; Cooper et al. (1996).
5. See Crouch (2006), p. 167 et seq.
6. See Greenwood and Empson (2003), p. 909 et seq.
7. See Pinnington and Morris (2002), p. 207.
8. See Kaiser and Kampe (2007).
9. See Brock et al. (1999), p. 68 et seq., p. 105 et seq., p. 183 et seq.
10. '(...) we would hypothesize that the P^2 archetype is more dominant among continental European firms, where state regulation of professional sectors has inhibited market development, than in the Anglo-American context.' (Pinnington and Morris 2002, p. 207)
11. See Pinnington and Morris (2002), p. 195; Greenwood and Hinings (1988), p. 309, who already state that 'Archetypes (...) will have to be sensitive to institutional contexts and differences'. It is therefore astonishing that they participate in generalisations such as in Brock et al. (1999).
12. See Jarausch and Cocks (1990), p. 20.
13. See Schmitz (1997), p. 13.
14. See Kirkpatrick and Ackroyd (2003), p. 739 et seq. who criticise applying the concept on the public sector in particular.
15. '(...) that professional firms in some sectors that are more market oriented in their values, such as accounting, will have more comprehensively embraced the MPB form while architecture (...) remains wedded, (...) to the P^2 form of organization. Other market-based professions, such as law, are likely to fall between these extremes (...). Likewise, professional organizations facing market-type pressures, such as those in general medical practice partnerships in the health sector, may well mimic MPB characteristics (...). But again, their values may not be consistent with these innovations' (Pinnington and Morris (2002), p. 207).
16. See Kirkpatrick and Ackroyd (2003), p. 733 et seq.

References

Achleitner AK, Charifzadeh M (2001) Handbuch Investment-Banking, 2., rev. and enl. ed., Gabler, Wiesbaden

Adams GA, King LA, King DW (1996) Relationships of job and family involvement, family social support, and work-family conflict with job and life satisfaction. In: Applied Psychology 81(4):411–420

Adamson I (2000) Management consultant meets a potential client for the first time. Qual Market Res 3(1):17–26

Adler PS, Kwon SW (2002) Social capital. Acad Manage Rev 27(1):17–40

Aharoni Y (1997a) Changing roles of state intervention in services in an era of open international markets. State University of New York Press, Albany, NY

Aharoni Y (1997b) Management consulting. In: Aharoni Y (ed) Changing roles of state intervention in services in an era of open international markets. State University of New York Press, Albany, NY, pp 153–179

Aharoni Y (1993a) Coalitions and competition, Routledge, London

Aharoni Y (1993b) Globalization of professional business services. In: Aharoni Y (ed) Coalitions and competition. Routledge, London, pp 1–19

Alavi M, Leidner DE (2001) Review: knowledge management and knowledge management systems. MIS Q 25(1):107–136

Albert U, Silverman M (1984)) Making management philosophy a cultural reality. Personnel 61(1):12–21

Albrecht K (1988) At America's service. Dow Jones-Irwin, Homewood, IL

Aldrich H (1979) Organizations and environments. Prentice-Hall, Englewood Cliffs, NJ

Allen NJ, Meyer JP (1990) The measurement and antecedents of affective, continuance and normative commitment to the organization. J Occup Psychol 63:1–18

Allen TD (2001) Family-supportive work environments: the role of organizational perceptions. J Vocat Behav 58(5):414–435

Allen TD, Herst DEL, Bruck CS, Sutton M (2000) Consequences associated with work-to-family conflict. J Occup Health Psychol 5(2):278–308

Alvesson M (1993) Cultural-ideological modes of management control: theory and case study of a professional service company. In: Deetz SA (ed) Communication yearbook 16. Sage Publications, Newbury Park, CA

Alvesson M (1995) Management of knowledge-intensive companies. Walter de Gruyter, Berlin

Anand N, Gardner HK, Morris T (2007) Knowledge-based innovation. Acad Manage J 50(2): 406–428

Anders SB (2002) Website of the month. CPA J August:17

Anderson SE, Coffey BS, Byerly RT (2002) Formal organizational initiatives and informal workplace practices: links to work-family conflict and job-related outcomes. J Manage 28(6):787–810

S. Kaiser, M.J. Ringlstetter, *Strategic Management of Professional Service Firms*, 189
DOI 10.1007/978-3-642-16063-9, © Springer-Verlag Berlin Heidelberg 2011

Appelbaum E, Bailey T, Berg P, Kalleberg AL (2000) Manufacturing competitive advantage. Ithaca, NY

Arthur JB (1994) Effects of human resource system on manufacturing performance and turnover. Acad Manage J 37:670–687

Aryee S, Srinivas E, Tan HH (2005) Rhythms of life: antecedents and outcomes of work-family balance in employed parents. J Appl Psychol 90(1):132–146

Astley WG (1985) Administrative science as socially constructed truth. Adm Sci Q 30(4):497–513

Atkinson J (1984) Manpower strategies for flexible organizations. Pers Manage 16(8):28–31

Badura B, Vetter C (2004) "Work-Life-Balance" – Herausforderung für die betriebliche Gesundheitspolitik and den Staat. In: Badura B, Schellschmidt H, Vetter C, Bäcker G (eds) Wettbewerbsfaktor work-life-balance. Betriebliche Strategien zur Vereinbarkeit von Beruf, Familie and Privatleben., Berlin, pp 5–17

Baer J, Stoll M (1999) Human resources management als Eckpfeiler der strategischen and operativen Geschäftsentwicklung. In: Müller-Stewens G (ed) Professional service firms, Frankfurt am Main, pp 198–221

Bailey TH (2004) High Performance Arbeitssysteme and ihre Auswirkungen auf die Organisationsleistung and die Beschäftigten. In: Gruber H, Harteis C, Heid H, Meier B (eds) Kapital and Kompetenz. Wiesbaden

Baker W (1990) Market networks and corporate behavior. Am J Sociol 96(3):589–625

Baltes BB, Briggs TE, Huff JW, Wright JA, Neuman GA (1999) Flexible and compressed work-week schedules: a meta-analysis of their effects on work-related criteria. J Appl Psychol 84(4):496–913

Balzer A, Student D (2002) Operation Big Mac. Wirtschaftswoche 32(11,02):52–63

Balzer K (2000) Die McKinsey-methode. Vienna

Bamberger I (1998) Strategische Unternehmensberatung. Wiesbaden

Bandura A (1979) Sozial-kognitive Lerntheorie. Stuttgart

Barabási A-L (2003) Linked. New York, NY

Barrett FD (1978) Creativity techniques. Adv Manage J 43(1):25

Baschab J, Piot J (2005) The professional services firm bible. Hoboken, NJ

BDU (2005) Facts & Figures zum Beratermarkt 2004, Bundesverband Deutscher Unternehmensberater BDU e.V. Bonn

Beauregard TA, Henry LC (2009) Making the link between work-life balance practices and organizational performance. Hum Resour Manage Rev 19(1):9–22

Becker BE, Huselid MA (1998) High performance work systems and firm perfromance. Res Pers Hum Resour Manage 16:53–101

Becker BE, Huselid MA, Pickus PS, Spratt MF (1997) HR as a source of shareholder value. Hum Resour Manage 36:39–47

Becker U, Schade C (1995) Betriebsformen der Unternehmensberatung. Z betriebswirt Forsch 47(4):327–354

Bedeian AG, Burke BG, Moffett RG (1988) Outcomes of work-family conflict among married male and female professionals. J Manage 14(3):475–491

Benkenstein M, Güthoff J (1996) Typologisierung von Dienstleistungen. Z Betriebswirt 66(12):1439–1510

Benkenstein M, Steiner S (2004) Formen von Dienstleistungsinnovationen. In: Bruhn M, Stauss B (eds) Dienstleistungsinnovationen. 1. Aufl. Wiesbaden, pp. 27–46

Benkhoff B (1997) Disentangling organizational commitment. Pers Rev 26:114–131

Berry LL, Parasuraman A (1992) Service-marketing. Frankfurt am Main

Bian Y (1997) Bringing strong ties back in. Am Soc Rev 62(3):366–385

Bigley G, Pearce J (1998) Straining for shared meaning: problems of trust and distrust. Acad Manage Rev 23:405–421

Bloom S (1984) Effective marketing for professionals services. Harv Bus Rev 62(5):102–110

Blyler M, Coff RW (2003) Dynamic capabilities, social capital, and rent appropriation. Strateg Manage J 24(7):677–686

Bone S (1995) Word of mouth effects on short-term and long-term product judgements. J Bus Res 32:213–223

Boselie S, Paauwe J, Richardson R (2003) Human resource management, institutionalization and organizational performance. Int J Hum Resour Manage 14(8):1407–1429

Bouncken R (2001) Transfer, Speicherung and Nutzung von Wissen bei Dienstleistungsunternehmen. In: Bruhn M, Stauss B (ed) Dienstleistungsmanagement Jahrbuch 2001. Wiesbaden, pp 205–223

Boxall P (2003) HR strategy and competitive advantage in the service sector. Hum Resour Manage J 13(3):5–20

Boxall P, Purcell J (2000) Strategic human resource management. Int J Manage Rev 2:183–203

Boyar SL, Maertz CP Jr, Pearson AW (2005) The effects of work–family conflict and family–work conflict on nonattendance behaviors. J Bus Res 58:919–925

Breipohl S (2004) Personalauswahl, Personalentwicklung and Karrierewege in der Strategieberatung – am Beispiel Bain & Company. In: Raff R, Brauner DJ (eds) Berufsziel Unternehmensberater. Sternenfels, pp 109–116

Brett JM, Stroh LK (2003) Working 61 plus hours a week: Why do managers do it. J Appl Psychol 88(1):67–78

Brinker B (1998) Strategische Herausforderungen im Investment Banking. Wiesbaden

Brock DM, Powell MJ, Hinings CR (1999) Restructuring the professional organization. London

Brown JL, Cooper DJ (1996) Strategic alliances within a big-six accounting firm. Int Stud Manage Organ 2:59–79

Brown JL, Cooper DJ, Greenwood R, Hinings CR (1996) Strategic alliances within a big-six accounting firm. Int Stud Manage Organ 26(2):59–79

Bruhn M (2000) Qualitätssicherung im Dienstleistungsmarketing – eine Einführung in die theoretischen and praktischen Probleme. In: Bruhn M, Stauss B (ed) Dienstleistungsqualität: Konzepte – Methoden – Erfahrungen. Wiesbaden, pp 21–48

Bruhn M, Georgi D, Treyer M, Leumann S (2000) Wertorientiertes relationship marketing. Die Unternehmung 54(3):167–187

Bruhn M, Homburg C (2000) Handbuch Kundenbindungsmanagement, 3., rev. and enl. ed. Wiesbaden

Bürger B (2004) Qualität als Differenzierungsmöglichkeit auf dem Markt für professionelle Dienstleistungen. In: Ringlstetter M, Bürger B, Kaiser S (eds) Strategien and management für professional service firms. Weinheim, pp 141–162

Bürger B (2005) Aspekte der Führung and der strategischen Entwicklung von Professional Service Firms, 1. Wiesbaden

Burke RJ (2006) Organizational culture. In: Jones F, Burke RJ, Westman M (eds) Work-life balance. Hove, pp 235–260

Burt RS (1997) The contingent value of social capital. Adm Sci Q 42(2):339–365

Burt RS (1992) Structural holes. Cambridge, MA

Büschmann J (1999) Wirkung von Reputation zur Reduktion von Qualitätsunsicherheit, Diskussionsbeitrag der Katholischen Universität Eichstätt – Wirtschaftswissenschaftlichen Fakultät Ingolstadt, Nr. 123. Ingolstadt

Carlson DS (1999) Personality and role variables as predictors of three forms of work–family conflict. J Vocat Behav 55:236–253

Caroli TS (2007) Unternehmensberatung als Sicherstellung von Führungsrationalität? In: Nissen V (ed) Consulting research. Wiesbaden, pp 109–126

Carpenter D, Esterling K, Lazer D (2003) The strength of strong ties: a model of contact-making in policy networks with evidence from US health politics. Rationality Soc 15(4):411–440

Carr AE, Li-Ping Tang T (2005) Sabbaticals and employee motivation: benefits, concerns, and implications. J Educ Bus 80(3):160–164

Casper WJ, Weltman D, Kwesiga E (2007) Beyond family-friendly: the construct and measurement of singles-friendly work culture. J Vocat Behav 70(3):478–501

Castan B (1997) Die Partnerschaftsgesellschaft. Bielefeld

Chambers E, Foulon M, Handfield-Jones H, Hankin SM, Michaels EG (1998) The war for talent. McKinsey Q 3:44–57

Chaston I (1998) Self-Managed teams. Br J Manage 9(1):1–12

Choo CW, Detlor B, Turnbull D (2000) Web work. Dordrecht

Christopher M, Payne A, Ballantyne D (2004) Relationship marketing – creating stakeholder value. Oxford

Clark SC (2000) Work-family border theory. A new theory of work-family balance. Hum Relat 53(6):747–770

Cohen D, Fields G (1999) Social capital and capital gains in Silicon Valley. Calif Manage Rev 41(2):108–131

Coleman JS (1988) Social capital in the creation of human capital. Am J Sociol 94:95–120

Coleman JS (1991) Grundlagen der Sozialtheorie. Munich

Coleman JS (1990) Foundations of social theory. Cambridge

Connor D (1989) Increasing revenue from your clients. New York

Connor M, Hooks K, McGuire T (1999) Gaining legitimacy for flexible work arrangements and career paths: the business case for public accounting and professional service firms. In: Parasuraman S, Greenhaus JH (1999) Integrating work and family: challenges and choices for a changing world. Praeger, pp 154–166

Cook J, Wall T (1980) New work attitude measures of trust, organizational commitment, and personal need non-fulfilment. J Occup Psychol 53:39–52

Cooper DJ, Hinings CR, Greenwood R, Brown J (1996) Sedimentation and transformation in organizational change. Organ Stud 17(4):623–647

Cross RL, Parker A (2004) The hidden power of social networks. Boston, MA

Crouch C (2006) Complementarity and fit in the study of comparative capitalisms. In: Morgan G (ed) Changing capitalisms? Oxford, pp 167–189

Davenport TH, Probst GJB (2002) Knowledge management case book, 2nd edn. Erlangen

Dawes PL, Dowling GR, Patterson PG (1992) Criteria Used to Select Management Consultants. Ind Mark Manage 21:187–193

Day E, Barksdale H Jr (1994) Organizational purchasing of professional services. J Bus Ind Mark 9(3):44–51

Deci EL, Ryan RM (2000) The "What" and "Why" of goal pursuits. Psychol Inq 11:227–268

Deci EL, Ryan RM (1985) Intrinsic motivation and self-determination in human behavior. New York, NY

DeFillippi RJ, Arthur MB, Parker P (2003) Internet odysseys: linking web roles to career and community investments. Int J Hum Resour Manage 14(5):751–767

deGraat E (2007) Kennzahlen and Kosten-Nutzen-Relationen zur Bewertung familienfreundlicher Maßnahmen in Unternehmen. In: Esslinger AS, Schobert DB (eds) Erfolgreiche Umsetzung von Work-Life Balance in Organisationen. Strategien, Konzepte, Maßnahmen., Wiesbaden

Dex SSF (1999) Business performance and family-friendly policies. J Gen Manage 24(4):22–37

Dikkers JSE, Geurts SAE, Dulk LD, Peper B, Taris TW, Kompier MAJ (2007) Dimensions of work-home culture and their relations with the use of work-home arrangements and work-home interaction. Work Stress 21(2):155–172

Dill P, Hügler G (1997) Unternehmenskultur and Führung betriebswirtschaftlicher Organisationen: Ansatzpunkte für ein kulturbewußtes Management. In: Heinen E, Fank M (eds) Unternehmenskultur. Munich, pp 141–209

Diller H (1995) Beziehungsmanagement. In: Tietz B (1995) Handwörterbuch des Marketing. Stuttgart

Dincher R, Gaugler E (2002) Personalberatung bei der Beschaffung von Fach- and Führungskräften. Mannheim

Dirks K, Ferrin D (2001) The role of trust in organizational settings. Organ Sci 12:450–467

Ditillo A (2004) Dealing with uncertainty in knowledge-intensive firms. Account Organ Soc 29:401–422

Donaldson L (2001) Reflections on knowledge and knowledge-intensive firms. Hum Relat 54(7):955–963

Drago R, Golden R (2006) The role of economics in work-family research. In: Pitt-Catsouphes M, Kossek EE, Sweet S (eds) The work and family handbook. Multi-disciplinary perspectives methods, and approaches. Mahwah, NJ, pp 267–282

Ebers M (2003) Geleitwort. In: Maurer I (ed) Soziales Kapital als Erfolgsfaktor junger Unternehmen. Wiesbaden

Eikhof DR, Warhurst C, Haunschild A (2007) Introduction: What work? What life? What balance? Critical reflections on the work-life balance debate. Empl Relat 29(4):325–333

Eisenhardt KM, Brown SL (1999) Wie Sie Ihr Geschäftsportfolio flexibel gestalten. Harv Bus 21(6):72–85

El-Murad J, West DC (2004) The definition and measurement of creativity. J Advert Res 44(2):188–201

Empson L (2000) Merging professional service firms. Bus Strat Rev 11(2):39–46

Empson L (2001a) Introduction. Hum Relat 54(7):811–817

Empson L (2001b) Fear of exploitation and fear of contamination. Hum Relat 54(7):839–862

Endress M (2002) Vertrauen. Bielefeld

Eriksson K, Vaghulg AL (2000) Customer retention, purchasing behavior and relationship substance in professional services. Ind Mark Manage 29:363–372

Ferguson C (1996a) "Selling" professional services. Manage Decis 34(4):19–23

Ferguson C (1996b) "Selling" professional services: a practical approach – Part I. Manage Decis 34(3):49–54

Fernandez RM, Castilla EJ (2001) How much is that network worth? social capital in employee referral networks. In: Lin N, Cook K, Burt RS (eds) Social capital, New York, NY, pp 85–104

Fey G (2005) Kontakte knüpfen und beruflich nutzen, 3., neu bearb. Aufl. Regensburg

Filiatrault P, Lapierre J (1997) Managing business-to-business marketing relationships in consulting engineering firms. Ind Mark Manage 26:213–222

Fink D, Knoblach B (2004) Strategien für Strategen. In: Nippa M, Schneiderbauer D (eds) Erfolgsmechanismen der Top-Management-Beratung. Heidelberg, pp 79–102

Fitzgerald L, Johnston R, Brignall S, Silvestro R, Voss C (1994) performance measurement in service businesses. London

Fombrun CJ (1996) Reputation. Boston, MA

Fombrun C, Shanley M (1990) What's in a name? Acad Manag J 33(2):233–258

Frey BS (1997) Markt and motivation. Munich

Friedman SD, Greenhaus JH (2000) Work and family – allies or enemies? What happens when business professionals confront life choices. Oxford

Friese M (1998) Kooperation als Wettbewerbsstrategie für Dienstleistungsunternehmen Wiesbaden

Fritz W, Effenberger J (1996) Strategische Unternehmensberatung. Braunschweig

Frone MR (2003) Work-family balance. In: Quick JC, Tetrick LE (eds) Handbook of occupational health psychology. Washington, DC, pp 143–162

Frone MR, Russell M, Cooper ML (1997) Relation of work-family conflict to health outcomes: a four-year longitudinal study of employed parents. J Occup Organ Psychol 70:325–335

Frone MR, Yardley JK (1996) Workplace family-supportive programs: predictors of employed parents' importance ratings. J Occup Organ Psychol 69(4):351–366

Galanter M, Palay T (1990) Why the big get better. Va Law Rev 76(4):747–811

Gargiulo M, Benassi M (2000) Trapped in your own net? Organ Science 11(2):183–196

Gauger J (2000) Commitment-Management in Unternehmen am Beispiel des mittleren Managements. Wiesbaden

Gaugler E (1992) Personalberatung. In: Gaugler E, Weber W (eds) Handwörterbuch des Personalwesens. Stuttgart, 1608–1620

Giardini A, Kabst R (2008) Effects of work-family human resource practices. A longitudinal perspective. Int J Hum Res Manage 19(11):2079–2094

Gillmann JP, Ruud TF (2002) Performance Measurement in Professional service firms, 1. Aufl. Wiesbaden

Glückler J (2001) Internationalisierung der Unternehmensberatung – Eine Exploration im Rhein-Main-Gebiet, Institut für Wirtschafts- and Sozialgeographie. Johann Wolfgang Goethe-Universität Frankfurt, Frankfurt am Main

Glückler J, Armbrüster T (2003) Bridging uncertainty in management consulting. Organ Stud 24(2):269–297

Gmür M (2003) Die Ressource Personal and ihr Beitrag zum Unternehmenserfolg. In: Martin A (ed) Personal als Ressource. Munich, pp 21–52

Goff SJ, Mount MK, Jamison RL (1990) Employer supported child care, work/family conflict, and absenteeism: a field study. Pers Psychol 43(4):793–809

Granovetter MS (1974) Getting a job: a study of contacts and careers. Cambridge MA

Granovetter MS (1973) The strength of weak ties. Am J Sociol 78(6):1360–1380

Grant-Vallone EJ, Donaldson SI (2001) Consequences of work-family conflict on employee well-being over time. Work Stress 15(3):214–226

Grawitch M, Trares S, Kohler J (2007) Healthy workplace practices and employee outcomes. Int J Stress Manage 14(3):275–293

Gray JT, Hinings CR, Malhotra N, Pinnington A, Morris T (2001) Internationalisation and change in professional service firms. New Zealand

Greenhaus JH, Beutell NJ (1985) Sources and conflict between work and family roles. Acad Manage Rev 10(1):76–88

Greenhaus JH, Collins KM, Singh R, Parasuraman S (1997) Work and family influences on departure from public accounting. J Vocat Behav 50(2):249–270

Greenwood R, Empson L (2003) The professional partnership. Organ Stud 24(6):909–933

Greenwood R, Hinings B, Brown J (1990) The 'P2 form' of strategic management: corporate practices in professional service firms. Acad Manage J 33(4):725–755

Greenwood R, Hinings CR, Brown J (1994) Merging professional service firms. Organ Sci 5(2):239–257

Greenwood R, Hinings C (1988) Organizational design types, tracks and the dynamics of strategic change. Organ Stud 9(3):293–316

Greenwood R, Hinings C (1993) Understanding Strategic Change. Acad Manage J 36(5):1052–1081

Griess HA, Zinnert M (1997) Der Versicherungsmakler: Position and Funktion aus rechtlicher and wirtschaftlicher Sicht. Karlsruhe

Grönroos C (1984) A service quality model and its marketing implications. Eur J Mark 18(4):36–44

Grönroos C (1982) An applied service marketing theory. Eur J Mark 16(7):30–41

Grönroos C (2002) Quo vadis, marketing? Marke Rev 3:129–146

Gröpel P, Kuhl J (2006) Having time for life activities: life balance and self-regulation. Z Gesundheitspsychologie 14(2):54–63

Guest DE (1997) Human resource management and performance. Int J Hum Resour Manage 8(3):263–276

Gulati R, Higgins MC (2003) Which ties matter when? Strat Manag J 24(2):127–144

Gummesson E (1979) The marketing of professional services. Eur J Mark 13(5):308–318

Gummesson E (1988) Quality strategy in professional service firms, paper presented at the EIASM workshop on strategies in service industries, European Institute of Advanced Studies in Management, Brüssel, 06.-07.05. (1998)

Gupta B, Iyer LS, Aronson JE (2001) Knowledge management. Ind Manage Data Syst 100(1):17–21

Halpern DF (2005) How time-flexible work policies can reduce stress, improve health, and save money. Stress Health 21(3):157–168

Hamel G (1991) Competition for competence and inter-partner learning within international strategic alliances. Strat Manage J 12:83–103

Hammer LB, Bauer TN, Grandey AA (2003) Work-family conflict and work-related withdrawal behaviors. J Bus Psychol 17(3):419–436

Hansen MT (1999) The search-transfer problem. Adm Sci Q 44:82–111

Hansen MT, Nohria N, Tierney T (1999) What's your strategy for managing knowledge? Harv Bus Rev 77(2):106–116

Harding CF (1990) Ten rules for better networking. J Manage Consul 6(1):41–44

Harrington B, James JB (2006) The standards of excellence in work-life integration. In: Pitt-Catsouphes M, Kossek EE, Sweet, SA (eds) The work and family handbook: Multi-disciplinary perspectives methods, and approaches. Mahwah, NJ, pp 665–683

Hart CWL, Schlesinger LA, Maher D (1992) Guarantees Come on Professional Service Firms. Sloan Manage Rev 33(3):19–29

Hartog Den DN, Verburg RM (2004) High performance work systems, organisational culture and firm effectiveness. Hum Resour Manage J 14(1):55–78

Hauschildt J, Salomo S (2007) Innovationsmanagement, 4., überarb., erg. and aktualisierte Aufl. Munich

Hentschel B (1992) Dienstleistungsqualität aus Kundensicht. Wiesbaden

Herbig P, Milewicz J, Golden J (1994) A model of reputation building and destruction. J Bus Res 31:23–31

Herbold I (2002) Personalberatung and executive search. Sternenfels

Heskett JL, Sasser WE, Schlesinger LA (1997) The service profit chain. New York, NY

Hill C (1988) Corporate control type, strategy, size and financial performance. J Manage Stud 25:403–418

Hinings CR, Greenwood R, Cooper DJ (1999) The dynamics of change in large accounting firms. In: Brock DM, Powell MJ, Hinings CR (eds) Restructuring the professional organization. London, pp 131–153

Hirsch PM, Levin DZ (1999) Umbrella advocates versus validity police. Organ Sci 10(2):199–212

Hitt MA, Biermant L, Shimizu K, Kochhar R (2001) Direct and moderating effects of human capital on strategy and performance in professional service firms. Acad Manage J 44: 13–28

Hofbauer G, Schweidler A (2006) Professionelles Produktmanagement. Erlangen

Hoffman KD, Bateson JEG (1997) Essentials of services marketing. Fort Worth, TX

Holmlund M (2004) Analyzing business relationships and distinguishing different interaction levels. Ind Mark Manage 33:279–287

Höselbarth F (2000) Aspekte des beruflichen Wechsels von Beratern. In: Höselbarth F (ed) Die Berater. Frankfurt am Main

Huselid MA (1995) The impact of human resource management practices on turnover, productivity, and corporate financial performance. Acad Manage J 38:635–672

Ichniowski C, Shaw K, Prennushi G (1997) The effects of human resource management practices on productivity. Am Econ Rev 87:291–314

Inkpen AC, Tsang EWK (2005) Social capital, networks, and knowledge transfer. Acad Manage Rev 30(1):146–165

Iyer VM (1998) Characteristics of Accounting Firm Alumni Who Benefit Their Former Firm. Account Horiz 12(1):18–30

Iyer VM, Bamber EM, Barefield RM (2000) CPA firms' marketing strategies. J Prof Serv Mark 21(1):1–7

Iyer VM, Day E (1998) CPA firm alumni as a marketing ressource. J Prof Serv Mark 17(2):17–29

Jäger W, Jäger M (2004) Talente finden und binden. Personal 2:11–15

Jansen D (2003) Einführung in die Netzwerkanalyse, 2., erw. Aufl. Opladen

Jansen D, Weber M (2004) Helping hands and entrepreneurship – supporting newly founded firms. In: Dowling M, Schmude J, Knyphausen-Aufsess D (eds) Advances in interdisciplinary European entrepreneurship research. Münster, pp 57–79

Jarausch K, Cocks G (1990) Introduction. In: Cocks G (ed) German professions, 1800–1950. New York, NY, pp 3–8

Jeschke K (2002) Marketingmanagement für Unternehmensberatungsleistungen. In: Mohe M (ed) Consulting – Problemlösung als Geschäftsmodell. Stuttgart, pp 243–261

Johannisson B (1995) Entrepreneurial networking in the Scandinavian context theoretical and empirical positioning. Entrepren Reg Dev 7(3):189–192

Jones C, Hesterly WS, Fladmoe-Lindquist K, Borgatti SP (1998) Professional service constellations: how strategies and capabilities influence colworkative stability and change. Organ Sci 9(3):396–410

Jones F, Burke RJ, Westman M (2006) Work-life balance. Hove

Kaiser S (2001) Entwicklung von Humanressourcen, 1. Aufl. Wiesbaden

Kaiser S (2004) Humanressourcen-management in professional service firms. In: Ringlstetter M, Bürger, B., Kaiser, S (eds) Strategien and management für professional service firms. Weinheim, pp 163–184

Kaiser S, Ringlstetter M (2005) Die Interaktion von Anwendern und Beratern als strategischer Erfolgsfaktor. In: Kirsch W, Seidl D, Linder M (eds) Grenzen der Strategieberatung. Eine Gegenüberstellung der Perspektiven von Wissenschaft, Beratung und Klienten. Bern: Haupt Verlag

Kaiser S (2007) Sozialkapital in der betriebswirtschaftlichen Forschung: Status quo and Zukunft. In: Lang R, Schmidt A (eds) Individuum and Organisation: Neue Trends eines organisationswissenschaftlichen Forschungsfeldes. Wiesbaden, pp 131–156

Kaiser S, Kampe T (2007) Archetype theory and contingency factors: the case of german law firms. European group of organisation studies (EGOS) Colloquium. Vienna

Kaiser S, Paust R (2004) Der Einsatz hochqualifizierter externer Mitarbeiter im Unternehmen. Der Betriebswirt 45(3):30–36

Kerr G, Way SA, Thacker J (2007) Performance, HR practices and the HR manager in small entrepreneurial firms. J Small Bus Entrepren 20(1):55–68

Kindermann H (2006) Grundlagen des organisationalen Beschaffungsverhaltens. In: Werani T, Gaubinger K, Kindermann H(Hg): Praxisorientiertes business-to-business-marketing. Wiesbaden, pp 17–28

Kirchmeyer C (2000) Work-life initiatives. In: Cooper CL, Rousseau DM (eds) Time in organizational behavior. Chichester, pp 79–93

Kirkpatrick I, Ackroyd P (2003) Archetype theory and the changing professional organization. In: Organization, H. 10(4), S. 731–750

Kirsch W (1990) Unternehmenspolitik and strategische Unternehmensführung. Munich

Kohr J (2000) Die Auswahl von Unternehmensberatungen. Munich

Koka BR, Prescott JE (2002) Strategic alliances as social capital. Strat Manage J 23(9):795–816

Kor YY, Leblebici H (2005) How do interdependencies among human-capital deployment, development, and diversification strategies affect firms' financial performance? Strat Manage J 26:967–985

Kossek EE, Friede A (2006) The business case. In: Pitt-Catsouphes M, Kossek EE, Sweet SA (2006) The work and family handbook. Multi-disciplinary perspectives methods, and approaches. Mahwah, NJ, pp 611–626

Kotler P, Connor R (1977) Marketing professional services. J Mark 41(1):71–76

Koza MP, Lewin AY (1999) The coevolution of network alliances. Organ Sci 10(5):638–653

Kraft T (2002) Personalberatung in Deutschland and in der Schweiz. Bern

Krieger F (09 Mar. 2007) Arbeit soll wieder schmecken. Financial Times Deutschland

Kühnel S (2004) Wissensorganisation in Professional Service Firms: Perspektiven aus der Wirtschaftsprüfung, Rostock zugl. St. Gallen

Landau E (1969) Psychologie der Kreativität. Munich

Langusch L (2004) Vertrauen: Aufbau, Verstärkung and Difmerger vor dem Hintergrund der Virtrualisierung von Unternehmen. Munich

Leana CR, Buren HJ (1999) Organizational social capital and employment practices. Acad Manage Rev 24(3):538–555

Lee MD, MacDermid SM, Williams ML, Buck ML, Leiba-O'Sullivan S (2002) Contextual factors in the success of reduced-load work arrangements among managers and professionals. Hum Res Manage 41(2):209–223

Lenz H, Schmidt M (1999) Das strategische Netzwerk als Organisationsform internationaler Prüfungs- and Beratungsunternehmen. In: Engelhard J (ed) Kooperation im Wettbewerb. Wiesbaden, pp 113–150

Lesser E (2000a) Knowledge and social capital. Boston, MA

Lesser EL (2000b) Leveraging social capital in organizations. In: Lesser E (ed) Knowledge and social capital. Boston, MA, pp 3–16

Lewicki R, Bunker BB (1996) Developing and maintaining trust in work relationships. In: Kramer RM (ed) Trust in organizations. Thousand Oaks, CA, pp 114–139

Lewis D, Weigert A (1985) Trust as a social reality. In: Social Forces, Jun 85, 63(4):967–985

Litrico JB, Lee MD (2008) Balancing exploration and exploitation in alternative work arrangements: a multiple case study in the professional and management services industry. J Organ Behav 29(8):995–1020

Lorsch JW, Tierney TJ (2002) Aligning the stars: how to succeed when professionals drive results, vol 1. Boston, MA

Løwendahl BR (1992) Global strategies for professional business service firms. Philadelphia, PA

Løwendahl BR (1997) Strategic management of professional service firms. Copenhagen

Løwendahl BR (2005) Strategic management of professional service firms. Copenhagen

Løwendahl BR, Revang O, Fosstenlokken SM (2001) Knowledge and value creation in professional service firms. Hum Relat 54(7):911–931

Luhmann N (1989) Vertrauen: Ein Mechanismus der Reduktion von Komplexität (Erstausgabe 1968). Stuttgart

Lyness KS, Thompson DE (1997) Above the glass ceiling: a comparison of matched samples of female and male executives. J Appl Psychol 82(3):359–375

MacDuffie JP (1995) Human resource bundles and manufacturing performance. Ind Relat Labor Rev 48:197–221

Maister DH (1982) Balancing the professional service firm. Sloan Manage Rev 24(1):15–29

Maister DH (1997) Managing the professional service firm, 2nd edn. New York, NY

Maister DH (2003) Managing the professional service firm. New York, NY

Malos SB, Campion MA (2000) Human resource strategy and career mobility in professional service firms. Acad Manage J 43(4):749–760

March JG (1991) Exploration and exploitation in organizational learning. Organ Sci 2(1):71–87

Marks SR, MacDermid SM (1996) Multiple roles and the self: a theory of role balance. J Marriage Fam 58(2):417–432

Marsden PV (2001) Interpersonal ties, social capital, and employer staffing practices. In: Lin N, Cook K, Burt RS (2001) Social capital, New York, NY, pp 105–125

Mattila AS (2001) The impact of relationship type on customer loyalty in a context of service failures. J Serv Res 4(2):91–101

McEvily B, Perrone V, Zaheer A (2003) Trust as an organizing principle. Organ Sci 14:91–103

Mertins K, Heisig P, Vorbeck J (2003) Knowledge management, 2nd edn. Berlin

Meyer JP, Allen NJ (1991) A three-component conceptualization of organizational commitment. Hum Resour Manage Rev 1(1):81

Miller D (1987) Strategy making and structure. Acad Manage J 30:7–32

Mills PK, Hall JL, Leidecker JK, Margulies N (1983) Flexiform: a model for professional service organizations. Acad Manage Rev 8(1):118–131

Mitchell VW (1994) Problems and risks in the purchasing of consultancy services. Serv Ind J 14(3):315–339

Mizruchi MS, Galaskiewicz J (1994) Networks of interorganizational relations. In: Wasserman S, Galaskiewicz J (1994) Advances in social network analysis. Thousand Oaks, CA, pp 230–253

Moran P (2005) Structural vs. relational embeddedness. Strat Manage J 26(12):1129–1151

Morner M (1997) Organisation der Innovation im Konzern. Wiesbaden

Morris ML, Madsen SR (2007) Advancing work-life integration in individuals, organizations, and communities. Adv Dev Hum Resour 9(4):439–454

Morris T, Pinnington A (1999) Continuity and change in professional organizations: evidence from British law firms. In: Brock DM, Powell MJ, Hinings CR (eds) Restructuring the professional organization. London, pp 200–214

Müller-Stewens G (1999) Professional service firms, 1. Aufl. Frankfurt am Main

Müller-Stewens G, Drolshammer J, Kriegmeier J (1999) Professional service firms. In: Müller-Stewens G (ed) Professional service firms. Frankfurt am Main, pp 11–157

Müller-Stewens G, Lechner C (2003) Strategisches Management, 2., rev. and enl. ed. Stuttgart

Nahapiet J, Ghoshal S (1998) Social capital, intellectual capital, and the organizational advantage. Acad Manage Rev 23(2):242–266

Nahapiet J, Ghoshal S (2002) Social capital, intellectual capital, and the organizational advantage. In: Choo CW, Bontis N (ed) The strategic management of intellectual capital and organizational knowledge. Oxford, pp 657–697

Nederstigt P (2005) Unternehmensberatungen. Karriere 2:32

Netemeyer RG, Boles JS, McMurrian R (1996) Development and validation of work-family conflict and family-work conflict scales. J Appl Psychol 81(4):400–410

Nissen V (2007) Consulting research. In: Nissen V (ed) Consulting research. Wiesbaden, pp 3–38

Nohria N, Eccles RG (1994) Face-to-face. In: Nohria N (ed) Networks and organizations. Boston, MA, pp 288–308

Nonaka I, Takeuchi H (1995) The knowledge-creating company. New York, NY

Nonaka I, Takeuchi H, Mader F (1997) Die Organisation des Wissens. Frankfurt(Main)

Ofek E, Sarvary M (2001) Leveraging the customer base. Creating competitive advantage through knowledge management. Manage Sci 47(10):1441–1456

Oelsnitz von derD, Hahmann M (2003) Wissensmanagement. Stuttgart

Ostendorp A (2007) Möglichkeiten für KMU and Großunternehmen bei der Umsetzung eines Trends. Life Balance als Beitrag zu einer Kultur der Unterschiede. In: Esslinger AS, Schobert D (eds) Erfolgreiche Umsetzung von Work-Life Balance in Organisationen. Strategien, Konzepte, Maßnahmen. Wiesbaden, pp 187–211

o.v. (04 Jan. 2002) Individuality in a merger of equals, Financial Times

Paauwe J, Boselie P (2005) HRM and performance. Hum Resour Manage J 15(4):68–83

Payne A, Poulfelt F (1992) Marketing of management consulting firms. Acad Manage Proc pp 160–164

Penley JA, Tomaka J (2002) Associations among the big five, emotional responses, and coping with acute stress. Pers Individ Differ 32(7):1215–1228

Pennings JM, Lee K (2002) Social capital of organization. In: Leenders RTAJ, Gabbay SM (eds) Corporate social capital and liability. Boston, MA, pp 43–67

Perry-Smith JE, Blum TC (2000) Work-family human resource bundles and perceived organizational performance. Acad Manage J 43(6):1107–1117

Perry-Smith JE, Shalley CE (2003) The social side of creativity. A static and dynamic social network perspective. Acad Manage Rev 28(1):89–106

Peterson M (2001) Wissensmanagement in der strategischen Unternehmensberatung, 1. Aufl. Wiesbaden

Pfeffer J (1994) Competitive advantage through people, press in paperback. Boston, MA.

Pinnington A, Morris T (1996) Power and control in professional partnerships. Long Range Plann 29(6):842–849

Pinnington A, Morris T (2002) Transforming the Architect. Organ Stud 23(2):189–210

Pinnington A, Morris T (2003) Archetype change in professional organizations. Br J Manage 14:85–99

Podolny JM (1993) A status-based model of market competition. Am J Sociol 98(4):829–872

Podolny JM (1994) Market Uncertainty and the Social Character of Economic Exchange. Adm Sci Q 39(3):458–48

Polanyi, M (1966) The tacit dimension. Doubleday & Co., New York, NY

Post HA (1996) Internationalization and professionalization in accounting services. Int Stud Manage Organ 26(2):80–103

Powell W, Koput K, Bowie J, Smith-Doerr L (2002) The Spatial clustering of science and capital. Reg Stud 36(3):291–305

Probst G, Raub, S, Romhardt K (2006) Wissen managen, 5., überarb. Aufl

Quinn JB, Anderson P, Finkelstein S (1996) Das Potential in den Köpfen gewinnbringender nutzen. Harv Bus Manager 18(3):95–104

Rammert W (1988) Das Innovationsdilemma. Opladen

Ranson S, Hinings C, Greenwood R (1980) The structuring of organizational structures. Adm Sci Q, 25:1–17

Rantanen J, Pulkkinen L, Kinnunen U (2005) The big five personality dimensions, work-family conflict, and psychological distress: a longitudinal view. J Individ Differ 26(3):155–166

Rasiel EM, Friga PN (2001) The McKinsey mind. New York, NY

Reischauer C, Schlesinger C (2005) In bester Gesellschaft: Capital, no. 5

Richter J, Stähler G (2003) Talente im Visier – Vom traditionellen Recruitment zum Talent Relationship Managemtn. In: Peitz A, Pfeffer R (eds) Perosnalauswahl International, Symposion, Düsseldorf, pp 165–189

Richter K, Hammer P (2003) Das Ende der Patriarchen. Werben Verkaufen 43(9):28–31

Ringlstetter M, Bürger B (2003) Bedeutung netzwerkartiger Strukturen bei der strategischen Entwicklung von Professional Service Firms. In: Bruhn M, Stauss B (eds) Dienstleistungsnetzwerke. Wiesbaden, pp 113–130

Ringlstetter M, Bürger B (2004) Strategische Entwicklung von Professional Service Firms. In: Ringlstetter M, Bürger, B., Kaiser S (eds) Strategien and Management für Professional Service Firms. Weinheim, pp 283–305

Ringlstetter M, Bürger B, Kaiser S (2004) Eine Einführung in die Welt der Professional Service Firms. In: Ringlstetter M, Bürger B, Kaiser S (eds) Strategien and Management für Professional Service Firms. Weinheim, pp 11–32

Ringlstetter MJ (1997) Organisation von Unternehmen and Unternehmensverbindungen. Munich

Ringlstetter MJ, Morner M (2000) creating value in corporate groups. In: Dahiya, SB (eds) The current state of business disciplines. Rohtak, pp 1469–1486

Ringlstetter M, Kniehl A (1995) Professionalisierung als Leitidee eines Humanressourcen-Managements. In: Wächter H (ed) Professionalisierte Personalarbeit? Munich, pp 139–161

Robbins SP (2001) Organisation der Unternehmung, 9. Aufl. [der amerikan. Ausg.]. Munich

Roberts EB (1987) Generating technological innovation. New York, NY

Rose G, Glorius-Rose C (1995) Unternehmungsformen and-verbindungen, 2nd edn. Köln

Rothbard NP, Dumas TL (2006) Research perspectives: managing the work-home interface. In: Jones F, Burke RJ, Westman M (eds) Work-life balance. Hove, pp 73–89

Rottloff A (2004) Networking. Bindlach

Ryoo J (1990) Adverse selection, reputation, and firms in professional service markets, CARESS Working Paper, Nr. 92–28, Philadelphia, PA

Schade C (1996) Marketing für Unternehmensberatung. Wiesbaden

Schade C, Schott E (1993) Kontraktgüter im Marketing. Marketing-ZFP 15:15–25

Schirmer F (1992) Arbeitsverhalten von Managern. Wiesbaden

Schmitz G (1997) Marketing für professionelle Dienstleistungen. Wiesbaden

Schneewind KA, Kupsch M (2007) Patterns of neuroticism, work-family stress, and resources as determinants of personal distress. J Individ Differ 28(3):150–160

Schobert DB (2007) Grundlagen zum Verständnis von work-life balance. In: Esslinger AS, Schobert DB (eds) Erfolgreiche Umsetzung von work-life balance in organisationen. Strategien, Konzepte, Maßnahmen, Wiesbaden, pp 19–33

Schreiner G (1998) Organisatorische Fähigkeiten. Munich

Schubert FM (2001) Transnationales Management im Investment Banking: Entwicklung eines Management-Modells für die Führung von weltweit agierenden Investment Banken and seine Implikationen für deutsche Universalbanken. Köln

Schumpeter JA (1931) Theorie der wirtschaftlichen Entwicklung, 3. Aufl., unveränderter Abdruck der 2., neubearb. Aufl. Leipzig

Scott MC (1998): The intellect industry. Profiting and learning from professional service firms. Chichester

Scott MC (2001) Professional service firm. Chichester

Seabright MA, Levinthal DA, Fichman M (1992) Role of individual attachments in the dissolution of interorganizational relationships. Acad Manage J 35(1):122–160

Seligman ME, Csikszentmihalyi M (2000) Positive psychology. An introduction. Am Psychol 55(1):5–14

Sertoglu C, Berkowitch A (2002a) Ehemalige als Waffe im Wettbewerb. Harv Bus Manager 24(6):8–9

Sertoglu C, Berkowitch A (2002b) Cultivating ex-employees. Harv Bus Rev Juni):20–21

Seufert A. Seufert S (1998) Wissensgenerierung and -transfer in knowledge networks. iomanagement 1998(10):76–84

Shah N, Kraatz MS (2002) Changing Patterns of Personnel Flows: The Emergence of Lateral Hiring Among Corporate Law Firms, Paper zum Workshop Professional Service Firms, University of Alberta, Edmonton, AB (Canada) 15–17 Aug. 2002.

Shapero A (1985) Managing professional people. New York, NY

Sherer PD (1995) Leveraging human assets in law firms: human capital structures and organizational capabilities. Ind Labor Relat Rev 48(4):671–691

Smith J, Gardner D (2007) Factors affecting employee use of work-life balance initiatives. N Z J Psychol 36(1):3–12

Solomon M, Surprenant C, Czepiel J, Gutman E (1985) A role theory perspective on dyadic interactions. J Mark 49(1):99–111

Spar DL (1997) Lawyers abroad. Calif Manage Rev 39(3):8–28

Stauss B (1995) "Augenblicke der Wahrheit" in der Dienstleistungserstellung. Ihre Relevanz and ihre Messung mit Hilfe der Kontaktpunkt-Analyse. In: Bruhn M, Stauss B (eds) Dienstleistungsqualität. Wiesbaden

Stoeva AZ, Chiu RK, Greenhaus JH (2002) Negative affectivity, role stress, and work-family conflict. J Vocat Behav 60(1):1–16

Strambach P (1995) Wissensintensive unternehmensorientierte Dienstleistungen. Münster

Stutz HR (1988) Management-consulting. Bern

Sundbo J (1997) Management of innovation in service. Serv Ind J 17(3):432–455

Süss C (2001) Führung in mittelständischen Konzernen. Lohmar

Sutton KL, Noe RA (2005): Family- friendly programs and work-life integration: More myth than magic. In: Kossek EE, Lambert SJ (eds) Work and life integration. Organizational, cultural, and individual perspectives. Lawrence Erlbaum Associates, Mahwah, NJ, pp. 151–169

Sveiby KE, Lloyd T (1990) Das Management des Know-how. Frankfurt

Sydow J (1995) Netzwerkorganisation: Interne and externe Restrukturierung von Unternehmungen. Wirtschaftswissenschaftliches Studium 24(12):629–634

Sydow J (1992) Strategische Netzwerke. Wiesbaden

The American Lawyer (2008) Vol. October

The Boston Consulting Group (2005) Move On 2006. Karriere, No. 12

Thiehoff R (2004) Work Life Balance mit Balanced Scorecard: Die wirtschaftliche Sicht der Prävention. In: Kastner M (ed) Die Zukunft der Work Life Balance. Wie lassen sich Beruf and Familie, Arbeit and Freizeit miteinander vereinbaren. Kröning, pp 409–436

Thiesse F (2001) Prozessorientiertes Wissensmanagement: Konzepte, Methode, Fallbeispiele, Bamberg zugl. St. Gallen

Thompson CA, Beauvais LL, Allen TA (2006) Work and family from an industrial/organizational psychology perspective. In: Pitt-Catsouphes M, Kossek EE, Sweet SA (eds) The work and family handbook. Multi-disciplinary perspectives methods, and approaches. Mahwah, NJ, pp 283–307

Thompson CA, Beauvais LL, Lyness KS (1999) When work-family benefits are not enough: the influence of work-family culture on benefit utilization, organizational attachment, and work-family conflict. J Vocat Behav 54(3):392–415

Thompson CA, Prottas D (2005) Relationships among organizational family support, job autonomy, perceived control, and employee well-being. J Occup Health Psychol 10(4):100–118

Tidd J, Izumimoto Y (2002) Knowledge exchange and learning through international joint ventures. Technovation 22:137–145

Tillmanns U, Jeschke K (2000) Erfolgsfaktor client loyalty. Frankfurt am Main

Toppin G, Czerniawska F (2005) Business consulting. London

Tordoir PP (1995) The professional knowledge economy. Dordrecht

Tsai W (2000) Social capital, strategic relatedness and the formation of intraorganizational linkages. Strat Manage J 21(9):925

van Doren D, Smith L, Biglin R (1985) The challenges of professional services marketing. J Consum Mark 2(2):19–27

van Well B (2001) Standardisierung and Individualisierung von Dienstleistungen, 1. Aufl. Wiesbaden

Vopel O (1999) Wissensmanagement im Investment Banking. Wiesbaden

Wagner M (2004) Business networking im internet, 1. Aufl. Wiesbaden

Walker G, Kogut B (1997) Social capital, structural holes and the formation of an industry network. Organ Sci 8(2):109

Walker K, Ferguson C, Denvir P (1998) Creating new clients. London

Wallace JE (1995) Organizational and professional commitment in professional and nonprofessional organizations. Adm Sci Q 40:228–255

Watson I (2003) Applying knowledge management. San Francisco, CA

Way SA (2002) High performance work systems and intermediate indicators of firm performance within the US small business sector. J Manage 28:765–785

Weber B (1996) Die fluide Organisation. Konzeptionelle Überlegungen für die Gestaltung und das Management von Unternehmen in hochdynamischen Umfeldern. Bern

Wegener B (1987) Vom Nutzen entfernter Bekannter. Kölner Zeitschrift für Soziologie and Sozialpsychologie 39:278–301

Weisbord ES (1990) Determinants and effects of growth strategy in corporate law firms. Acad Manage Proc 37:42–46

Wells D (28 Jun. 2005) Wined and dined by Wall Street, Financial Times

Westlund H, Bolton R (2003) Local social capital and entrepreneurship. Small Bus Econ 21(2):77

Whitefield K, Poole M (1997) Organizing employment for high performance: theories, evidence and policy. Organ Stud 18:745–764

Widmer U, Brun J (1999) Knowledge management in der professional service firm. In: Müller-Stewens G (ed) Professional service firms. Frankfurt am Main, pp 235–258

Wierda-Boer HH, Gerris JRM, Vermulst AA (2009) Managing multiple roles. Personality, stress, and work-family interference in dual-earner couples. J Individ Differ 30(1):6–19

Willke H (1996) 0Systemtheorie 1. Grundlagen, 5. Stuttgart

Wilson JR (1991) Mund-zu-Mund-Marketing. Landsberg

Wittenreich W (1966) How to buy/sell professional services. Harv Bus Rev 44(2):127–138

Wittenreich W (1969) Selling – A perquisite to success as a professional. Philadelphia, PA

Wollburg R (2004) Wissensmanagement in einer internationalen Anwaltssozietät. In: Ringlstetter M, Bürger B, Kaiser S (2004) Strategien and management für professional service firms. Weinheim, pp 217–227

Worpitz H (1991) Wissenschaftliche Unternehmensführung?, 1. Aufl. Frankfurt am Main

Wright PM, Dunford BB, Snell SA (2001) Human resources and the resource based view of the firm. J Manage 27:701–721

Wright PM, McMahan GC, McWilliams A (1994) Human resources and sustained competitive advantage. Int J Hum Resour Manage 5:299–326

Yasbek P (2004) The business case for firm-level work-life balance policies. A review of the literature. Labour Market Policy Group, Department of Labour, Wellington. Online verfügbar unter, zuletzt geprüft am

Young L (2005a) Marketing the professional services firm. Chichester

Young L (2005b) Professional services marketing. Market Lead 31:47–50

Zabala I, Panadero G, Gallardo LM, Amate CM, Sánchez-Galindo M, Tena I, Villalba I (2005) Corporate reputation in professional services firms. Corp Reputation Rev 8(1):59–71

Zedeck S, Mosier KL (1990) Work in the family and employing organization. Am Psychol 45(2):240–251

Zeithaml VA (1981) How consumer evaluation processes differ between goods and services. In: Donnelly JH, George WR (eds) Marketing of services. Chicago, IL, pp 186–190

Zucker LG (1986) Production of trust: institutional sources of economic structure, 1840–1920. Res Organ Behav 8:53–111

About the Authors

Stephan Kaiser is Full Professor for Human Resource Management and Organization at the Universität der Bundeswehr Munich (Germany) and Visiting Professor at the Ingolstadt School of Management (Catholic University of Eichstaett-Ingolstadt, Germany), where he also received his doctorate and habilitation. His present main research issues are knowledge-intensive work, professional services, human resources and organization. He is author and editor of various books and publishes in international journals on the topics of organization, innovation and knowledge management.

Max Ringlstetter is Professor and Chair of the Department for Human Resources and Organization at the Ingolstadt School of Management (Catholic University of Eichstaett-Ingolstadt, Germany). He studied economics at the University Munich, where he also attained a doctorate and his habilitation. His main points of research lie in the areas of professional service firms and organization. In practice he worked – among other companies – for McKinsey & Co. and Strategma – Institute for Applied Strategic Studies. He is chair of the Institute for Corporate Development in Munich.

About the Co-authors

Adrian Bründl studied economics at the Ingolstadt School of Management (Catholic University of Eichstaett-Ingolstadt, Germany). He was research assistant at the Department for Human Resources and Organization. His research interest and practical experience lie in the areas Professional Service Firms and energy industry.

Bernd Bürger is head of the Strategic Planning and Analysis Department with Allianz Global Risks. Before he joined Allianz, he worked as freelance consultant and as research associate with the Department for Human Resources and Organization at the Ingolstadt School of Management (Catholic University of Eichstaett-Ingolstadt, Germany). His research and dissertation concentrated on the management and the development of Professional Service Firms.

Tim Kampe is head auditor of the auditing and consulting company HLB Dr. Stückmann & Partner, Bielefeld. Prior to that, he worked as research associate at the Department for Human Resources and Organization at the Ingolstadt School of Management (Catholic University of Eichstaett-Ingolstadt, Germany) and as consultant in the area personnel management for several years. In the context of his research and his dissertation he focuses on management challenges of Professional Service Firms.

Tilo Polster studied economics at the Ingolstadt School of Management (Katholische Universität Eichstätt-Ingolstadt, Germany) and at the university Modena e Reggio Emilia (Italy). Since 2007 he is a graduate at the Department for Human Resources and Organization at the Ingolstadt School of Management (Catholic University of Eichstaett-Ingolstadt, Germany). His main research focus is 'Innovations in Management Consultancies'.

Cornelia U. Reindl studied education sciences and psychology majoring in business and education at the University Munich (Germany). Since 2008 she is research assistant and PhD student at the Department for Human Resources and Organization at the Ingolstadt School of Management (Catholic University of Eichstaett-Ingolstadt, Germany). Her main point of research is human resource management and in particular 'Work-life Integration'.

Martin L. Stolz studied economics at the Ingolstadt School of Management (Katholische Universität Eichstätt-Ingolstadt, Germany) and at the university Modena e Reggio Emilia (Italy). Since 2007 he is a graduate at the Department for Human Resources and Organization at the Ingolstadt School of Management (Catholic University of Eichstaett-Ingolstadt, Germany). His main research focus is the 'Work-Life Balance in Management Consultancies'.

Simon A. Woll studied education sciences and economics at the universities of Regensburg (Germany) and Fribourg (Switzerland). Since 2008 he is research assistant and PhD student at the Department for Human Resources and Organization at the Ingolstadt School of Management (Catholic University of Eichstaett-Ingolstadt, Germany). His main point of research is human resource management and in particular 'Integrative Forms of Competence Management'.

Index

Lightning Source UK Ltd.
Milton Keynes UK
04 December 2010

163812UK00006B/35/P